IMPOSSIBLE TO FAIL

HOW TO GUARANTEE YOUR SUCCESS

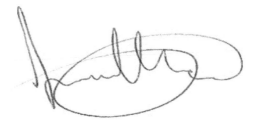

RON MALHOTRA

Interior design: Ida Jansson

National Library of Australia Catalogue-in-Publication data:
Impossible to Fail/ Ron Malhotra
Success/Self-help

ISBN: 978-0-6486645-6-7 (hc)
ISBN: 978-0-6486645-7-4 (sc)
ISBN: 978-0-6486645-8-1 (e)

This book is dedicated to all my brothers and sisters in the world, who have an open mind, an ambitious heart and a fiery spirit.

I know if you have the above three elements, you have everything you need to design the life and lifestyle you desire.

I hope this book can provide a little assistance and inspiration on your winner's journey.

CONTENTS

INTRODUCTION

What if I told you, you can assure your success?

That you are guaranteed to succeed in any endeavour you want.

That you can have the results you desire.

That you can achieve your goals – whether they relate to your health, finances, peace of mind, relationships, or career/business.

What if I promised that by applying the principles, insights, and strategies contained within this book you are virtually guaranteed exponential results in any area you desire.

What if I shared insights so transformational, profound and researched, that they will transform you from the inside out?

What would you do?

Would you do what it takes?

You are probably thinking, 'What's the catch?'

Well, there is one. Two, to be precise. I have deliberately put these caveats in this introduction so if you decide they are unreasonable you can stop reading now and save your time.

First, you must follow the principles, concepts, and strategies that I have laid out in this book. After all, expecting to land at the top of the mountain without climbing it would be bordering on insanity.

And secondly, be open-minded about concepts where relevance is not immediately obvious, or if they challenge your existing worldview. Do not reject an idea that is new to you until you have applied it without scepticism for a reasonable amount of time.

That's all I ask.

Humans are more resourceful than we realise. We are the only species on the planet that can create at will. We are the only species who can influence our circumstances. We are the only species who can solve complex problems. Despite this, the vast majority find themselves stuck – without choices and confused.

Why is this? There is no simple answer, but my intent for this book is to demystify some of the causes and provide you with solutions so you can step into the person you know in your heart you were meant to be. Charles Kettering, famed inventor and head of research for GM once said, 'A problem well-stated is half-solved.' And that is where we sometimes need to start – with a definition.

I know there are many books on motivation, inspiration and positive psychology already out there, so why read *Impossible to Fail*?

You are more than a body and a mind. *Impossible to Fail* will help you to realise your potential. It will enable you to understand your true powers and give you an integrated and holistic approach to unleash these inner powers so you can create the life and lifestyle you truly desire.

Most success-based literature is incomplete because it either:
- does not consider all the internal factors that lead to self-mastery (the most fundamental pre-requisite to complete success)
- does not consider all the external factors that lead to the understanding of the material world
- does not integrate the physical with the spiritual
- does not teach well-researched laws, principles and strategies which have their roots in science as well as philosophy
- does not teach applied and proven tactics
- teaches theories, which are one or two dimensional, and lacking holistic perspectives.

I have been a voracious student of success for over a decade. Not just a student who delves into theories, but a practitioner of all I have learnt.

Because I am both teacher and practitioner, I have the conviction to preach what I have learnt and applied. I test everything to achieve real outcomes before sharing my theories and practices.

I have studied many schools of thought, from traditional psychology, neuroscience, philosophy and metaphysics, to behavioural finance, achievement science, epigenetics, spirituality, and more. Why? Because I found myself on an insatiable journey to figure out why most people struggle to create the life and lifestyle they want.

There are three primary reasons for this:
- not having a total understanding of self (we are not just a mind and a body, we are also a heart and spirit)
- not having a total understanding of natural and universal laws (most of life is simply cause and effect)
- not understanding the fundamentals that drive the financial, economic, and commercial system (we are spiritual beings having a physical experience, therefore we must master, not bypass the physical world).

MY STORY

I was born in India to a middle-class family. I do not recall many happy moments from my early childhood, or indeed, much at all from this time, but I do remember being poor and not having peace of mind. Most people around me were struggling and suffering.

There was a lot of talk about spirituality and God from people around me, but looking back, I realise it came from a place of fear, lack and scarcity. From an early age, I remember not feeling understood and not understanding the way in which people talked about certain things. For example, I couldn't understand why we had to go to school when hardly anyone around me seemed happy or successful. I struggled at school and was rarely able to pay attention due to emotional dramas at home. I later realised the education system and culture did not educate, it served to indoctrinate.

When I was a young boy we migrated to Melbourne, Australia. I recall feeling excited about the move because I always enjoyed heavy metal and rap music. I felt that in the West there would be more opportunities for self-expression. I remember the morning we arrived, driving to my auntie's place: the streets were desolate and quiet in a way I had never experienced before. The sounds of India were nowhere to be heard. Melbourne was far from the bustling metropolis I had imagined. I recall feeling numb all over; the life, country and family I had known, was no longer.

While I enjoyed the higher level of freedom in Australia, I still struggled to fit in. The issue was not cultural or racial because I was never subjected to any serious racism. It was more that I felt the vast majority of people thought and behaved in a way that was devoid of individual thinking. Everywhere I looked I saw people blindly following a system. At school I fell in with the wrong crowd and moved in with a bunch of guys who were broke and doing drugs.

At the age of twenty, I lived in a commission house and could barely afford my rent. I'll never forget the smell of drugs, smoke and dirty clothes that lingered in every area of the house. I struggled to pay my bills. I was so broke I couldn't even afford to buy an iron for my clothes. Most nights my dinner was cereal with milk and a banana – the cheapest dinner I could afford. I remember working so hard to pay my bills, but still couldn't afford to move out of the cockroach-infested place. They would sometimes crawl down the curtains and creep into my bed, waking me from my sleep. The daily feeling of barely scraping by was all too familiar.

I had no formal education. I couldn't even finish a certificate due to emotional stress. I had no confidence. I hardly saw my family. I didn't know how to dress or conduct myself. I found out the hard way I had no real friends. One day I came home to find police cars parked on my street, conducting a drug raid. The guys I lived with hid the drugs in my room. I was interrogated by the police and I told them the drugs were not mine and belonged to my housemates. Fortunately for me, the police took my word and I escaped any legal consequences.

But my relief was short-lived. Defending myself was seen as a betrayal by my housemates. I remember walking into the lounge room and looking into the faces of five angry guys who were high on drugs and wanted to teach me a lesson. What followed was ten minutes of brutal punches, kicks, and metal dumbbells thrown at me while I lay on the floor in the foetal position. When I finally got to my room and looked at my face in the mirror, I did not recognise myself. I couldn't hold back the tears. My face was swollen in so many places. I felt alone, betrayed and hurt. I felt a deep sense of shame about my life and I promised I would never put myself in that situation again. That was the day I committed to becoming totally financially independent so I could choose to live life on my own terms.

By the time I was thirty, I'd acquired financial education, millions of dollars' worth of assets, an esteemed corporate position and some formal education. But … I still wasn't fulfilled or inspired, and I felt like an imposter. I had secured a position in a prestigious wealth management organisation's private bank, which allowed me to buy what I thought was the home of my dreams – a 50 sq. ft. mansion. I drove prestigious European cars, wore $3,000 suits and expensive Swiss watches, and had all the other trappings you would expect of a person who was doing well financially.

I enjoyed my work because I loved learning about money. But even though I was doing something I excelled at, I knew I was *not* operating in my absolute zone of inspiration. I felt lost. Little things made me angry and frustrated. Some days I would come home and get into arguments with my wife for petty reasons. I remember thinking there was something wrong with me. How could I feel like this when I had everything a person could ever want?

I was considered to be the epitome of success by many, yet deep down I knew there was something missing and out of alignment. Everyone thought I was doing great, but I felt hollow inside. As Tony Robbins says, success without fulfillment is the ultimate failure.

I remember lying in bed and thinking I needed to walk away from whatever I had built in order to find my true path. I knew this would require me to walk away from the trappings of success and rebuild everything, so that my career or business would support my life and my highest values. I needed to invest in myself and my development, to learn new skills, and potentially build a business that was aligned to my greater purpose. To seek opportunities providing full expression and fulfillment, without compromising on my values and financial abundance. I didn't want to be one of those people who loved what they did but were always broke.

But I no longer wanted to be a slave to my career or money.

I'll never forget my wife's face when I told her I was going to sell our beautiful home and rent another. The image is etched into my mind forever; sadness creeping over her eyes as the realisation hit – the home we had bought would be no longer. Despite her pain, she said nothing and gave me unconditional support.

Most property agents were reluctant to lease out properties to me because I had no recent rental history and I had quit my job. Due to lack of choice,

I settled for a basic home, a quarter of the size of my mansion, with not even a fraction of the luxury fittings and furniture I had become accustomed to. I'm not expecting sympathy because I was still better off than a lot of people in the world, but the point I'm trying to make is that when you have built something substantial, it can be hard to walk away from it all and take a risk when you don't need to take one.

When we drove into the garage of our new rental property, my wife broke down. This was the first time she openly expressed her sadness to me. She was scared, concerned and worried that her family would think I was having an early midlife crisis, but she continued to believe in me. Not once did she question my decision. At this moment I knew failure was not an option.

I was conscious not to deny my financial responsibilities and continue to aim for financial abundance because I was pragmatic enough to know that I would require sufficient financial resources in order to make a significant impact with my life. There was no way I was going to let my wife's sacrifice and complete devotion to my aspirations and dreams be in vain.

Again, I understand this might be a first world problem for many, but there's a point behind my actions. Sometimes you need to have the willingness to seek your greater purpose by walking away from what you have and feeding your dreams more than your fears, despite the risk and uncertainty. It's easy to carve a new path when you have nothing. It's a little more difficult to walk away from fancy titles, job security and material assets, especially when you have worked so hard to get to that point.

The core issue, as I later discovered, was that I was not operating out of my zone of genius. I was not serving my greatest purpose, or living in full expression. I had not unleashed my creativity. I was not living by my highest value or maximising my potential, and I was not making the difference I truly wanted. After all, how could I do any of those things when I hadn't even truly worked out who I was?

Mark Twain said: 'The two most important days in your life are the day you are born and the day you find out why.'

Previously, my entire identity was based around my occupation, appearance, nationality, culture, education and media conditioning.

Eventually I was able to overcome these issues and challenges. I was able to discover who I truly was and successfully design the life and lifestyle I desired.

Today, I live a life of purpose, passion and meaning. I'm mentally at peace, physically fit and healthy, and have a loving wife and daughter and meaningful relationship with my few close friends. The lessons I learnt in my earlier life and my self-determination have resulted in me achieving global influence. I have businesses aligned to my passion, purpose, values and strengths; I have an enviable lifestyle with global experiences and a high level of financial security, which allows me to continue to invest in my growth as well as in new ventures. All this allows me to live by my highest value of legacy and significance.

I'm fortunate I eventually discovered the purpose of my existence.

I want to enable you to do the same, so you too can design a holistically successful life and lifestyle for yourself and your family: a life that will allow you to leave a positive footprint in the world by serving your highest purpose. Throughout *Impossible to Fail* I hope to educate, empower and enable you to do the same so you can guarantee your success.

What I will share in *Impossible to Fail* are time-tested and proven principles, strategies and tools to enable you to design the life and lifestyle you truly want to live. I'm living proof that you can still create the life of your dreams despite experiencing significant psychological pain, defeats, setbacks, challenges, rejections and criticisms. By following this time-tested way of thinking and living, you too can craft and live your ideal life and lifestyle.

Self-mastery can only come from self-control, which can only come from self-awareness. The problem with self-awareness is that you don't know what you don't know. So how can you fix it?

Most people make their decisions from a place of fear, not from their dreams and aspirations. We are programmed to think more about what can go wrong, instead of what can go right. That's what our scarcity based middle-class culture has done to most of us.

The leading cause of people's fear is ignorance. I'm not referring to ignorance around skills, doing one's job, or professional, skill-based or academic education. I mean ignorance about:

- how life works
- how you work
- how the universe works.

In this book, I'll take you through the entire process to help you understand what you need to *know*, what steps you need to *apply*, and how you need to apply these steps to *guarantee* your success in virtually all areas of your life. You will learn how to think, how to gain control over your emotions, how to direct your actions, and how to create the results you want.

Clarity leads to power and until you are crystal clear on who you are, what you want and what success means to you individually and personally, you do not have a proper basis for making the right decisions for yourself.

At times, my tone may seem a bit harsh, but please know that my intent is to serve you through the truth. You can't be a sensitive snowflake if you want to succeed. You want to be a diamond. And diamonds only shine after they have been rubbed, polished and cut, over and over again. I will be your inconvenient mentor, your trusted guide and your well-wisher. I care about your results more than I care about your emotions. As we progress through the lessons, you will see why your feelings cannot be the only guide to your decisions, because feelings can distort your perceptions.

Throughout this book, you will learn many important concepts and their applications. Surface level comprehension of information does not cause sustainable transformation. Until you have understood, engaged with and absorbed the knowledge at a deep level, and blended that knowledge with physical actions and experience, it will not translate into habitual behaviours. Your habits will simply overrule and override what you learn and what you think you know.

Ultimately there is only one determinant of what you know: YOUR RESULTS IN THE LONG TERM.

Sure, things may happen to you in the short term that are out of your control, but in the long term, it cannot be denied that a person who consistently fails to produce the outcomes they truly want, has either the wrong knowledge, wrong perception of the knowledge, or is engaging in the wrong application of the knowledge.

See, I told you I would be hard on you. But only because I want to enable you to create the life you have always wanted.

If you are a good person who has experienced misfortune, you might feel a little bitter. If you have worked hard but haven't been able to design the life of your dreams, you might feel doubtful. If you have always strived to do the right thing by people but you've been lied to, taken advantage of, or been deceived, you might feel cynical.

The fact is, most of us have been taught how to make a living, but not how to make a life.

You see, there are certain LAWS that govern life.

There are PRINCIPLES that govern how we think and act and the results we produce.

And there are STRATEGIES that govern what level of abundance or scarcity we attract.

Ignorance or misunderstanding of these principles, laws and strategies can cause unnecessary struggle and suffering.

I'm not claiming that *Impossible to Fail* will eliminate struggle and suffering from your life. I'm claiming that if you follow the lessons in *Impossible to Fail*, struggle and suffering will be short-lived and it will never defeat you.

If success were simply the ability to design the life and lifestyle you truly want to live, would you consider yourself successful? If you are like most people, you probably wouldn't.

But that is all about to change.

Finally, you hold in your hands the key to holistic success. Success in the areas of peace and fulfillment, relationships and influence, inspirational and purposeful work, financial and commercial abundance and health and well-being.

You may not be able to control everything that happens in your life, but the good news is, you don't need to.

You only need to learn how to influence things, because you can influence a lot more than you think.

Are you ready to live a life of opportunity, abundance and fulfillment? Are you ready to maximise your potential?

Are you ready to become the highest and best version of you?

Let's GO! Let's GUARANTEE your personal success.

CHAPTER 1
Define your own success

'Success becomes inevitable when you understand the process of success and are willing to go through the process.'

Have you ever wondered what success is?

What exactly is it that would make you feel successful?

What would need to happen in five years from now for you to look back and feel happy with your progress?

You see, vague ideas about success lead to vague outcomes in life. Defining your success is the start and the foundation of where the magic happens. Unless you understand *what* you are aiming for, your chances of attaining it are very slim. You cannot hit a target that you cannot see, so not knowing what you want can result in you making decisions that do not make you happy. Wrong jobs, wrong partners, wrong friends, being in the wrong situations or wrong events, and doing things for the wrong reasons

– these are some examples. Each time you decide without clarity, you risk moving further and further away from what truly makes you feel successful and fulfilled.

Success for you is different to what success is for other people. Defining your success includes understanding where you are now, what you want out of life, why you want it, and understanding your life mission.

Most never stop to think about what they truly want. Many just blindly chase money or career success without ever questioning what would truly make them feel successful, happy and fulfilled.

So, when people don't know what they truly want and why they want it, they end up making decisions based on what everyone else is doing, or they get persuaded into situations, jobs or relationships because of other people's opinions. Think about it. If you don't have a clear idea of what it is that you want, the basis of your decisions will be other people's opinions, cultural and religious orientation, influences, and the media.

There's a man I know who keeps going from job to job in a profession that he's not passionate about. This is because he has never fully understood how he wanted to live his life, or defined success in a way that was meaningful to him. He prefers spending time camping and motorcycle riding, but because of his chosen career he gets little time to do these things, even though he makes decent money. Now, isn't that the whole point of having money? Isn't it to live the life you want? Don't you think it defeats the purpose when someone is unable to live the life they want, despite making a decent income?

Life's too short to unconsciously follow career paths and life decisions without having clarity of what makes us feel successful and happy. Remember my story? That's what happened to me, which is why I want you to become conscious about what success means to you.

Think about this: are you someone who is happier with more time than more money? Are you someone who lives in the city but craves the quiet country life? Do you prefer to stay in and have a nice meal but your partner is outgoing and likes to socialise? All these situations are simply a consequence of not being deliberate about decisions, and you can't be deliberate when you lack clarity about what you truly want.

This chapter is about helping you come to your unique definition of success, away from a mentality of racing and competing with others. Remember, what you want in life has nothing to do with other people's opinions.

What is success for you?

Everyone's definition of success is different. However, all human beings innately want to be more, do more and have more, and we all want to be successful. But what is success? In this section, I'll explore the definition of success and why it's important to know what makes you feel successful, and share what I consider, is the Universal definition of success.

How's this?

'Success is the ability to design the life and lifestyle one truly wants to live.'

Simple. Now, how many people do you think meet their own definition of success?

The primary reason why most people do not get what they *want* out of life is because they've never specifically decided *what* they want out of their life.

When you truly know what you want, you concentrate your mental energy and focus on this. This activates the part of your brain responsible for identifying opportunities that will take you closer to your desires. You know, much like when you decide to buy a certain kind of car. That decision activates your brain and you start to see that type of car everywhere. The cars were always there, but because the mind was not switched on (due to a lack of specific direction), those cars fell in your blind zone. So, when you truly know what you want, and you've defined it very specifically, your brain automatically goes to work for you. I'll delve deeper into this concept in Chapter 10.

While I can appreciate that everyone's definition of success is different, there is one thing no one will disagree on. And that is; success is doing what you want, when you want, and with whom you want. Now it's impossible for anyone to do what they want, when they want, with whom they want 100 per cent of the time. However, as I'm sure you will appreciate, if there were two people and one of them spent 70 per cent of their life and time doing what they wanted, when they wanted, with who they wanted, while the other did this for only 20 per cent of their life and time, it could be easily argued that the first person is more successful. This is why it's so important to know what it is that you truly want.

As we progress further, I'll share why you need to know where you are *now* before you can identify how to get where you want to go. For now, think about success, and then answer the following question as truthfully as possible. Based on the definition of success above, are you truly successful? Write your answer down. Write down why you believe you are successful or why you believe you are not. You don't need to share your answer with anyone, but write it down.

Where are you now?

Before you can figure out where you need to go and what it will take to get there, you need to figure out exactly where you are right now.

Before you can plan for your success, you need to define your current reality. This helps us understand the gap between where we are and where to be. But it also helps us identify areas of personal deficiency that need the most work and priority for us to become successful.

Time for a life diagnosis. On a scale of one (lowest) to ten (highest), rate yourself on these key areas:

- health and fitness
- meaningful relationships
- satisfying career
- personal finances
- peace of mind
- personal growth.

Be completely honest with yourself when completing your life diagnosis. This helps you understand the gap between where you are and where you want to be.

Now that you know where you are, let's get to the heart of what you want.

What do you genuinely desire?

What do you genuinely desire? The number one prerequisite to success is knowing what you want combined with a burning desire.

Knowing what you want + burning desire

In his book *Think And Grow Rich*, Napoleon Hill talks about desire being the first step towards achieving success. Desire is much more than a hope and a wish. A burning desire becomes the fuel that keeps us going even when we are struck by challenges. Think back to a time when you had a burning and sustained desire for something. You'll find that in most cases you actually ended up achieving what you were after, provided your desire was strong and you sustained that desire for a period of time.

Desire is the catalyst for high performance.

So, what do you want? What makes you truly happy? What would you choose to do with your time if all your financial commitments were taken care of?

Imagine that you have the innate ability to achieve anything you desired. What do you want to *be*? What do you want to *have*? And what do you want to *do*?

What do you want in your career right now? In your health and fitness, your family or relationships, and your finances?

When we have consistent desire, our ability to find solutions is also enhanced. We all possess a keen desire for certain things and a lukewarm desire for other things. Therefore, it is important to aim for things where we have a genuine desire, rather than aiming for things based on other people's opinions.

Tip: choose the desires that come from a deeper place inside you. Desires that only serve the ego are difficult to attain and even when the object of desire is achieved, it leaves us feeling unfulfilled.

The reason why desire equals success is because we are unable to sustain an intense desire for things we do not truly want. A lot of people will say they want more money, when in fact, it is not money they desire, but the freedom of flexibility they're craving. This is why you will see people who say they want money, but because they lack intense desire, they never end up attaining financial success. They've never worked out *why* they want the money.

Activity: Set a timer for three minutes. Without thinking too much, make a list of what you want in your life. Next, go through this list; for each item, ask yourself, 'Is this something I want? Is it a lukewarm desire? Or is this a real and burning desire?' Finally, cross out everything except those you have a genuinely burning desire to achieve.

Now, let's talk about the reasons your *why* is much more important than your *how* at this stage, when it comes to achieving what you truly want.

Why do you want what you want?

Why do you want what you want? If your why is strong enough, the how is less important.

Do you want to know how to find out what you love and to love what you do? Figure out your *why*. Later in *Impossible to Fail*, you'll learn why you don't need to work out the *how* yet. It is only necessary to figure out the *why* at this stage.

> *'He who has a why to live for can bear almost any how.'*
> **–Friedrich Nietzsche**

As kids, most of us are curious. The older we become, the more we turn away from the why questions and start to focus on the how questions. How do I become wealthy? How do I get out of debt? How do I start my own business?

However, these questions will not provide you with the preliminary ammunition you need for success. In fact, they will discourage you, and make you quit before you get started. The *how* is useless, as well as elusive, without the why. The *why* will give you the energy, inspiration and resourcefulness to source the *how*. When you want to quit, it will be your *why* that provides meaning for your actions, which further creates an intense desire for the success you want.

People who achieve great things are those who are more driven by their why than their how. Ask yourself these questions:

- Why do you want success?
- Why do you work?
- Why are you reading *Impossible to Fail*?
- Why do you want to be more informed?
- Why did you get married (or why are you in a relationship)?
- Why do you want freedom?
- Why do you want financial security?

Asking good questions of yourself and others is the only way to find the right answers. Everyone automatically seeks solutions, but before you know where to look, you first need to come up with the right questions.

As I mentioned earlier, if your reason to become successful is coming from a place of ego (so you can accumulate more or occupy more), I'm sorry to say your odds of total success are slim. You have to know what fuels your passion. You have to know what you're fighting for. When life gets tough, when you want to quit, when people disappoint you, you will run out of motivation unless you are clear on your *why*.

So, the real question is, what is your *why*? What has captured your heart? Is it your family? Is it freedom? Do you want to make a difference? What are the three reasons or people in your life that are worth striving for? What's your *why*?

Your *why* will give you a sense of purpose; it will make you inspired and even make you inspiring. It will make you a better human and a better leader. It will make you persevere. It will make you relentless. It will make you mentally tougher. So, have a cause that captures your heart.

Did you know that Apple only has a 6 per cent market share in the United States? And less than 3 per cent market share worldwide? By no stretch of the imagination is Apple a leading manufacturer of computers. However, Apple leads the computer industry as the most established and dominant brand. It was not Apple's computers that made them famous. It was the story behind their business that took the world by storm. Their *why* allowed them to deliver the technology and customer experience they are well known for.

I want to share a story with you. Dave and John are best friends. Dave plays soccer for his school but is not highly motivated. Dave's coach believes he has potential and tries to motivate him to achieve it, but Dave seems satisfied to do the bare minimum. One day, John has a car accident in front of Dave, and dies in his arms. The coach expects Dave to take time off to grieve the loss of his best friend, but the opposite happens. The next week, Dave is on the field early, putting a massive effort into his practise. He's serious about winning, he tells the coach, and when the big game comes, Dave plays like his life depends on it. Afterwards, the coach says, 'What's happened to you? I've never seen you play like this.' And Dave tells him, 'When John was dying in my arms, he told me to play a great game and win the trophy. So I did.' Dave played his best for John, believing that John was looking down on him from heaven. John was Dave's *why*, the spark that lit the fire inside him and pushed him to achieve success.

Now, I am going to share my *why* with you.

Why I do what I do

My parents earned ordinary incomes throughout their working lives. Unfortunately, despite years of hard work, they didn't achieve any of their goals and dreams. Over the years, I saw this trend repeated time and time again with most other people around me.

Seeing my parents and others suffer became the catalyst for learning everything I could about the human mind, success, and, of course, wealth and business. I was obsessed with learning why so few people in the world succeeded in designing their ideal life and lifestyle, the majority never achieving their dreams or having the opportunity to make a difference.

Over time, I learnt how ignorance in some areas resulted in struggle and suffering regardless of hard work or good hearts. I learnt how the right education helped people become mentally resourceful, emotionally agile and acquire financial resources. And I realised that it's not the lack of money, but the loss of dignity and choice that hurts people the most.

I wanted to see my parents and others thrive, not just survive. My biggest deprivations became my biggest aspirations. That's why what I do is more than just a career choice to me.

Helping people avoid the common mistakes, assisting them with the right strategies and knowledge, and then seeing them on the path to business and financial success (and make a difference), gives me tremendous satisfaction.

In the following section, you will use the answers to 'Why do you want what you want?' and translate them into a life mission statement to guide and direct your journey towards becoming a successful person.

What is your life mission statement?

'The two most important days in your life are the days you were born and the day you figure out why.'
Mark Twain

What is your mission in life? To answer that, think of the one thing that will make you feel your time here on earth will make a difference. It could be something simple.

Having a personal life mission statement brings focus, clarity and purpose to your life. For US President John F. Kennedy, it was putting man on the moon. For Thomas Edison, it was to create an invention people needed, while for Einstein, it was to solve the mystery about space and time. Author and motivational speaker Jack Canfield's mission is to inspire and empower people to live their highest vision in a context of love and joy. And my mission is to help people attain personal and financial success, so they can add value to others' lives, contribute to causes they care about, and make a difference to the world.

A lot of corporations have a mission statement. Essentially, it is a brief description of *what* they want to accomplish and *why* they want to accomplish it. The mission statement serves as a compass to guiding the company's operations.

For individuals, having a life mission statement can be inspirational and motivational. Having one gives you direction in life, making other decisions easier. Your life mission statement will help you decide things like, where to live and work, which career path to pursue, what industry you want to work in and what you want to specialise in, what your values are, and the kind of books, TV shows and movies that feed your soul. Your life mission statement can guide your daily actions, and if something derails you, can get you back on track.

Professor Zoltan Takacs is someone who is following his life mission (I talk about him more in my previous book, *The Success Answer*). As a young boy, he was fascinated by snakes. Now an expert in toxins, he has travelled to more than a hundred countries where he has caught thousands of reptiles to collect their venom for screening. To do this, he drives small planes, scuba dives, and sleeps in the middle of rainforests and deserts if he has to. He has overcome constant obstacles, from infections to crocodiles, civil wars to landslides. Even pirates. He's been jailed, chased by elephants, sprayed with cobra venom, and bitten about six times by snakes. He does all this despite being allergic to venom.

Why would he put his life at risk like this? It's because of his life mission statement, which is to push toxins into medical use. Why? Because toxins have yielded about a dozen medications, some that have saved lives. For example, if someone has a deadly heart attack, three drugs exist that might save their life. Two of these drugs have been derived from reptile venom. To Professor Takacs, it's worth the immense danger he faces, to explore the many hundreds of thousands of different venomous animals that may have potential as medication. He does whatever it takes to succeed. What an inspiration!

Now, I want you to identify the one thing that will make you feel like your time on earth has made a difference. What were you born to do? Who does this impact? What do you need to change in your life in order to align with your life mission?

Here are my examples:
- I was born to help people learn how to change their daily actions to save the wildlife on this planet.
- I was born to teach underprivileged children to learn to read so that they can become successful in life.
- I was born to become a successful entrepreneur to ensure a comfortable lifestyle and more options, and then allow me to become a philanthropist for cancer research.
- I was born to help young couples who want to buy their first home, and teach them how to select a home, how to manage their credit rating and how to get their loan approved and use debt wisely.
- I was born to start a sustainable farm to grow organic produce to help people have vibrant health.

You get the idea?

What we have covered in this chapter

In this chapter we covered:
- What is success for you?
- Where are you now?
- What do you genuinely desire?
- Why do you want what you want?
- What is your life mission statement?

What do successful people do? Well, they know what success they want. They know where they're at. They know why they want that success and they have some sort of a guiding philosophy for their lives.

Having clear answers to the above questions is foundational to your success. It may take time to come up with the responses, but don't worry. Just do the best that you can. Some things will become clearer as you progress through *Impossible to Fail*. You can always come back to any question if you're not totally clear. Having said that, make sure you do spend enough time reflecting on each question – don't lightly skim over them.

> *'Eight hours of sleep and eight hours of work will help you survive. What you do in the remaining eight hours can help you thrive.'*

CHAPTER 2
Understanding your beliefs

'Yes, I'm defiant. I believe that you and I are here to be successful, and I'm uncompromising about that.'

Take a few minutes to reflect on these questions.
- Do you truly believe that you can be successful?
- Do you truly believe that you can have anything you want?
- Do your behaviours reflect your beliefs?
- Are your beliefs in alignment with your goals?

I'm sure you've all heard sayings like, 'What you believe, you can achieve.' But beliefs are far more in-depth and powerful than that. In this chapter, I'll cover what beliefs are, where they reside, how they are formed, neuroplasticity and how beliefs can change, the integration between beliefs and behaviours, and perception versus reality.

Our beliefs are more powerful than we think

Understanding what beliefs are is the beginning of a shift in your success journey. What we believe becomes our reality. Therefore, it is important that your beliefs, at the deepest unconscious level, are supportive of who you want to be and what you want to accomplish.

Here are a few more questions:

- Do you feel others are responsible for your actions and circumstances?
- Do you feel that no matter what you do, you never seem to get what you want?

If someone doesn't have clarity about their beliefs, they end up living an unfulfilling and unsuccessful life. They could be going from one job to another. They could find themselves in situations they don't want to be a part of because they keep repeating their destructive patterns. Despite doing all the right things, they may feel they are not making sufficient progress.

When people are clear about their beliefs, and their beliefs support what they desire in life, they can make better decisions in line with who they are and what they want. They have better control over their situation in life because they understand the mechanics behind decision-making, hence they achieve success with much less effort. As a result, they feel more in control of their destiny by forming self-empowering beliefs.

What would it mean if you could replace your unconscious beliefs with empowering ones? Why would that help you have more control over your life? How could this information help you in crafting a proactive rather than reactive life?

Perception versus reality

'We do not see the world as it is. We see the world as we are.'
Rabbi Shemuel ben Nachmani

Your beliefs are the filters through which you see the world.

You probably already know that perception influences reality. That your world is not made of what you see, but what you believe.

Basically, beliefs are deeply formed opinions. In most cases, these opinions are not based on proven facts, yet they have the ability to guide our decisions and how we see life. Over the years, people have believed many things that have determined their thinking and behaviours, and it has since been proven that many of those old beliefs were not even necessarily true. For example, one belief in the last hundred years that has controlled people's thinking, perception, and behaviours was that IQ was fixed. If a person truly believes that, and has a limited IQ, will they reach out for opportunities? And then there's the belief some people hold that men are superior to women, which then guides their actions. If a man carries this belief at a very deep level, how would he act towards a woman?

I remember a time when my business partner Caroline and I met with a male real estate agent to talk about a potential collaboration. Caroline was taking notes through the conversation (she is brilliant at capturing notes). Fifteen minutes into the conversation, the man looked at Caroline and then me, and said, 'I can see that your secretary is great at taking notes.' It was his belief that women work in subservient roles to men. Needless to say, the collaboration never went ahead.

And then there's the belief that was popular in the eighties, that to get ahead, you needed to work hard. Yes, hard work is definitely a prerequisite to success, but it's not the only prerequisite. More and more these days, I hear of research that highlights smart and efficient work, rather than just hard work.

The list goes on. Here are some examples of commonly held beliefs people have had over time (and some still do):

- Smoking is good for you.
- Soft drinks are good for you.
- The world is flat.
- War is the only way to achieve peace.
- The customer is always right.
- Weightlifting is only for men.
- You need to work out at least an hour to get fit.
- The way to get ahead is to get good grades, go to university, and get a stable job.
- You need money to make money.
- Everything that needs to be invented has been invented.

How many of these beliefs have been proven wrong?

We now know there's more to a customer and organisation dynamic than saying the customer's always right. Once upon a time, you would walk into a gymnasium and see men doing strength training and women on treadmills or doing cardio-based exercises. Now more and more women are doing strength and endurance training. Research is showing that short workouts can produce the same outcomes as a long workout. Many successful entrepreneurs, millionaires and billionaires haven't gone through the traditional academic system. Time is more important when it comes to making money – if you put off creating wealth and investing until you have a lot of money, you can miss opportunities in investment markets. And look at how much has happened since Charles H. Duell said in 1899, 'Everything that can be invented has been invented.'

How many beliefs do you think you're personally carrying that may not be true, but at an unconscious level dictate your thinking and behaviours?

Are you even aware of these beliefs? Is it possible they are dominating your actions without you even being conscious of them?

Do they limit your progress and keep you ignorant? Are your beliefs leading you down a path of mediocrity or failure?

One way to know whether your deep-rooted beliefs are supporting you or not is to look at your life and your answers, and ask, 'Am I where I deserve to be?' If your answer is no, your undetected beliefs may not be aligned with your desires.

One thing you need to understand is that your current life is in many ways a reflection of your belief system (the collection of all the beliefs you carry), so your desires and willpower have little chance of winning against your belief system. Why? Because your unconscious beliefs can exert control that is thousands of times more powerful than what you consciously desire.

Personal development training is not only about teaching you new things, it is also about helping you get rid of old things that may be holding you back.

Often our beliefs form a perceptive layer through which we interpret what is happening around us. Imagine seeing the world through lenses that distort your view of reality. This is what's happening with a lot of people. This is why Anaïs Nin said, 'We don't see the world as it is, we see it as we are.'

If you wear blue-coloured glasses, everything will look blue. But it doesn't mean it is blue. Your perceptions, acquired through opinions, beliefs and unexamined experiences, are those glasses through which you view *your* world.

Beliefs are very powerful. In the field of epigenetics, American developmental biologist Dr Bruce Lipton pioneered work showing the connection between the energy of beliefs and the behaviour of cells at physiological level. But before we can talk about what *your* beliefs are and how to change them, we must first start with where beliefs reside and why it's important for you to understand this.

Where beliefs reside

Before we can even begin to change our beliefs, we must first understand where beliefs reside. You cannot understand beliefs unless you understand the mysterious working of the mind. Psychologist Pierre Janet originally came up with the theory that the mind has two components. Neuroscience will tell you there are more than two components in the brain, but we're not talking about the brain here. The brain is simply a broadcasting device and an organ. The mind is a whole lot more. In philosophy, theology, even science, whenever reference is made to the mind, they're essentially talking about the mental faculties of our conscious and subconscious mind, like memory, perception, intuition, imagination, will and reasoning, all of which can be strengthened with training and used intelligently to get quick and effective results.

The conscious mind is the thinking mind, whereas the subconscious mind is the feeling mind. The brain, which is the centre of the nervous system, coordinates our movements, thoughts and feelings. But these are put forth or felt through the mind. We all use the mind to think, feel and respond. The mind refers to a person's understanding of things and also their conscience. Mind also refers to a person's thought process. Dr Caroline Leaf, who has researched the human brain with particular emphasis on unlocking its vast untapped potential, determined that thinking is the *activity* of the mind, that is, the mind is what the brain *does*, so the mind works through the brain.

Our conscious beliefs can have as much of an impact on our life as our subconscious beliefs. In fact, I would argue that our subconscious beliefs can easily override our conscious beliefs. There is a story of a woman who was terribly allergic to the pollen from certain spring flowers. Because of this, her family took her to another part of the country to live where those particular flowers didn't grow. One year, they had to return to their original hometown and on the way there the plane made an unscheduled stop. The woman, thinking they had landed at her hometown, immediately broke out in hives and had such a difficult time breathing that flight staff became concerned. When she was told she was not yet in her home city, she began to breathe normally and the hives disappeared. Her mistaken belief became a kind of self-fulfilling prophecy, which created changes in her body that led to her physical discomfort.

Beliefs are known to create a placebo effect in our bodies, which can result in both psychological and physiological changes. Why do you think our breathing automatically becomes heavy when we are angry and light when we are relaxed? Can we do damage to our bodies through the way we think and what we believe? You bet.

Our subconscious mind is the basis of life and supports many of our life functions without any conscious thought. It controls our breathing, blood circulation, heartbeat, and so on. But much of the time we feed our subconscious mind with negative thoughts and limiting beliefs, and because the subconscious mind cannot tell the difference between real and imagined events, it ends up acting on our belief as if they were true.

So now that we know where our beliefs reside, let's move on to the question, 'How are beliefs formed in the first place?'

How beliefs are formed

You are not your beliefs.

Most of the time, the belief system we have adopted and inadvertently embraced has come from our conditioning – our childhood and our external environment. We have adopted many of our beliefs unconsciously. Why? Up until a certain age we have no ability to reject or choose ideas, meaning that pretty much anything said repetitively by a person of authority (or anyone around us), bypasses our conscious mind and becomes a part of our unconscious conditioning.

Activity: Firstly, write down two current beliefs that you have about money, then two about relationships and two about business and health. Secondly, try to identify where these beliefs came from. Thirdly, ask yourself if changing your current beliefs would improve your life. Finally, write down two beliefs in the area of money, relationships, business and health that would serve you and not limit your progress.

There is a reason I want you to write out the answers. Writing will cause you to think, which will then create images in your mind. As these images are created, it will stir emotions, which will then cause you to act. So, make sure that you write down your responses before moving on.

Once you've done that, we'll take a look at one of psychology's most significant findings: neuroplasticity.

Neuroplasticity and changing beliefs

Now that you understand that your beliefs affect how you think, feel and act, the question shifts to, 'Are the beliefs that I am carrying supporting or hindering my success?'

Lasting success comes from making decisions based on what is true and real, not what is false and made up. For example, someone who desires more money, but unconsciously carries a belief that having a lot of money would make them seem greedy or money-hungry, is likely to spend money as quickly as they make it in order to avoid being labelled money-hungry or greedy. If you identify that your beliefs are not constructive, and that they were shaped by family, education, or religious influences, you can change them.

One of the most significant findings in psychology in the last twenty years is that individuals can choose the way they think. For a long time, it was believed that human brains could not change. However, the science of neuroplasticity has confirmed the brain's ability to change in response to experiences. In essence, the theory of neuroplasticity is that we can consciously change the way we think. This means our brain can adapt, and due to our ability to be self-reflective and conscious, we can override any of the program beliefs in our mind by practising awareness.

The first step to changing beliefs is to identify what they are and then replace them with beliefs aligned with what we want and who we wish to become. When I was young, I believed that money was scarce and this belief resulted in me aiming small. Back then, I had not come to the realisation that I could make as much money as I wanted. When people unconsciously believe that there is limited money, they don't even consider how they can generate more. They simply say things like 'I don't have money' and they draw a line at that. That's why hidden beliefs can be so dangerous.

But the market produces billions of dollars each day and one day I thought, 'Why can't I have as much as I want?' I changed my belief and then worked out how to attract and generate more money.

How do you change your beliefs? Well, start by identifying what they are and which ones need to be changed, then replace old limiting beliefs with new enabling ones.

I mentioned the placebo effect earlier. A placebo is anything that seems to be a real medical treatment but isn't actually real. It could be a pill, a shot, or some other type of fake treatment. What all placebos have in common is that they do not contain an active substance meant to affect or impact our health.

Supported by scientific evidence, the placebo effect shows that positive beliefs promote positive outcomes. The question is not whether placebos work, but how they work. Positive beliefs can help patients with illnesses get better and negative beliefs can cause a sick person to get worse. The American Medical Association reported a case where a patient was able to fight off his cancer for a period of months when he was falsely advised that there was a pill available to heal his tumour. What he was given was a powdered pill with no medicinal qualities whatsoever. However, due to his belief that the pill cured his tumour, the tumour healed. Sadly, when he later he found out the pill was a placebo his tumour returned in a matter of days, and he died.

This is not to suggest that all beliefs work in this way, but to illustrate the power of beliefs and the impact they have on your life, mind and body. All this said, having conscious or superficial knowledge of your beliefs does not necessarily change your behaviours and results. It takes more to integrate your beliefs with your behaviours.

Integrating beliefs and behaviours

Let's talk about how you can integrate beliefs and behaviours. All personal breakthroughs begin with a change in beliefs. When you acquire new knowledge, your brain starts to create a new network of neural pathways. But simply acquiring knowledge does not change the mental programming that's already in place.

The existing programming is a result of thoughts and feelings that you have engaged in over and over again, over a long period of time. This results in creating a set of wiring in your brain that gets you to think, feel and act in predictable ways, which are all emerging from hidden beliefs carried at a deep level.

So, when you become aware of new information, it merely sits in the conscious part of your mind. The knowledge fails to change behaviours because the old mental programming is still dominant. You can read a book, go to a seminar or hear a motivational speaker and be confronted with new truth and facts, but it doesn't necessarily cause a permanent transformation. If information and knowledge alone fixed people's issues and raised awareness, the average person would be healthy, wealthy and wise. According to the World Health Organisation, worldwide obesity has nearly tripled since 1975 and one in four people are affected by a mental disorder. Additionally, Bloomberg estimated that about half the world population do not even have a financial net worth of $1,000USD. This clearly demonstrates that despite more and more information being available, people are still struggling in many key areas of their life.

Think of how many times you have witnessed people saying or doing things they know they shouldn't. Why do they do this, even though they know better?

Never before in the history of the world has the average person had access to the amount of information that is now available through the Internet. Yet, despite that, we are seeing record levels of depression, anxiety, performance problems, divorce, financial stress, bankruptcy, and business failures.

Information does not transform behaviours until we have created an integration of what we believe and how we behave. This integration can be facilitated through repetition of mental activity, which creates new neural structures to replace the old ones.

Information is not a driver of permanent change. It is only through *repeatedly thinking and feeling new thoughts* that we stop living from the past and start strengthening new neural connections in our brain. Over a period of time, this changes our behaviours to align with our dominant thoughts and feelings.

How would changing your beliefs help you change your life results? How could you use this information to identify why people don't do what they know they should be doing?

What we have covered in this chapter

In this chapter we covered:
- perception versus reality
- where beliefs reside
- how beliefs are formed
- neuroplasticity and changing beliefs
- integrating beliefs and behaviours.

What do successful people do? Successful people are aware of their beliefs and choose beliefs that serve them. They focus on what they have control over and move on when circumstances are beyond their control. They do not let an adverse event in one area of their life seep into other areas of their life.

I hope you have a better understanding of your beliefs and how they impact your life, and most importantly, how they may be hindering you from having the success you want.

'Mixed intentions, lack of clarity and conflicting beliefs, erode confidence and result in procrastination.'

CHAPTER 3
Understanding the power of your mind

*'The thinking that is keeping you struggling, is the same
thinking that will keep you from taking the action
that is necessary to break out of that struggle. That
is the paradox of the mind. The first step to mental
freedom is to understand this.*

Do you find yourself thinking negative thoughts? Do you find yourself in jobs, financial situations, events or relationships that are not ideal? Do you allow your fears to get in the way of your dreams? Do you struggle to achieve results?

It's one thing to read that minds are powerful, but do you fully understand what this means? To explore this further, this chapter covers how the mind works, how results are formed, how your unconscious powerhouse works, dealing with fears, fixed mindset versus growth mindset, and mind bugs that prevent people from becoming successful.

Most people never discover the power of their own mind, which often leads them to remain in a state of struggle. Why? Most people do not understand the difference between cause and effect.

Circumstances are never the cause. They are the effect. The outcome. The root cause of this effect and how you experience or understand it, is the mind. When people try to change their circumstances by fixing the effect, it does not work (or only works temporarily). It's the equivalent of somebody trying to become fit by joining a gym, not realising that if they do not intrinsically value health, vitality and appearance, they will not have the long-term drive to sustain their motivation. The only permanent way to transform life results is to go to the root cause – and the root cause is always the mind and the way we think.

When it comes to life success and achieving desirable outcomes (whatever they may be for you), action is important. However, action without the right mindset is not ideal. When it comes to results, 80 per cent of our results can be attributed to our mindset, paradigms and awareness. Tony Robbins, the great personal development legend, once said: 'Success is 80 per cent psychology and 20 per cent mechanics.' Isn't that a profound statement?

So, as Lao-Tzu said, 'If you correct your mind, the rest of your life will fall into place.' Renowned psychologist William James puts it like this: 'The greatest discovery of my generation is that a human being can alter his life by altering his attitudes of mind.' The message of these statements is something most, if not all, philosophers and personal development authorities worldwide agree on: when you correct your mind, you can correct your life.

How the mind works

If you ask the vast majority of people how the mind works or how it looks, it's likely you'll get a blank stare. But understanding the way your mind works is the single most important thing that you can do to create life success.

The mind is an activity not a thing, therefore not many people have a clear-cut picture to work with that explains its mental functions. Remember, the mind is not the brain, although it primarily works through the brain. We tend to think in pictures because pictures bring order to the mind – so it does help to have a picture of the mind. Without one, it is difficult to conceive the workings of this most powerful force. For instance, when you think of your car, images of your car flash across the screen of your mind. The brain cells that contain this image are activated by the thought.

Picture your mind as having two levels: the conscious and the subconscious. The top level – the conscious mind – thinks and reasons. This is where free will resides. It's where ideas are accepted and rejected and where you choose what to think. It's important to understand this because what you choose to think will eventually determine your life outcomes.

Over time, thoughts relating to fear, confidence, pain, pleasure, scarcity or abundance (which either originate in the conscious part of your mind or are accepted uncritically through outside influences), may be transferred to the lower level, the subconscious mind.

The subconscious mind is your primary powerhouse. It is your feeling mind. It has no ability to accept or reject ideas and no concept of time. Read that again. It expresses itself through words, decisions and actions. Repetitive thoughts or feelings become ingrained in this part of your mind. Over time, these thoughts and feelings become habits. We start thinking, feeling and acting without any conscious thought.

Your body is the most visible and obvious part of you, but it's simply a physical representation of your *self*. It's also the channel through which the mind expresses itself. Your body will act and behave in ways consistent with ideas, beliefs or feelings embedded in the subconscious. For example, our breathing naturally changes when we are stressed or excited – we don't consciously make this happen.

So, how does our mind work? The conscious mind reasons, thinks, chooses and rejects. But it switches off when strong feelings are triggered, and switches on the subconscious mind, the feeling mind. The conscious mind is the mind through which we use our senses of hearing, seeing, smelling, touching and tasting; the subconscious mind is where our worldview, beliefs, habits, values and our self-concept live. It's where our programming lies. The conscious mind thinks, but the subconscious mind executes its programming through mental and physical actions.

Back to cause and effect ... behaviour causes results we see through our conscious mind, but the behaviour is the secondary cause of an outcome. The primary cause (or the root cause), is in the subconscious mind. Your conditions, circumstances and environment have no bearing on your future, unless you let them.

When it comes to success, your state of mind is paramount. Your mind is either in a disorganised and confused state or a precise and corrected state. It will predominantly be in one state or the other. You cannot attract success unless order prevails in your mind first.

How you are creating your current outcomes

Results are determined by actions, decisions and behaviours. Successful people are driven by their life's calling, so let's take a deeper look into how life outcomes are formed.

Read this statement over and over again:

> *'You cannot change your life results unless you change the way you think consciously and feel subconsciously, and they are both in alignment.'*

For the first thirty years of my life, I was conditioned to live from the outside in. I blamed my personal, professional and financial situations on my parents, bosses, politicians, the economy, and the girls I dated. Now I know that my mental and emotional disposition influenced my decisions and actions. Even when we decide not to make a decision, it is a decision, isn't it?

Think about it. What determines your decisions, behaviours, attitude and actions? Your feelings. And what causes you to feel a certain way? Your thoughts. But have you ever wondered where your thoughts originated? They come from your worldview, which is the context you apply when you think.

For example, one person's context may be this: 'To become successful I must be educated through traditional education and establish a career is through a stable and secure job.' Another person's context may be: 'The best way to establish a career is through entrepreneurship.' A third person may believe careers are for average thinkers. Each of us views life through our unique context and sometimes, when people believe their context is better or more credible it gives rise to disagreement and conflict with others.

When people are unhappy with their life results, they first try to modify their actions and behaviours. Perhaps they work harder or try a different approach. Perhaps they try to change the way they act or think. But this does not work, or if it works, it's only temporary. Why? Because actions are simply a consequence of feeling. Feelings are a consequence of thoughts. And these thoughts originate from a worldview or context.

In order to change our life results, we need to go back to our roots, back to our worldview or context. Back to how we see the world. Our individual mindset is the cornerstone of who we are and what we do.

The problem is, most people are unaware of how worldview works and how it controls their life results. They don't understand that their worldview drives everything they think and do. Too often, this critical concept is not only misunderstood, but completely dismissed. This is why most people in the world fail to achieve their ideal life or produce desirable outcomes.

Trying to identify and change your worldview can be difficult or even impossible. However, a proper understanding of the mind, along with guidance from a mentor who's been through the process, can help.

*'Until you make the unconscious, conscious, it
will direct your life and you will call it fate.'*
Carl Jung

I love that quote. Before we go further, take a moment to reflect on what Jung is saying. What do you think his intent was?

Now answer the following questions:
* When was one time you changed your actions, but your results didn't change?

- What worldview or perception do you think you needed to change instead?

How your unconscious / subconscious powerhouse works

'When you understand how your subconscious works,
you can go from chance to choice.'

Our subconscious convictions and conditioning dictate and control most of our actions, and therefore, most of our results.

As I covered earlier, the subconscious mind is the feeling mind where emotions are stored and our worldview lives. Our worldview governs our actions and results in the long term. It's made up of our belief system, our habits, our innermost and deepest values (whether we're conscious of them or not), and our self-concept.

Your results are a consequence of your behaviours and actions. Your behaviours and actions are a consequence of how you feel; how you feel is a consequence of how you think. Your thoughts are a consequence of your worldview and perceptions. Therefore, in order to change your results in the long term, simply changing behaviours and actions rarely works. Your worldview must be changed in line with the results that you seek. Unfortunately, most people believe that their results are outside of their control due to fate, luck or circumstances.

Self-awareness is the foundation upon which success is built. Where does it come from? As stated in Chapter 2, simply gathering knowledge does not change behaviours or results. If it did, the world would be a different place. The answer is insight. It is insight that helps us internalise, understand and apply the knowledge that results in long term and sustainable outcomes.

Most people live 'unconsciously' and are not aware they do this. They live from other people's habitual ways of thinking. But when you understand how paradigms work, you go from chance to choice. You go from being an unconscious observer of your results to becoming a conscious architect of your results.

'The more diligent you are with your conscious and subconscious processes, the more you can master your success.'

The good news is that we can change our worldview by being aware of our thoughts, beliefs and choices, and then changing them intentionally. We do this by managing our attention. Repeatedly and consciously diverting our attention and feelings to what we want is an effective way to change our mindset. It comes back to awareness. Once you become aware of the subconscious programming running beneath your conscious thinking, you're in a position to intervene and control your results.

For example, when I became aware that I was conditioned to seek job security, because of my belief that you need to have a lot of capital to start a business, I could see why I had never ever considered becoming an Entrepreneur. I later learnt that success in business doesn't come from resources, necessarily, but primarily from resourcefulness. I came to the conclusion that if I could learn the key skills that resulted in business success, that I would be able to create revenue and profitability through sales, instead of relying on external funding. My new belief has helped me build multiple businesses from scratch, without requiring external funding or debt, and now I teach young Entrepreneurs that if they can't make money, without getting money, they will not be able to make money if they get external funding.

How to deal with fears that are holding you back

Most of us repeatedly engage with thoughts of worry, fear and anxiety. In fact, for many it is the predominant emotional disposition throughout their waking hours, without even noticing it. When we worry or feel anxious, we are using our imagination, our most powerful mental ability, in the wrong way. We are using it to create mental images of what we don't want, and bringing an imagined negative future event forward. Since we do this habitually, we end up moving towards the exact circumstances that we don't want.

What we give attention and feed energy to in the metaphysical world is likely to show up as an event or a situation in our physical world. Why? Because the subconscious will automatically lead us to what we keep giving attention, and energy to.

For most of us, fear is a habit that has replaced inner confidence in our subconscious mind. Fear shows itself in the human body through frustration, impatience, anxiety, depression and procrastination. Fear haunts people, even in happy moments, and it prevents them taking action that allows them to grow and blossom. Over time, as it becomes a habit, it can dominate a person's life and become a major cause of unhappiness and inefficiency.

'The fear of failure itself creates the feeling of failure. This in turn creates further failure and it becomes a vicious trap. Stop over-feeding your fears and you will guarantee your success.'

More than anything else, fear leads to mediocrity, cowardice and failure. And when someone acts from a place of fear, it leads to inefficient outcomes because it strangles creativity, originality and individuality. Most people cannot think clearly and rationally when they're paralysed by fear. Once fear has been planted as a habit in the subconscious mind, it becomes part of our paradigm and produces thoughts and feelings of a consistent nature. This then becomes a self-fulfilling cycle, which becomes difficult to break from as time passes. But convincing yourself that your fears are not real will not break the pattern, until you understand how fear works, and you start to monitor your thoughts.

A part of the brain, called the amygdala (also called the reptile brain), is responsible for our flight or fight response. This response is triggered any time we're about to embark on something new to us. To protect us, the amygdala creates feelings of chaos and conflict, which show up as anxiety in our physiology if left unchecked. Remember, I said earlier that the body automatically follows the mind.

Let's look at this in more detail. Our mind is a product of our current conditioning and experiences and it gives us a certain way of thinking, feeling and perceiving life, as well as creating our worldview. When we try to accommodate or entertain an idea that contradicts our current conditioning, we experience conflict and confusion. We might perceive it as a threat and feel fear. This leads to doubt, worry, and irritation, which is also referred to as cognitive dissonance. At this point, the most comfortable thing to do is reject the new idea and stick with the current worldview or perception.

This happens every time we embark on a new idea, project or event. Changing this old way of thinking can only happen if you smash through the invisible wall standing between the old outcomes and the desired outcomes. You need to recognise that this is happening and resist the urge to retreat or defend your old worldview unless it is consistently supporting you to achieve the results you want.

See the diagram below of the comfort zone. What does it say to you?

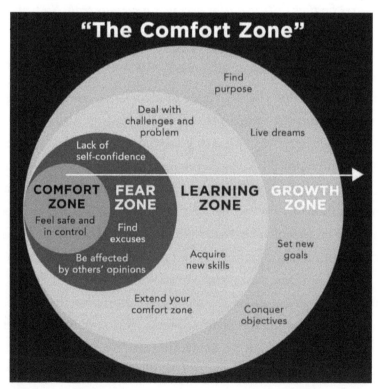

For most people, the easiest way to get rid of uneasy feelings is avoidance of things that make them feel fearful and conflicted. They don't realise that the uneasy feeling is the brain's protective response to alert them to a perceived danger.

When this happens, you can do two things. Firstly, remember that your fear is not real, but is the brain's primitive protection response designed to keep you safe. Knowing this means you don't have to be a slave to fear. Secondly, think back to times in your childhood when you had the same feeling, such as when you first learnt how to ride a bike, started a new school, went on a date, drove a car, or applied for a job. Children and young adults often seem more comfortable with acting despite fear, because they know they cannot grow and learn if they avoid these experiences. However, as we get older, many people give into their fears and stop taking actions or risks that are necessary for continued growth and learning.

Most fear is imagined. It is completely normal for you to feel this way. To paraphrase Franklin D. Roosevelt, courage is not the absence of fear, but the ability to act despite it. It has been said that over 90 per cent of our fears will never materialise. So, for a 10 per cent possibility of something going wrong, does it make sense for us to restrict going after what we desire in our heart and soul?

An understanding of the irrationality of fear is usually sufficient for us to not succumb to it, because understanding helps us get past this illusion and move towards our true goals, which lie just beyond our fears. With understanding, our feelings of worry, doubt, fear and anxiety disappear; when we are ignorant of how fear works, it's when we feel most anxious.

To become successful, it is important to act and take some level of risk despite our fear. This applies to entrepreneurship, leadership, business, money, relationships and life. World-renowned billionaire businessman Richard Branson says he had to take great risks to get *Student* magazine off the ground. These risks included calling big brands and big names like Mick Jagger and David Hockney for advertising, telling them that their rivals were already advertising and playing them off against each other. In an interview, Branson said, 'It was all great fun and we learnt so much about business by taking chances, getting things wrong, failing but getting up to give it another shot.'

You know my story. Due to my willingness to leave the nine-to-five work system, I was open to build and scale three businesses, two of which were scaled and went global. The only reason I now have businesses that serve my life and lifestyle is because I faced my fears directly and did not succumb to them.

Have you dealt with fear up until now? How will you deal with it now that you understand what fear is?

Now that you understand how fear works, why not do something that scares you this week and get through your fear barrier.

Fixed versus growth mindset

'Your mind is a force to be reckoned with.
How you use it can either make you or break you.'
Carol Dweck

Mindset was a simple idea discovered by world-renowned Stanford University psychologist, Carol Dweck. Through decades of research conducted on achievement and success, she hypothesised that when it came to success, it was not people's abilities and talents, but whether people approached their goals from a fixed or growth mindset.

People with a fixed mindset believe that basic qualities such as intelligence and talent are fixed traits. They have an underlying (and quite possibly, subconscious) belief that talent alone creates success. In other words, they may have a fixed and non-negotiable mindset, which can become a major impediment to success.

Do you know anyone who stubbornly holds on to worldviews or beliefs that are not serving them?

Are they living a successful life?

When those with a fixed mindset value inherent intelligence over effort, (consciously or not), it results in not taking enough initiative putting in the effort to develop themselves.

Contrary to this, people with growth mindsets *do not feel restricted by any factor.* They believe abilities can be developed through dedication and hard work. This is not to say they don't value intelligence and talent; it's that they don't believe brains and talents are the ultimate or only determinant of success. This type of thinking creates a mindset conducive to learning and persistence, which are essential qualities for great success.

A growth mindset person embraces challenges instead of avoiding them, persists in the face of setbacks instead of getting frustrated and giving up, and learns from criticism instead of being defeated by it. A growth mindset person sees effort as a path to development and mastery, instead of assuming that their potential is predetermined, and does not see their circumstances as permanent. And lastly, a growth mindset person finds lessons and inspiration in others' successes instead of feeling threatened. Having a growth mindset is important to achieve the success you want.

Steve Case of AOL and Jerry Levin of Time Warner were two CEOs with fixed mindsets who decided to merge their companies. Despite both being highly intelligent and having a lot in common, when the merged company ran into trouble each held on for personal power, instead of compromising and working together. The problems were workable, but because neither had a growth mindset they were unable to demonstrate flexibility in working together. The result? AOL-Time Warner ended in 2002 with one of the largest corporate losses in US history – almost one hundred billion dollars.

In the below lesson we're going to cover mind viruses and how they can stop you from living your best life.

Do you have mind viruses?

Have you ever wondered why some people still do not change their behaviours or show transformation in their life or results despite engaging in personal development, reading books, attending seminars, and watching inspirational videos?

Let me use the analogy of a computer (probably the closest invention to the human mind). Imagine you have a computer you've been using for years. You've used it to process, upload, and download information. Over the years, you have never serviced this computer. Would you agree there's a very high probability that the computer's performance has slowed down over the years? That it has potentially picked up some bugs and viruses? Now, imagine you're given new software to install in this computer. If the computer is full of viruses, will the software work successfully? It's unlikely. For the software to work in its optimum capacity, it would probably make more sense to first service the computer and eliminate existing viruses.

It's no different for our mind. Viruses for the mind include procrastination, ignorance, worry, self-doubt, fear and ego. These viruses typically prevent new information from working effectively. So, a lot of the time people who suffer these viruses of the mind and then engage in personal development training, fail to get desirable results. The mind is still riddled with viruses, so it can't work efficiently.

> *'You cannot be successful and continue to be a victim.'*
> **Maxine Waters.**

It's important to understand that success education is not only about acquiring new information and insights. It is also about removing and replacing the impediments to success.

Being aware of your mind viruses will help you identify behaviours that get in the way of thinking, feeling and acting in ways that support successful outcomes.

Reprogramming your mind

Learn how to reprogram your mind and you will have the key to your life.

Many of the ideas we have about life and how it works are erroneous. Most of what we believe about life and successfully creating results has never been tested in the real world, yet we still live our lives based on the premise that our perceptions of success and results is true. What we 'see' is not always the truth – often it is our version of the truth, which has been filtered through the belief systems that we carry.

Our subconscious mind will help us achieve anything we believe to be true.

But we need to remind ourselves that our beliefs are a part of our worldview, and we become, act, think and feel in accordance with what is programmed in our subconscious.

The good news is that we're not permanently stuck with a program that is unsupportive and not working for us. We are able to reprogram ourselves.

There are a number of tools we can use to do this. I have a morning ritual that helps align my thoughts, feelings and actions with my goals, and accelerates the rate at which I achieve my goals. I'll share that later, but here are some other ideas.

In his book *Think and Grow Rich*, Napoleon Hill talks about autosuggestion, which is basically positive self-talk. Positive self-talk works on the theory of displacement. Imagine you have a glass of dirty water and you put it under a tap, then start filling clean water into the glass. Eventually the dirty water will be displaced by the clean water. However, if you stop in the middle, the glass will still have traces of dirty water. That's why it's so important to use constant repetition to completely displace all of the negative programming that is not serving you.

When you replace unworkable thoughts with positive workable thoughts, you start to see a change in results. In information technology there is a term called G-I-G-O: garbage in, garbage out. If data fed into a computer is incorrect, when the computer is called upon to solve a problem the feedback or answer will also be incorrect. Likewise, if your personal programmer (your conscious mind) incorrectly inputs illogical, erroneous or unsupportive data, the translation of the data will be incorrect and this will start to show up in your results.

Also, it pays to remember that you cannot hold two opposing thoughts and beliefs at the same time. If you try to do that you will find that one belief will start to dilute the other belief.

You cannot believe something and doubt it at the same time.

Ralph Waldo Emerson once said, 'We become what we think about all day long.' We are walking, talking evidence of our programming. Positive self-talk is also called an affirmation, which means to validate and confirm. So, when you think a thought over and over again, you validate it and you end up confirming it as the truth. Remember, the subconscious mind has no deductive reasoning powers.

When solid foundational beliefs are created, by making a recording in the brain's neuron structure, it is processed through the subconscious mind. Once the mind has accepted it as an idea, then your thoughts, feelings and actions will automatically start to change to coincide with the idea you've impressed in your subconscious mind.

Visualisation is an effective tool you can use to reprogram your mind. Visualisation, or imagery, refers to the ability of the mind to see things in pictures. Earlier in this chapter, I said the mind thinks in images. With visualisation, we hold on to a thought to create a conscious, mental and emotional picture. Also referred to as applied imagination, visualisation is one of the most significant tools used for mindset change, and is used by actors and Olympic athletes regularly.

Arnold Schwarzenegger is a former Governor of California, multi-millionaire, actor, successful real estate tycoon, bodybuilder and five times winner of the Mr Universe title. He was asked, 'What is it that makes a person a winner and distinguishes those who succeed from those who fail?' His response was, 'It's all in the mind.'

Arnold has it made, but it wasn't always so. Once upon a time, Arnold had nothing going for him except the belief that his mind was the key to get everything he wanted.

'When I was very young, I visualised myself being and having what I wanted. Mentally I never had any doubts about it. The mind is really so incredible. Before I won my first Mr Universe, I walked around the tournament like I owned it. The title was already mine. I had won it so many times in my mind that there was no doubt I would win it. Then, when I moved on to the movies, the same thing. I visualised myself being a successful actor and earning big money. I could feel and taste success. I just knew it would all happen.'
Arnold Schwarzenegger

What makes it really interesting is that Arnold Schwarzenegger combined visualisation (vivid and clear images), with emotions, and a state of expectation.

Expectation is when you expect something and that state brings it into your reality even faster. Be honest, what do you really expect for yourself and your life? Expectation is a state of mind that does not doubt the desired result will be achieved. Visualisation is using your imagination to see yourself in a situation that hasn't occurred yet.

While most people use their imagination a lot, often they unconsciously use it for the wrong things. For example, when people worry they are using their imagination to think about things and outcomes they do not desire. People who worry constantly have reasons to worry because the exact mental pictures they mentally build keep showing up in their life. Further, by reinforcing the need to worry, what they worry about becomes a self-fulfilling prophecy.

Let's talk about how we can use affirmations and visualisation more effectively.

The first thing to do is affirm what you want with an intention statement. An intention statement is a statement of fact or belief written out in a personal, positive, present tense form, as though it is already a reality. When using an intention statement, you are saying, 'This is what I choose to be ...' (or do or have). It is a declaration of a specific desire. Intention statements are highly reliable and they work effectively where they affirm correctly.

If you listen to your self-talk, you will see concrete proof that intention statements work because they have brought you to where you are today. They either have allowed us to create what we desire or kept us from having what we desire. The key to making intention statements work is to ensure the desired intention is the true intention you set. Once an intention is installed in your subconscious mind, it is not easily removed and becomes a permanent part of your mental program until you remove it intentionally.

The key step for intention setting is to avoid making intention statements that conflict with your beliefs. Do not associate any negative feelings with what you wish to achieve. For example, if your goal is to lose weight and you think, 'Losing weight means I will have to give up my favorite food', then you're attaching a negative connotation to your intention statement. When you do that, the intention statement ceases to become effective. It is better to say, 'I'm successful' than, 'I don't want to fail.' It is better to say, 'I'm healthy' than, 'I don't want to be sick.'

The second part of affirmation is to picture the end result, also called constructing a virtual reality. Remember the theory of displacement I mentioned earlier? By picturing the end result, you are replacing the old picture with a new one. Try it. Picture yourself having or doing something you want and successfully achieving your desired result. Imagine yourself actively involved in the process.

The next thing to do is imagine the emotion that goes along with the accomplishment. Try to feel it. The subconscious mind responds to feelings more than it does to words. It doesn't respond any better to positive feelings than it does to negative feelings, it just responds to feelings. The more feeling you can put behind the thought the faster it will be impressed in your subconscious mind – feeling is crucial for impact. When you use affirmations, it's important to use the present tense, picture the end result and associate the affirmation with positive feelings and clear intention. You will start to manifest the affirmations or intentions as long as you reinforce them repeatedly. Remember, repetition is important, so if you state them only once in a while, they may not manifest.

If you simply read or state your intentions and affirmations, you can expect a 10 per cent success rate. If you also visualise the end result, you can expect about a 50 per cent success rate. But if you read, state your affirmations, picture the end result, and feel the emotion behind what you're picturing, your success rate will climb to about 80-90 per cent.

One more thing about affirmations – keep them short. They should be like a mantra, short and simple; easy to say, easy to repeat. I like to keep my affirmations to six to eight words.

When it comes to visualisation, there are two main conditions for success. One, always visualise your goal as if it's happening *right now*. Make it as real and detailed in your mind as possible. Two, visualise your goals at least once a day. Remember, there is power in constant repetition. Anything you put into your mind and nourish regularly with vivid images and emotions will produce results in your life.

Let me share with you a famous and well-documented experiment conducted by psychologist Alan Richardson. Students and basketball players were divided into three groups and tested for their ability to score baskets. Results were recorded. After this, the first group was directed to attend the gym every day for a month to practise shooting, while the second group was instructed not to practise at all. The third group was instructed to practise in a very different way – rather than set foot in the gym, group members were told to stay in their dorms and visualise themselves shooting, scoring and improving dramatically.

Each group was given a month to do as instructed and at the end of this time the three groups were tested again. The first group, which practised shooting every day, showed a 24 per cent improvement. The second group, which did not practise, showed no improvement at all. The third group, which used visualisation, improved equally well as first group.

Such creative visualisation is powerful, but it's far from magic. It involves working with natural laws that govern thoughts and energies and it's about being creative in interacting with our inner power. Properly directed, our imagination is one of the most dynamic faculties that we possess.

If you begin using visualisation straight away, you don't need to concern yourself with the specifics of how things will unfold. Remember, to turn on the lights you do not need to know how electricity works. Trust the process.

I love the quote by Lillian Whiting: 'When an object or purpose is clearly held in thought, its precipitation, in tangible and visible form, is merely a question of time. The vision always precedes and itself determines the realisation.'

I will now share with you my morning ritual. I have been doing this for years and it has helped me achieve a number of goals and consistently manifest the object of my desire. When I wake up in the morning, I start by emptying my mind with about ten minutes' meditation. This requires me to be relaxed and still, and also requires complete silence around me. When I'm trying to quiet my mind, I avoid thinking about anything and focus on my breath. If a thought comes into my mind, I gently bring my concentration back to my breath.

After meditation, I review my goals. Sometimes I rewrite them and sometimes I simply read them.

Then, I repeat affirmations consistent with my goals – I do this for about one to two minutes.

Finally, I visualise my goals with intensity and emotion (exactly as I have recommended earlier).

Try this process. But remember, as you work through the steps – relaxation, goals, affirmation, and visualisation – do it with an open heart.

Our hearts are powerful and have their own intelligence and that's why I recommend combining emotional association with visualisation. In Chapter 14, I will talk more about this heart intelligence, and why feelings (magnetic energy), and thoughts (electrical energy), are so powerful when they combine (creating electromagnetic energy).

We are powerful beings and we are creative beings. Are you finally starting to understand the creative powers you have and how you can use them to manifest the outcomes you desire? If not, review this chapter again so you have a thorough understanding of the principles discussed.

Answer the following questions:
- What life outcomes would have been different if you had understood the power of your mind better? What impact could these different results have had in your life?
- Do you feel defeated and lose hope when you have a setback, or do you see setbacks as inevitable challenges and sometimes even feel inspired by them?
- How can you see this information impacting your future results?

What we have covered in this chapter

In this chapter we covered:

- how the mind works
- how results are formed
- how the subconscious powerhouse works
- dealing with fears
- fixed versus growth mindset
- mind viruses
- practical strategies to reprogram your powerful mind.

What do successful people do? Successful people do not believe their qualities are fixed and they know they can develop any quality through effort and persistence. Successful people know they need to maintain constant awareness to avoid forming beliefs that would hijack their success. Successful people know not to label others based on their current situation, as circumstances are not permanent and can change. Successful people do not let their potential be determined by things outside of their control, such as physical characteristics, ethnicity or age, and other variables.

'If you don't consciously make choices that push you, scare you and inspire you, you will unconsciously make choices that will keep you fearful, stagnant and uninspired.'

CHAPTER 4

Discover yourself (truly knowing and understanding yourself)

'Don't forget you had your own dreams and vision before you got swayed by other people's opinions.'

Do you feel certain about your future? Are you completely clear about who you are and what you want out of life? Do you have crystal clarity on your values, strengths, passion and purpose?

Knowing who you are from the inside out is one of the most important parts of life success. You are more than your name, occupation, religion, cultural beliefs, or your educational orientation. In most cases, people have not picked these things for themselves. They have been inherited through cultural, media, religious, and educational conditioning.

Who you really are should be defined by something deeper: your purpose, passion, vision, values, strengths, and your goals.

Have you ever been in the presence of a person and sensed something very powerful about them, even if you have not spoken to them or do not know them? A person who comes across as congruent and coherent, aligned with their strengths, values, purpose, passion, and goals? A person who exudes a high level of confidence and effective decision-making?

Ever wondered why some people come across as naturally powerful? Chances are because they know who they are and their place in the world.

Unless you know exactly who you are, the basis of your decisions will always be what your family and friends say, as well as workplace or media influences. These decisions may lead you down the wrong path to situations, jobs, people and events that are not deeply fulfilling.

Discovering yourself includes:
- finding your definite purpose
- following your inner-guidance system
- knowing your strengths and values
- exploring your passion
- operating out of your zone of genius
- having a self-image aligned to who you really want to become.

Finding your purpose

In *Think And Grow Rich*, Napoleon Hill said one of the key qualities of highly successful people was a definite purpose in life.

Everyone has a purpose in life. Not everyone knows what theirs is.

Your purpose is your compass on your life's journey. Once you understand your purpose, you can dedicate your life to doing what you love to do. You will know what you're good at and will set goals and directions for your life decisions consistent with your purpose. Knowing your purpose will allow you to pursue your dreams easier and faster.

Without purpose, you're in danger of drifting along without knowing if any of the roads you choose are right or wrong. It's like a ship without a compass; even if it's a state-of-the-art vessel, it's still likely to sink.

Your purpose can fall into one or more of the following categories:

- career
- relationships and family
- civic duty
- spirituality.

For most people, it's career related.

Benjamin Franklin is often attributed with saying, 'Most men die at twenty-five and aren't buried until they're seventy-five.'

The quote means that most people give up on their dreams before they're thirty, and then they spend the rest of their lives drifting, living day-to-day and trying to get through the days and the weeks, rather than living a deliberate life filled with purpose and passion.

For the first thirty years of my life, I wasn't living my true purpose. And although I achieved great success in many areas, it came incrementally and slowly, and with a lot of frustration. To be honest, it felt like I was swimming upstream against the flow. When I finally discovered my purpose, I felt that I was taking quantum leaps towards the outcomes I really wanted in my life.

Until you're clear about your life's purpose, calling, mission or destiny, you will drift in life from day-to-day like I did. But once you find your purpose, you will be future-focused instead of getting caught up in today living with its worries and frustrations. You will start thinking excitedly about possibilities related to your mission and calling, which will create a higher level of energy and lower time-wastage on trivial tasks. When you're clear about and committed to achieving your life's purpose, you will propel your success in life.

So, how do you find it? Typically, your life purpose is something consistent with your natural gifts, talents and interests that you gravitate to effortlessly. It can be time-consuming to discover if you haven't spent time connecting with yourself and determining your natural interests and gifts. Many people have been conditioned to choose careers based on practical considerations such as security, money, longevity and status, and in doing so, they have found themselves locked into jobs and careers inconsistent with their true gifts, talents and calling. If you've made a career decision based on mind-thinking rather than heart-intelligence, it is quite likely that you feel unfulfilled and yearn to do what you were naturally born to do, despite any superficial success you've attained. That is what happened to me.

The Passion Test by Janet Bray Attwood and Chris Attwood talks about the effortless path to discovering your life purpose. The authors maintain that whenever you are faced with a choice, decision or opportunity, you should always choose in favour of your passion. So, one of the ways to determine your purpose is by first identifying your passion because your passion will lead you to (or hint at), your life's purpose. When you're truly passionate about doing something, you don't have to try too hard to give it attention. When challenges come up, they will not deter you, because it is something you have a natural desire to do.

The clearer you are about what you want to do, the more this will show up in your life. Your brain is happier when you're focused on doing things you love. Scientific research has proven that when you do things you love, your brain releases high levels of dopamine, endorphins and stress-reducing hormones. And now, science has also suggested that doing what you love boosts your immune system. In contrast, you're more likely to suffer headaches, migraines and other illnesses if you're drifting or chasing money without passion or purpose.

Ask yourself the following questions:
- Which things or conversations charge you up?
- What do you love talking about?
- What are you more likely to take risk with?
- What do you secretly dream of?
- What would you do for free?
- What sparks your creative juices?
- What are your unique strengths? (Ask your friends and family.)
- What are you naturally good at doing or gifted at?
- What is extremely important to you?
- What do you think you were born to do?

- What have your life experiences and the blend of all your good and bad experiences prepared you to do today?
- What makes you lose track of time or ignore your bodily needs like going to the toilet or eating or drinking?

Now, think of some instances in your childhood where you did things and felt like you were in your element. Remember those times you were doing something you loved and time seemed to go really quick? That is usually a hint about what you're meant to do.

Try not to think in terms of existing careers and job descriptions. Let your mind wander and think openly and freely. Just because there isn't a job description or an existing career for your current passion and interests doesn't necessarily mean there is no career for you. In fact, many people have designed their own careers in very specific niches based on the unique blend of experience, skills, talents, and strengths that they have.

William Bryant once said, 'Destiny is not a matter of chance, it is a matter of choice.'

It's not something to be waited for, but rather something to be achieved.

Next up, I'll talk about a concept called your inner guidance system. Knowing how to tap into this intuition is a secret successful people have used for many years.

Your inner guidance system

Imagine how confident, enthusiastic and secure you would feel, if you teamed up with a partner able to supply you with everything you need in life. Imagine this partner could give you solutions to your problems, point out exciting new opportunities, and show you what you could do about those opportunities, as well as provide you with wise and reliable advice when you need it.

Here's the thing: we already possess such a partner within us – it's called our intuition. It's interesting how many of us are conditioned to seek all solutions from outside, forgetting that by practising self-reliance, most answers, if not all, can be found within us.

Many great achievers – from business leaders and politicians to athletes and artists – trust and use their intuition to make key decisions. The ability to come up with inspired ideas, and make smart and wise decisions, is one of the main secrets of success. It is a hallmark of someone who has worked on their inner guidance system.

I've come across some very successful people who do this. There's one person I can't name, but he is a prominent and highly successful Australian I had lunch with once. He told me the primary basis for many of his decisions was going with his gut feel. He could not think of any major decision he had made without first checking within himself. That doesn't mean he didn't do due diligence, or didn't look at research or consult others; it means that he never allowed his decisions to be driven only by external knowledge, opinions, due diligence or measurable data. He's not the only one. Mozart said he tapped into his inner inspiration; Socrates said he was guided by his inner voice. Einstein, Thomas Edison, Guglielmo Marconi, Henry Ford are among the highly successful men and women who have attributed their success to their intuitive senses.

In the *Harvard Business Review*, Henry Mintzberg describes a study where he researched high-ranking corporate executives. He found most constantly relied on hunches to cope with problems too complicated for rational thinking. Not all problems had solutions in facts and figures or data. He concluded that success did not lie in the narrow-minded concept called rationality, but in a blend of clear-headed logic combined with powerful intuition.

When I had the original idea for The Successful Male movement, I understood that it was a movement that was needed, but it had to be executed in a particular way. Well-meaning friends, colleagues and experts gave me a lot of advice. Some advice was good, some was great, and some was average. But here's the thing: even when I thought the advice was good and I could have decided based on the person's expertise and their track record, I ultimately consulted my inner guidance system to make my decisions. Many of the decisions I made about The Successful Male were almost like a sixth sense. I knew in my heart that I had to do things a certain way; the movement had to look a certain way and have a certain feel. I believe that when we silently consult our inner guidance system, it can be amazing in guiding decision making.

Fast food tycoon Ray Kroc is another notable example of a businessman who made decisions against the advice of his lawyers and accountants around him. It was he who turned McDonalds into a franchise. He said he sensed in his funny bone it was a certain thing – and he was right. McDonalds is obviously a certain thing – it's one of the most successful franchise businesses in the world.

Paying attention to your inner guidance system will enable you to make better decisions and lead to more creative ideas and deeper insights. Sometimes your intuition will guide you to your destination or your goals in the smoothest and the fastest way possible. Those people who seem to be in the right place at the right time and have good things happen to them with uncanny frequency? They're not just lucky. They've developed an intuitive sense of what to do and when to do it. The inner guidance system that they tap into allows them to go beyond the obvious and consider fresh and innovative possibilities that probably didn't exist before.

When we act on ideas coming from intuition, rather than letting them slide, the probability of achieving success can be quite high. Your inner guidance system supplies you with a lot of information, as well as instructions on when and how to use that information. Cognitive specialists have studied how information flows through the brain, yet the brain only tells us a small fraction of what the mind takes in. Less than 1 per cent ever actually reaches our conscious awareness. It's staggering to think how much we are missing. Look at it this way: your conscious mind only knows and understands your personal experiences and knowledge, but sometimes your intuitive senses pick up frequency from a world that exists outside of your mind, much like a radio device has the potential to broadcast music or documentaries by picking up frequencies.

If you accept the fact that tapping into your inner guidance system is a wise strategy, there are a few steps that will help you do this.

Firstly, spend a few minutes affirming you do have a powerful mind, with a lot of answers and solutions already existing in your memory bank. Believe it. Have the emotional conviction to know this is true. Take note of the examples I have mentioned and look for more. Be intentional about this, because when you are intentional your attention will focus on tapping into your intuition. The good thing is, (and I know this by personal experience), the inner guidance system gets stronger with experience, recognition and use. The more you tap into it, the stronger it becomes. So, remind yourself over and over again of the existence and potential of your inner guidance system.

Next, clearly state what you're looking for, what goal you wish to achieve, what answers or solutions you are seeking, or what specific problems you would like to solve. For example, in a relaxed voice, tell your mind, 'This is a challenge I'm having.'. Then say, 'I command you to provide me an answer to this problem.' Repeat this as if instructing your mind. Don't let your conscious mind interfere, or allow yourself to feel pressure or confusion by trying to figure out the answers consciously.

Also, fill your mind with a sense of faith or expectancy that the correct answer will come to you. Confidence and faith are not just attitudes. They're vibrations of energy that will attract solutions and answers just as a magnet attracts metal filings. When your mind vibrates with the belief that answers are coming to it, those answers will naturally come. How do you do this? Imagine what you would feel like if you knew the answers and you already had the solutions. Do this before you receive the answer. Let your mind play with that mood in a very relaxed way. Try it before going to bed or when you first awake – if you think about it, the entire process only takes five to ten minutes. With constant practise, you will start to have epiphanies, ideas, 'a-ha' moments or hunches. Pay attention to those hunches because this is your inner guidance system trying to communicate with you.

A lot of our insecurity comes from the sense that we don't have all the answers. But if you're prepared to tap into your inner guidance system, you will find you sometimes have a sense of *knowing* that can guide you in making decisions.

Knowing your values

*'When your values are clear,
decision-making becomes easy.'*
Walt Disney

Our propensity to make bad decisions is significantly reduced when we understand what is important to us – or what our values are. Knowing your values is essential for discovering your purpose and revealing your destiny.

There are two types of values. The first primary, or natural, values refer to values we are born with. Science cannot explain why different things are important to different people and why we all do not all desire to do or have the same things. The things that are important to us from the time we become conscious are our primary values and we tend to naturally and willingly engage in activities that align with them.

The second type is acquired values, which are formed as a result of what we perceive to be missing the most in our childhood. Whatever you believe is missing in your life becomes important and therefore valuable to you. This may result in you spending your time, money and energy on the thing you perceive to be missing.

Sometimes we end up valuing that thing at the expense of other things. For example, if you perceive yourself as lacking love, then you will probably invest a lot of time examining methods to help you find love. Keep in mind that this doesn't mean you do lack love, but you *perceive* you do, and that's how it might become an acquired value. If you perceive that you lack friends or a social life, you may invest time and effort in finding ways to meet people.

We tend to focus our time and attention on what ranks highest on our values list, while giving less time to things we perceive to be of less value. No one wakes up in the morning wanting to be less successful, accomplished, knowledgeable, happy or enthusiastic. Innately, we all want to be more, do more and have more. It's a part of our essential human nature.

*'Put your hand on a hot stove for a minute, and
it seems like an hour. Sit with a pretty girl for an
hour, and it seems like a minute. That's relativity.'*
Albert Einstein

It's exactly the same thing with values. When we're doing something fulfilling, something that's important to us or makes us feel worthy, time flies. But, when we're doing something less inspiring, something we do not perceive to be of high value, time drags. That's why it's so important to identify your values if you want to live a fulfilled and inspired existence.

I have found that it is better to align your life, lifestyle, and career decisions to your primary values because it provides a sustained sense of fulfillment. Aligning your decisions and goals to acquired values can create a sense of achievement, but not always a sustained sense of fulfillment.

Although you may value many things, it's good to know your top three to five values. Those top values then become the basis of your decisions. When you are not clear on your values, you're making decisions based on hearsay, opinions, cultural conditioning, media, and current trends, but when you know your values there is consistency in your decision-making. This consistency leads to a high level of success.

How do you identify your values?

The first question to ask yourself is, 'How do I fill my space?' Look around your home, your room or your office. What have you surrounded yourself with? Books? Learning materials? Electronic gadgets? Photos of family and friends? Whatever they are, these items are indicative of what you value. We tend to surround ourselves with what is valuable to us.

The second question is, 'How do I spend my time?' When you have spare time, how do you use it? Do you learn something new or socialise or do physical activities? Once again, all of these things provide insight into what we value the most.

The third question is, 'How do I spend my energy?' What do you give your energy to? What activities do you do? Again, that is an indication of what you love and what energises you. These activities could be work related as long as this is something you're willingly doing. Think back over the past thirty days and reflect on where you've willingly poured most of your focus and energy.

Another question is, 'How do I spend my money?' People tend to exchange money for the things that they value the most. Do you find that you're spending more and more money on learning, or do you spend more on looking good? Maybe on clothes and accessories? Do you spend money on travel or meeting people or possessions or adventures? Again, all of these things are indicative of what you value the most.

The fifth question to ask is, 'Where am I most organised?' Where we are most organised is also indicative of what we value the most. For example, if you don't enjoy cleaning your dishes and you're disorganised when it comes to putting them away, obviously dishes or an organised kitchen are not of highest value to you.

Ask yourself the sixth question: 'Where am I most disciplined?' We tend to be more disciplined in areas consistent with our values, and less disciplined in areas not consistent with our values.

The seventh question is, 'What do I think about a lot?' What do you think about when you're by yourself or even with people? Do you think about sport? Entertainment? Love? Consumerism? Do you think about accomplishing things? Again, all of these things are an indication of what you value.

Now ask yourself, 'What do I talk to myself about? And what do I talk to other people about?' If you were to ask the three people you're closest with what you talk a lot about, their responses may reveal what you value. If you're talking a lot about people or about money, these things are indicative of your values.

When you're encouraged to set goals, what are the first three goals that come to mind? Are they about career? Money? Success? Better relationships? Or are they about more time, flexibility, or freedom? Whatever your top three goals are, these indicate the things you value the most.

Finally, ask yourself, 'Who inspires me and why?' The answer is a good indication into what you value. If you find yourself being inspired by people like Elon Musk, Richard Branson or Steve Jobs, it's quite possible you're inspired by business or entrepreneurial success. If you find yourself inspired by people like Nelson Mandela or Martin Luther King (I'm highly inspired by them, as well as Malcolm X and Gandhi), then that means you're inspired by legacy, by creating a movement or inspiring people. Who inspires you is a good indication of what you value.

Clarifying our values is a refinement process. It's not too different from peeling away the layers of an onion. We start with what we have been taught to value and then we ask, are we valuing this because we perceive a lack, or because it's something we truly desire that makes us happy?

Regardless of the reasons behind them, knowing your values can significantly contribute to your success.

Understanding your strengths

I love this quote by Steve Jobs: 'Your work is going to fill a large part of your life, and the only way to be truly satisfied is to do what you believe is great work. And the only way to do great work is to love what you do. If you haven't found it yet, keep looking. Don't settle. As with all matters of the heart, you'll know when you find it. And, like any great relationship, it just gets better and better as the years roll on.'

When people want to become more successful, they typically try to identify and correct their weaknesses. In this lesson we're going to focus on your strengths, instead of your weaknesses, so you can leverage your strengths to create the life you want.

Previously, I covered the importance of determining your passion. But if you also seek to discover what your natural strengths are, decision making can become easy. If you choose a career that's in alignment with your passion, purpose, values, and strengths, imagine how successful you will be.

When it comes to our values, interests and passion, we can be pretty good at determining what they are without help. But when it comes to strengths, talents and skills, we sometimes require feedback from others. One of the first ways to identify your strengths is to contact three to five people – friends, family, colleagues – who know you extremely well. Ask them the following questions and tell them to be completely honest in their answers.

- What do you see as my strengths, talents and skills?
- What type of work or career do they think I would be best at (and why)?
- Do you think I have strengths I'm unaware of, and if so, what are they?

If you ask five people these questions and they have similar responses, there's a pretty good chance these responses indicate your strengths.

Here are some other questions to consider:
- Which subjects did you excel in at school?
- What did you like about those subjects?
- Which subjects or classes did you struggle with?
- What caused you to struggle with those subjects or classes?
- Which activities motivate and inspire you, and make you lose all concept of time?
- What type of activity feels natural or effortless to you?
- Are you aware of any hidden strengths or talents you haven't developed yet?
- Were you discouraged from developing any natural strengths or talents? If so, what are they?

In my case, I loved English grammar at school and looking at my career now, I do a lot of writing, speaking, training, and coaching. It makes sense that I have chosen a career that requires me to use my vocabulary, grammar, and speaking skills because it is in line with my strengths.

Now that you have done this exercise, is there any way to tie in what you've discovered about yourself to what you're currently doing in your life and what you would like to do in the future? What action can you take to incorporate more of your strengths, talents, and skills into your future job, career, or life in general?

Exploring your passions

I cannot stress enough the importance of understanding your underlying passion. If you can align your career path, calling, or vocation with passion, you can increase your success in quantum leaps.

These days, many people are disconnected with themselves, often to the point that they're uncertain about their passions in life. But when you are clear, what you want will show up in your life (to the extent that you have clarity).

Have you ever noticed that highly successful (and fulfilled) people almost always talk about what they love to do? If you ask them for good career advice, they're likely to tell you to do what you love, to perform at a high level of success and effectiveness.

In previous lessons we talked about the importance of purpose. But purpose is only the initial ingredient of success. Purpose by itself is not sufficient to bring you what you want in terms of success and fulfillment. You also need passion.

'Passion combined with purpose is a formidable combination.'

Numerous studies of highly successful people indicate a high correlation between passion, believing in a calling, enjoying a job and performing at a high level. Passion is very different from a goal. Passion is how you decide to live your life, whereas a goal is something that you aim for.

Some people assume that passion is an energetic or romantic, exciting, sexy emotion which has a broad appeal without any pragmatic implications. But passion is not just some nice-to-have soft skill. It has practical implications and significance for the outcomes and the success that you produce into your life.

Every individual in this world is unique. There is not one person who has the exact blend of purpose, passion, values, strengths, and goals as you. Once you completely understand this and identify your unique blend of gifts and talents, you do not need to compete with anyone else. Your passion is based on what you love in life: things that are important to you, that light you up when you're doing them or talking about them.

Author Mark C. Thompson interviewed dozens of corporate and government leaders around the world and concluded that there was one differentiating factor of successful leaders everywhere: passion. When work is aligned with passion, life can be joyful, delightful, exciting, and fulfilling. Research also shows that the brain is more productive and happier when we are focused on doing what we love. The more you focus on doing what you love, the more parts of the brain's limbic system where the destructive emotions of fear, anger, depression and anxiety reside are controlled. When this happens, we think more clearly because the learning centres in our brain light up. At the same time, the parts of the limbic system that generate positive chemical releases such dopamine, endorphins and a variety of stress-reducing hormones and neurotransmitters are turned up. Research also suggest that the more time we do things we love, things that make us feel alive, the more the immune system is boosted as those positive effects of the stress-reducing chemical releases flow through. And when we are passionate about something, we have more energy to pursue tasks.

I'm a passionate individual. I don't even consider embarking on projects I do not feel passionate about. There is a huge difference between the days when I was in a corporate job working just for money (or settling for jobs), compared to where I am today. Now, anything I do is completely aligned with my passion. My body produces a very high level of energy and I sleep only four to five hours a night (I'm not suggesting you do this); I rarely get tired and I pack a lot into every day. My mind produces an enormous amount of creativity. It doesn't mean that I'm exceptional or more capable than anyone else. It's simply a consequence of identifying my passion and choosing a career and calling aligned with it.

Unfortunately, many people are sceptical to the notion that passion and career can be connected. When people are confronted with another's passion and success, I've heard remarks like, 'Oh, that's easy for them, they've made it. It's not so easy for me because I have bills to pay.' What a lot of these people don't realise is that connecting work and passion is what made the others successful in the first place.

Yes, making this happen will require you to make some tough decisions – maybe some trade-off decisions, compromises or sacrifices. But I want you to consider this: if your work or career is not aligned with your passion, you will potentially spend 60 or 70 per cent of your life engaged in uninspiring work that fails to unleash your creativity.

Now, a lot of people will justify their choice of jobs or careers using extrinsic factors such as money, respect, position, status, convenience, and so forth. However, research shows these factors only provide short-term motivation. So, in the beginning, people get excited about the job with the good salary, location, title, perks, and so on. But in the long term, when they find themselves stuck in a career or job not aligned with their true passion, they feel a growing sense of frustration and stress, which eventually leads to disease, chronic fatigue syndrome, depression, anxiety, migraines, and more. They end up spending the money they're making on health and medical issues.

The problem with using logic only when it comes to career choice, is that once you have made that choice and lived with it for a while, you might find it enormously difficult to radically shift the course and dramatically change your career. But if you also consider passion when making long term choices, and consider intrinsic factors (like belonging, contributing, strong feelings, causes you believe in, relationships, and other intangible or measurable things), then that assists with long-term motivation. I'm not suggesting that extrinsic factors are not important in career selection, just that they alone are not sufficient when choosing your career or calling.

When you choose work based on extrinsic and intrinsic factors *and* passion, you place yourself in a position for best performance, for an extended period of time. Accept that you're unlikely to become rich or famous or lead an organisation within the first few years – it can often be a long slog before people attain many of their external goals, even in some of the most lucrative careers. Why do I say this? If it's going to take time slogging, determination, and persistence, wouldn't it be better to choose something you enjoy? In the short-term, external motivators will help, but the rewards will soon lose their appeal. And when you're involved in the day-to-day grind, external rewards fail to motivate us to perform at our best capacity.

Many people say things like: 'I would love to do something aligned with my passion, but I don't have the luxury'; 'I'm too pressed for money or time'; or 'I desperately need a job.' All of this is understandable. We all have responsibilities and obligations in regards to paying bills and taking care of loved ones. But you want to be careful not to adopt a belief system and mindset that traps you in a vicious cycle, one in which you stop considering what you enjoy because it's easier to avoid having to make tough decisions. Yes, it can take time to determine what your passion is, but it is absolutely worthwhile. Figuring out what you're passionate about and aligning that with your career has little downside, but a lot of upside. When you're passionate about your work, you operate from a place of hopes and dreams, rather than fears and insecurities.

I regularly encourage people to write down what they're passionate about, but many give up on the exercise if they can't immediately see how they can pursue their passion. I'm going to ask you to do this in a moment, but when you do, don't worry about the *how*, just think about the *what*. As you progress through *Impossible to Fail*, we will talk about how the mind works to find solutions, thinking outside the square and constructing neurons in your frontal lobe area to work out logical paths to an outcome. But for now, when you're trying to determine your passion, don't be afraid of thinking big and don't over-analyse it. In their book *The Passion Test*, authors Janet Bray Attwood and Chris Attwood suggest that passion comes out of your heart's impulse and what comes out of your heart is more likely to be the truth than what you analyse mentally and intellectually. For those who choose to play it safe, remember this – you could potentially end up living your whole life from a place of less enthusiasm, energy, creativity, excitement, and passion. When you operate from that space, it's unlikely that you'll play the big game in life.

I am passionate about:
- running a global movement that can transform the lives of millions of people
- having a global impact
- developing myself as a world-class leader

- financial success (because I understand what money can and can't do for people)
- spiritual and deep growth
- connecting with people.

So, ask yourself the following: What would you do with your time if you were living your ideal life? Make a list of at least ten things.

And now, here are some other questions to reconnect you with your passion. I've used the word reconnect deliberately. When we are young, we know what we naturally gravitate towards and what we enjoy, but as we grow up we make more intellectual decisions and disconnect with the feelings that come from our heart. This is especially prevalent for men.

Write down the answers to these questions:

If you only had one year to live, how would you spend it? What does that answer tell you about what you enjoy and what you're really passionate about?

- If you had enough money to do whatever you wanted, what job or career would you choose?
- If you knew success was guaranteed, what career path would you pursue?
- Which accomplishments would like to tell your children and grandchildren about? How would you explain your career and life choices?
- If someone asked you how to find their passion, what would you tell them?

Now let's look at how you see yourself affects the decisions you make and the results you produce.

How do you see yourself?

How you see yourself is more important than how others see you.

This doesn't necessarily equate to how you see yourself physically, although that may be a part of it. What I'm referring to is self-concept – how you see yourself physically and mentally, and how you perceive your personality and place in the world. Your self-concept is critical to success because it is linked to your self-esteem and confidence. It is about how you feel about yourself and how you believe others see you. These are closely related – if you have a poor opinion of yourself, your self-esteem when interacting with people will also be affected. Self-concept affects your behaviours, thinking, and how you connect with others. People will respond to you either positively or negatively, according to how you present yourself. And how you present yourself will always be consistent with how you see yourself.

You have to understand that your evaluation of yourself will, in most cases, determine how others evaluate you. Your evaluation is embedded in thoughts and beliefs that you have about yourself, which may be distorted or inaccurate and come from cultural orientation, childhood conditioning, and multiple other factors.

Maxwell Maltz wrote an excellent book called *Psycho-Cybernetics* in 1960 in which he observed the impact of a strong self-image and its ability to achieve goals, success, and happiness. Maltz says we are engineered as goal-seeking organisms. We are built to conquer our environment, solve problems, and achieve goals. But if we have no goals, or our goals have no meaning, we go around in circles, feeling lost, aimless, and purposeless. We feel that life is not worthwhile, but what this means, is that we have no personal goals that are worthwhile.

How do you see yourself? Successful? Accomplished? Charismatic? Confident? Influential? Do you see yourself as struggling? Unhealthy? Average? Socially awkward? The answer will carry through in your thoughts, feelings, and behaviours, meaning that you will live out that image that's embedded into the subconscious part of your mind. It is nearly impossible for people to outperform their own self-concept.

Think about how someone would act if they saw themselves as an 'average suburban dad'. What would they wear? How would they talk? How would they present themselves? What kind of opportunities would they pursue? What kind of risks would they take? What kind of magazines would they read? Now, contrast that with someone who views themselves as a visionary world leader. How would they act? How would they dress? How would they speak to people? Do you see that self-concept affects everything you do?

Your self-concept also places an invisible barrier to your accomplishments. Imagine a person who sees themselves as average applying for high paid job. Imagine a person who sees themselves as unattractive approaching a person they considered more attractive. Imagine a person who places low self-worth on themselves starting an entrepreneurial venture – will they do it with enthusiasm and confidence? If you undertake a task inconsistent with your self-concept, your mind will trigger the cybernetics mechanism. The cybernetics mechanism is similar to ducted heating systems in homes, where a thermostat is set and triggered once the temperature in the room drops. If you're about to take on a challenge, risk or action that's inconsistent with your self-concept, your mind triggers the cybernetics mechanism and gets you to engage in self-sabotaging behaviours. Once this happens, you can't successfully accomplish the task.

It is so important that before you embark on a challenge that is far greater than your self-concept allows, you work on developing a self-concept that is healthy and successful, as well as conducive to, and in alignment with, what you want to accomplish.

Most people are not really aware of their own self-concept. They act in a way consistent with the self-concept they don't understand and then wonder why they're not getting the results a successful person should get.

The good news is that you can set or change your self-concept, regardless of your age. This process starts with awareness about your current thoughts and moves on to retraining your mind, to remove mention of, or focus on, any negative statements or thoughts about yourself. Negative thoughts and words shrink and restrict our self-concept, so do not pay too much attention to the failures of your past or think about the limitations of the future. Instead, think about the present moment and who you're going to become.

When you start to build a self-concept conducive to who you want to become, over time you will embed that new self-image in your mind. Once that self-concept is embedded into the deepest part of the subconscious mind, your brain and body will automatically engage in actions and behaviours to match that self-concept. It starts with being aware of what you say about yourself, so you can make the effort to change it. Your subconscious mind will know what to do, but it needs to be directed in a way that brings you success and happiness. Your success depends on doing this. If you don't work on this, you'll chip away at your confidence and cause self-doubt, but if you make a conscious effort you can release fears about self-doubt and failure, and embrace success. So, work on your beliefs to ensure they coincide with the healthy and successful self-concept that matches the person you want to be.

Here are ten exercises to improve your self-concept:

1. List what you like about yourself. This list may include your appearance and personality, but it can also include your skills and talents.

2. Change your negative thoughts to positive ones by focusing on the positive and letting go of the negative things in your past.

3. When someone compliments you, write it down. Do not deflect the compliment – this happens when you believe the compliment is inconsistent with your self-image.

4. Use positive affirmations such as *I'm capable, I'm successful, I'm a leader, I'm a world-class consultant* (fill in the blanks with whatever it is you do for a living). Affirmations, if repeated regularly, will help you build a new self-image.

5. Observe the feelings that make you question yourself, like self-doubt. But don't react to the feeling. Simply ask yourself whether the feeling is accurate and consider why the feeling has been triggered.

6. Make changes to aid success, for example in your clothing, appearance and behaviours. Consider modelling people

who are successful in the areas that you wish to be successful in. You don't have to emulate them, just observe how they interact with others, how they dress, how they handle complex situations, and so on.

7. Accept things about yourself that are true and learn to think about them in a positive way. If someone thinks that you're strange, remind yourself that strange behaviours also have some positives. Remember, we choose how we perceive certain behaviours in ourselves, and many times, we tend to perceive messages from others to be negative ones. Try to see the positive in things that you may not necessarily consider positive about yourself. Also, accept criticism constructively so you can move forward and improve yourself.

8. Get fit and healthy. You will look and feel better. The psychological benefits of exercise are well known. Try not to be ashamed of your body. Instead, appreciate and look after it. Remember, your body is where you live and it allows you to experience so much. So many people are ashamed and critical of their body. Instead, be grateful for your body.

9. Don't be limited by your current internal image. Step outside of it and break free. It doesn't have to control you or keep you down. Acting differently will change how others respond towards you, but it takes time to change the inside. Some people say, 'Fake it till you make it.' I say, have faith until you make it. Faith means believing that once you have embedded a positive self-concept, your behaviours and actions will automatically change to become consistent with that self-concept.

10. Read inspiring books and surround yourself with supportive people. Doing this boosts self-esteem and confidence, as well as skills for communication, all of which helps you build a positive self-concept.

In 1900, William James, one of America's earliest and greatest psychologists, said: 'The greatest discovery of my generation is that a human being can alter his life by altering his attitudes of mind.' Remember, the results you're achieving in life now are a direct reflection of your current self-concept. When you make positive changes to that, improvements will automatically be reflected in your results through the changes in your behaviours and actions.

Finally, try this visualisation exercise: Imagine your life is a movie. You are the director, producer, actor, and financer. What does your life-movie look like? What kind of movie is it? What is the plot like? What is the journey like? And what would you like the ending to be? Remember, you are the main character, not a supporting actor. You are the star and the writer of the story.

My life-movie is an inspirational one. A feel good movie. It's about a man who goes from being a struggling employee to an inspiring global speaker and mentor.

Visualising activities will help you *feel* what it could be like to design a life consistent with a successful self-concept – the person you want to become and the life you want to have.

What we have covered in this chapter

In this chapter we covered:
- finding your purpose
- following your inner guidance system
- knowing your values, understanding your strengths
- exploring your passions
- developing a successful self-concept.

In the next chapter, I'll cover some foundational achievement fundamentals.

> *'If you are lacking energy, there is a pretty good chance that you are lacking passion.'*

CHAPTER 5
Foundational achievement fundamentals

*'People who overlook, reject or ignore you are not meant
to be a part of your success journey.'*

Success is something almost everyone wants and spends a lifetime hoping for. Some never find it, while others realise it early in life. In today's super-competitive marketplace, high achievers follow a systematic approach to their success. There are certain achievement principles you need to understand to lay a strong foundation for life success. These principles are time tested and applied by hundreds and thousands of men and women to achieve a brighter future. The fundamentals in this chapter can take you as far as you dare to dream.

These fundamentals may be simple, but they're effective. It's important to understand that achievement fundamentals are not about gimmicks, hollow solutions or magic bullets. They are proven and time tested.

Accepting total responsibility for your situation

'You must take personal responsibility. You
cannot change the circumstances, the seasons,
or the wind, but you can change yourself.'
Jim Rohn

One of the most pervasive myths in our culture today is that we are somehow entitled to a great life. That somehow, somewhere, someone – not us – is responsible for our results, circumstances, and success.

The real truth is this: there is only one person responsible for the life you are living. You guessed it. That person is you.

In order to become successful, you have to embody the perspective of taking 100 per cent responsibility for everything you experience in your life. Now, what happens a lot of the time is that we either take part responsibility, or in many cases, we take no responsibility. But even when you are not directly responsible for something that happens to you, by taking it on, or by acting like you are 100 per cent responsible, you end up empowering and differentiating yourself.

When you take 100 per cent responsibility for your results, achievements, the quality of your relationships, health and fitness, income and debts, feelings, and actions, you start to feel empowered instead of overwhelmed because you understand that control over your life lies with you.

Taking 100 per cent responsibility for your life has two components. The first component is taking ownership of your behaviour and its consequences. Until responsibility is accepted for actions and failures, it is difficult to develop self-respect. It is also difficult to gain respect from others. All people make mistakes, poor choices and fail to act when they know they should. Even when we don't make a decision, we make a choice. But you're not the first person, and neither will you be the last, to fall short in the personal behaviour department. From time to time, we all do it.

The second component of taking 100 per cent responsibility is indirect responsibility. It involves moving beyond yourself and acting to help situations around you – you know, that call for assistance that you are not directly responsible for. In this case, the key is not that you feel you're taking it on, but you feel there is something you can do about it in a way that attracts respect and attention. Accepting responsibility, both personal and indirect, helps define character. When the moment comes to choose responsibility, what you do or don't do, tells others who you really are.

Avoiding responsibilities only works to your advantage in the short term. You may get away with keeping your mouth shut about something you've done, blaming someone else, or not having to deal with the consequences of your actions. Make no mistake, eventually this poor choice will catch up with you, and most times, it will cause more pain and failure than if you had stepped up to the situation when it happened and did something about it.

> *'When you blame others, you*
> *give up your power to change.'*
> **Robert Anthony**

The consequences of not taking responsibility can be quite severe. Repeated shirking of responsibility impacts self-esteem, because our minds and hearts know we're continuing to absolve ourselves. It eats away and causes self-doubt. Eventually self-respect is lost, and when that happens, we start to act in ways that end up in loss of respect from others as well.

If you look around, you'll find it's common for people to blame others, such as bosses, friends, parents, media, clients, economy, governments, or company policy. Some people even blame their lack of money on astrological charts. We don't think twice when we're holding something or someone else responsible for the situation we're in, because it's such acceptable behaviour. I used to be like that – always looking to blame someone or something else for my problems – until it dawned on me that *I* was the root cause of all my problems. And while I blamed others, nothing changed for me.

There's a difference between responsibility and blame. Taking responsibility is positive and empowering, while blaming ourselves is negative and disempowering.

If you are serious about having more success in your life, it's time to stop looking outside yourself to explain why you don't have the life and results you want. Ultimately, *you* create the quality of your life and your results. You. No-one else. And to achieve major success in life, to achieve the things that are meaningful to you, you have to assume 100 per cent responsibility for your life. Nothing else will do.

Doing this, will put you in the minority of people perceived as reliable, with strong character and integrity. Over time you'll be elevated to more responsible positions in life requiring you to make decisions and perhaps even lead others.

Taking 100 per cent responsibility also means giving up your excuses. If something doesn't turn out as planned, ask the following:
- How did I create or contribute to that situation?
- What was I thinking?
- What were my beliefs while I was engaged in that situation?
- What did I say?
- What did I not say that could have helped me get a better outcome in that situation?
- What could I have done differently to get a different outcome?

'E + R= O'
Jack Canfield

Jack Canfield, America's number one success coach, talks about a powerful formula called 'E + R= O', or 'Events + Responses = Outcome.' E means the *events* of our life, R is our *responses*, and O refers to the *outcome* we experience. Canfield says this formula is an easy way to understand we have control over our feelings and reactions to situations and others, and when we do understand this, it gives us more power. In other words, it is more profitable to consider how we are creating what we're experiencing through our thoughts, feelings and behaviours. Over years of studying success principles and interviewing thousands of successful people, Canfield found that people exercised E + R= O, whether they were aware of it or not, achieved a much higher level of success than people who avoided responsibility. He concluded that it's not *what* happens to us, but how we *respond* to what happens that ultimately determines our results in the long term.

Sometimes things happen that derail us or put short-term barriers on the path to success. However, when our long-term success is affected, it is never the event that determines where we end up. It is always our response to that event. Things happen. There's not a person in the world who doesn't have to go through tough situations or deal with difficult partners or bosses. Everyone feels incompetent, or let down or disappointed at some point. Everyone can describe situations where they failed or didn't get their desired results. Some of the world's top achievers came from disadvantaged backgrounds and faced many challenges.

In their famous 'Cradles of Eminence' study, Victor Goertzel and Mildred G. Goertzel, investigated the home backgrounds of three hundred highly successful people – men and women who most people would recognise as being brilliant in their fields. People like Franklin D. Roosevelt, Helen Keller, Winston Churchill, Albert Schweitzer, Clara Barton, Gandhi, and Einstein. The intensive investigation yielded some very surprising findings:

- As children, three-quarters were troubled either by poverty, by a broken home or by rejection or dominating parents.
- Seventy-four of eighty-five fiction or drama writers and sixteen of the twenty poets experienced intense psychological drama through their relatives or parents.
- Physical handicaps such as blindness, deafness or crippled limbs categorised over one-quarter of the sample.

And, yet from such poor circumstances, these people had great success in life.

Ultimately, if our life events determined our results, we would never hear rags-to-riches stories, or read about Paralympians or people from underprivileged backgrounds who achieved greatness. But there are many examples of people who have succeeded despite all odds. Why? Because their results were not determined by *what* happened to them, but how they *responded* to what happened.

Reflect on this for a moment: If you took just 10 per cent more responsibility for your life, what would you do with that extra 10 per cent? Would that mean eating one less junk food item pear week, especially if you're trying to lose weight or be healthy? Could you fit in ten minutes of meditation a week? Or exercise once or twice a week? Would you spend an extra hour with your spouse or contact a relative or friend who's important to you? Or would you start saving a percentage of your income each week or each month?

Taking 10 per cent more responsibility can lead to a better outcome for you. How? Fill in the blanks to the following questions with action items – things you would *do*:

- If I took 10 per cent more responsibility for the attainment of my goals, I would …
- If I took 10 per cent more responsibility for my relationships, I would …
- If I took 10 per cent more responsibility towards my finances, I would …

Filling in the blanks means reinforcing the benefits. Rather than this exercise staying a passive thought, you are embedding the importance of this concept in your mind and taking proactive steps to practising this important principle.

The biggest success killer

Now I'm going to talk about something a bit touchy: the curse of being average and why you need to embrace excellence instead of mediocrity.

The biggest success killer is identifying with being average and accepting mediocrity as your way of life. Mediocrity is a personal choice. It's a conscious or unconscious choice to be less than you can be. Without understanding the difference between success and mediocrity, we all risk accepting things are way below our potential and leading a very average life.

As I said, mediocrity is the personal choice to be less than you can be. The Macquarie Dictionary defines mediocre as 'of middling quality; of only moderate excellence; neither good nor bad; indifferent; ordinary'. Synonyms include undistinguished, commonplace, everyday, and the phrase 'run of the mill'. What is wrong with mediocrity? Well, mediocrity never stands out. It's just passable and it does not result in significant changes and improvements in our own or others' lives. There are seven billion people on the planet so if you really want to stand out, you must understand what mediocrity is, avoid it like a plague, and understand that anything to do with being average and ordinary is not going to cut it.

So why is mediocrity acceptable? How do people end up living such mediocre, average, ordinary lives and be okay with it? Speaking from experience, I think it begins with the choice not to push beyond what already is. After all, if you're comfortable with the status quo and feel that everything is fine, why change it? The underlying belief says, 'I do not need to be excellent. I have chosen not to step out of my comfort zone because stepping out of my comfort zone will require me to push the envelope and that's going to make me feel uncomfortable.'

Some say mediocrity is a cultural problem, some say it's a status problem, and others say it's a background problem. But really, it's the avoidance of getting out of your comfort zone, and it's fuelled by the fear of the unknown. The reality is, everyone at a deep level wants the best life can deliver, but they settle for mediocrity (and even rationalise and defend mediocrity), because at a deep level they do not truly believe they can have a high level of success.

We know from research that no one really enjoys crawling in life and living in mediocrity. If you want to test this theory, ask someone who says, 'I'm okay, I'm satisfied, I'm happy with my current income or my current situation', one simple question. Ask them, 'If someone was to give you a mortgage-free beach house worth two or three million dollars, would you accept it?' Now, you'll find most people will say 'yes', if they're being honest.

So, if they want it, why have they settled for less? Well, if they've settled for less they have a deep belief (and most of the time it's an unconscious belief), that they cannot have more so they've settled for the ordinary and the average. One of the symptoms of mediocrity-based thinking is playing the games of life, success, career progression or financial freedom, just enough to not lose the game.

Here I want to make a distinction between playing to win versus playing not to lose. Imagine watching your favourite sports team play. You're up in the grandstands and you watch your team putting an effort, but just enough so they don't lose. Would you be disappointed with that performance? I'm sure you would be if you were a passionate supporter and they only put in average effort. You would be disappointed that you spent money and time supporting the team and they did not make a wholehearted effort to win.

When teams play not to lose, the outcome is likely to be, at worst a loss, and at best a draw. Look around and you'll see this is how most people play the game of life. They're constantly lining up their ducks and they aim, aim, aim, but never fire. To make it worse, they use mediocrity-based language or rationalisation to justify why they're supposedly happy to live like this. I heard someone say once, 'Rationalising is rationing-lies.' It makes sense. When we start to say, '..if I was a little bit younger'; 'I would've done this if I didn't have a mortgage'; 'I would've done this if I was in this position or in that position'; 'if I lived in that country'; 'if I had the right education,' or 'if I was the right culture I would've done this,' these rationalisations are simply excuses used to justify settling for an average position in life. We rationalise because it hurts to accept that we didn't reach out for our true potential.

*'The choice is yours. You can steer the course you
choice in the direction of where you want to be
– today, tomorrow, or in a distant time to come.'*
W. Clement Stone

The most successful people in the world are risk-takers. As soon as they identify an opportunity, they move quickly and make something happen. This initiative is a special quality that sets them apart from less-successful people. They do not suffer from analysis paralysis (which can become a habit). People who are not prepared to accept mediocrity are willing to try different approaches to reach their goal. They throw mud at the wall, knowing that if they throw enough, some will stick. Instead of focusing on failure, they focus on the result. They don't have time to focus on approaches that didn't work. Did you know that successful people make decisions fast and change them slowly? Unsuccessful people do the opposite. The faster people move, the more energy they have; the more different things they try, the more likely they are to succeed. Successful people have this attitude that says, 'There is always a way', 'I will find a way' and 'I will succeed.'

People who accept mediocrity and being average or ordinary often say things like, 'It's not good to obsess' and 'Life is all about balance.' Now, you're probably thinking, what's wrong with balance? Isn't balance a good thing? Yes, of course it is, but when we make balance the objective, we often do it at the expense of diluting energy towards a cause or desirable outcome.

Mediocrity-based language also shows up when people say 'Don't be greedy,' or 'You can't have it all.' For me, success has never been about *one* thing, achievement, dream, or goal. I've always wanted a lot of things for myself. Someone said to me once, 'You can't have your cake and eat it' and my response was, 'Well what's the point of having cake if I can't eat it?' What does 'you can't have your cake and eat it' even mean? To me, those words have never made sense.

So, watch out for conformity-based behaviours and language that is aligned with being average and settling for mediocrity. Other examples include 'going with the flow' and 'I'm just very laid back.' I'm not sure being laid back is a compliment. The first thing I think of is the saying, 'Only dead fish go with the flow.' When we're trying to achieve success, we're not meant to go with the flow, we're not meant to be laid back. And then there's, 'I'm just the guy next door' or 'the girl next door'. You can see the belief-system behind this language is that of mediocrity.

People have been told that it's okay to settle for less, rather than being obsessed with their dreams because obsession is seen to be a bad thing. When you're obsessed with a good cause, when you're passionate about your craft, when you don't want to settle for anything less than successful, you may be seen by others as abnormal, greedy, obsessive, self-serving, or even someone that's never satisfied, so some of the advice you may get from mediocre people might include:

- 'Slow down. Life is to be enjoyed.'
- 'Don't work too much/too hard. Take it easy.'
- 'Be grateful – someone else is worse off than you.'
- 'Life is short.'
- 'Money/success isn't everything.'
- 'Bigger isn't better.'

What's interesting is that most people who say these sorts of things are obsessed with something themselves, such as comfort, being 'normal' or unmotivated or purposeless, or with sticking to doubts that prevent them from playing big.

Ever noticed that the person who says 'Success isn't everything' is actually the person who has none? This type of advice is dispensed freely. You have to be careful not to embrace or entertain this type of advice. People will try to persuade you to give up so they feel better about giving up on their dreams and goals. Now, that doesn't mean they're bad people –they're just misinformed about success and its benefits. Always remember that those with the smallest goals will have the biggest problems.

Mediocrity as a formula works for no one, no matter how much you try to make sense of it. Unhappy people can't teach you how to be happy. Poor people can't teach you how to become wealthy. Someone in a failed relationship can't tell you how to make a relationship work.

Look at successful people like Steve Jobs, Martin Luther King, Bill Gates and Muhammad Ali. They are not superheroes because of their talents – they became superheroes because of their obsession, complete non-acceptance of mediocrity, and unshakeable dedication. They didn't just play the game, they were obsessed with winning the game. To make world-class income, you have to be world class in your skills.

Time for some self-reflective writing. How do most people act when they don't know what their goals are or when they are not achieving their goals? What do they do and say? What does it indicate to you when people make rationalising statements about their lack of goal setting or results? Now think about some other mediocrity-based language you have heard. Write down two or three sayings you hear in your workplace, family or social networks.

For the next step, I want you to write a short passage about how getting out of mediocrity and becoming really successful would impact your life? Just fifty words, or maybe a hundred. Include examples of times you have lied to yourself about success, or when you have used rationalising language to convince yourself that success is not everything.

Think about how much time you spend on wasteful activities like watching TV, drinking, oversleeping, or having long lunches and meetings with no agenda. Write down what these activities are so you can see what is distracting you from becoming successful and keeping you in the mediocrity zone.

Finally, write down your definition of middle-class and how middle-class people act. None of this is meant to be derogatory towards the middle-class, but it's to highlight that middle-class syndrome is based on an acceptance of being less than we can be. To me, middle-class generally means having a reliable job with average-to-decent pay and a fairly comfortable home in an average or above-average suburb, being able to afford healthcare, just enough time off for holidays once or twice a year, and having some money growing in a retirement fund.

The way I see it, being middle-class is failing to provide real freedom for anyone, and settling for middle-class only ensures a life of fear and constant worry. Entrepreneur Grant Cardone gives us some statistics around how deep this epidemic runs in the US. One study suggested that somewhere between 62 and 76 per cent of Americans live pay-check to pay-check, even those in what used to be solid, reliable, middle-class jobs with middle-class incomes. Half of the US population is on some form of government assistance. Ninety-two per cent of small businesses make less than $250,000USD a year and 67 per cent don't even break even. There is over 1.3 trillion dollars worth of college debt and 30 per cent of college graduates, despite this debt, do not work in the field they studied. Seventy per cent of middle-class Americans are disengaged in their jobs. The US is one of the most powerful countries in the world, so you can imagine that if this is what's happening there, things won't be a lot better in many other countries. It's a worldwide epidemic.

A lot of people in the middle-class find themselves stuck, with heavily taxed income because many do not invest or they don't run businesses. As a wealth planner, I see a lot of people and I get to know their financial situation quite intimately, and in Australia, which has one of the highest incomes in the world and supposedly one of the best lifestyles in the world, most people retire with very little money. It is estimated that about 80 per cent of Australians retire with less than $150,000, despite thirty or forty years in the workforce. And, in the US at the time of writing this book, I believe there are over fifty million people under the poverty line, which represents roughly 16 per cent of their population. So, if middle-class typically represents a lot of the mediocrity-based thinking you hear, it stands that the middle-class is under a lot of pressure now. With new trends of jobs being outsourced and technology replacing jobs, the old system is no longer working.

In addition, people are living longer and longer. When people run out of money in the first five or ten years after retirement, then they'll find themselves living a life of struggle with few options in the later years of their lives. This is why it's incredibly important for people not to just *get by* but to think big from the start. Thinking big now is going to make you comfortable enough to fund your lifestyle for thirty to forty years after you stop working due to retirement or ill health. Thinking small is not an option for those who desire to guarantee their success.

If you're just getting by and not even putting 10 or 20 per cent of your salary away or investing consistently, it's because you have, from a very early age, been conditioned to play small. You've accepted average thinking and you're content to play at a level where you're playing the game of life not to lose.

Is that what you want?

Now that you know all about the biggest success killer, I sure hope you're going to avoid average like the plague.

In the next section, we're going to learn about the law of compounding development and how small actions can lead to incredible results.

The compounding development effect

In this section, I'll talk about the law of compounding development and how you can use this law to achieve success.

The compounding development effect is a very powerful success concept, one of the most legitimate I have come across. Everywhere you look these days, people are offering quick solutions, tips, and tactics in blogs and articles to become more successful, wealthy, sexy, or to lose weight. Realistically, there is no quick fix when it comes to sustainable success. Of course, it is possible for people to lose weight or make money quickly; however, it's not possible for people to sustain that instant level of success, wealth, or ideal weight without an understanding of the law of compounding development.

The compounding development effect, also called the compound effect, is probably based on the most time-tested fundamental principle of success. The formula for the compound effect is this:

'Small, Smart Choices + Consistency
+ Time = RADICAL DIFFERENCE'
Darren Hardy, *The Compound Effect*

Publisher of *Success Magazine* and author Darren Hardy says the compound effect is the principle of reaping huge rewards from a series of small but smart choices. This particular strategy works in any area, whether you're trying to improve your finances or wealth or anything else. It doesn't really matter.

One example of the compounding development effect is compound interest (referred to as the eighth wonder of the world by Einstein). At my wealth seminars, I sometimes ask my audience this question: 'If you had the choice between a million dollars today or having one cent that simply doubles for the next thirty-one days, which option would you pick, and why?' Of course, most people can tell it's a trick question. But here's the thing: I ask people to make a choice and tell me why they made that choice. Most people, if actually confronted with these choices, would probably succumb to instant gratification and take the million dollars. Very few people, if any, would opt for the one-cent option. And yet, if they did take the one-cent option and allowed that money to double every day for the next thirty-one days only, that one cent would be worth 10.7 million on the thirty-first day.

For someone who doesn't understand the compound effect and its applications, it is very probable that they would regret their decision even if they did opt for the one-cent option. Do you know why? Because, if they did go for that one-cent option, even on the twenty-sixth day, that money would only be worth three hundred and thirty-six thousand. They would be likely to stop and say, 'Oh, I should've gone with the other option. I'm sitting here on the twenty-sixth day and my money is only worth three hundred and thirty-six thousand dollars', not realising that in the final five days that will leap to 10.7 million. From day one to day twenty-six, the money grows at very small increments. This is one reason most people do not become wealthy – they do not understand the compound effect.

Here's another example of how the compound effect works in real life. In my primary occupation as a wealth advisor, when I talk with people about money one of the things I explain is that compound effect, when it comes to money, is called compound interest. What does this compound effect have to do with success? Everything. A big part of being successful is having the understanding and ability to make our money grow. But the compound effect works in many other areas.

Take healthcare. Imagine if you were talking to two people, and you asked one to increase their calorie intake by one hundred calories a day and the other to reduce their calorie intake by one hundred calories a day. After a few months, you might not observe much difference in their weight. But if that trend continued for a year, there would be a significant difference in weight. Those extra calories would carry on and then in one, two, three years you would start to see the aggravation of the compound development effect. The person who had the increased calorie intake would, after one, two or three years, have gained significantly more weight compared to a person who reduced their calorie intake.

So, the compound development effect works this way: if you're improving yourself in small, smart ways over time, you may not see much change for a while (or even give you that high you want to feel). But there will come a day when you will see massive improvements and results in your life. It works in reverse as well. If you neglect things you should not be neglecting, you may not see negative repercussions in the short to medium term, but in the long term things will go from bad to worse. It's like a windshield crack. When there is a crack on a windshield, you can prevent the crack from shattering the glass if you get it fixed quickly. But if you allow the crack to go unattended for a long period of time, it may get larger and larger, or shatter the glass. Problems, in many cases, do not start off as problems. Often they start as small symptoms, but then the symptoms become problems because of prolonged neglect.

What you have to remember is that when you trigger the compound effect, the changes take time and unfortunately a lot of people give up or do not follow through and persist. Most people unfortunately are looking for instant results, and when they do not see instant results, they ask, 'Why bother?' Quick-fix thinking, results in people not having the tenacity to follow through with things, because their mind is so conditioned to opt for the fastest and quickest solution. And if they can't find joy in the process, it gives them another good reason to quit.

Publisher of *Success Magazine* and author Darren Hardy claims the compound effect is the only process a person needs in order to achieve the ultimate level of success. Due to his position, he receives interviews and articles from thousands of experts, thought leaders, authors, and speakers who talk about success. Through his life and career experience, he has been able to distil and work out the common denominator of success for some of the world's most successful people. He warns people not to be tempted into the promises of quick success, saying that the path to success can be laborious, tedious and sometimes a very boring endeavour, but that having wealth, influence and becoming world-class is possible for anyone, if they follow through on what needs to be done.

Now, at this point you might be thinking, 'I'm not really interested in the long-term solution.' You're not alone. But once you understand, apply and commit to the compound developing effect, you'll start to see improvements and results in your life almost immediately. Of course, if you avoid hard work, commitment and discipline, you'll likely struggle with this concept. Just remember, if you're serious about success, anything that is worthwhile will take time and consistent effort. And if you have an aversion to consistent effort, unfortunately you are likely to become the next victim of a TV advertisement offering false hopes and promises of overnight success (and all you have to do is provide the details of your credit card). The best way to utilise the compounding development effect in any area of your life is by increasing your commitment levels. When you commit for the long term, you will outperform most people, as well as your own expectations.

So, the question is, where could you be applying the compound effect in your favour? Where is the compound effect working against you? One little change can have a significant impact on your results in the long term because of the ripple effect I talked about before. Remember, the most challenging aspect of the compound effect, is having to work consistently and efficiently before we see the payoff. Our grandparents knew this. They didn't spend the evening glued to the TV, watching infomercials about '$30K in 30 days' or a real estate kingdom in six months. Most of our grandparents would have worked long hours, possibly five, six, seven days a week, sun-up to sundown, using the skills they learnt in their youth. They were conditioned to understand that the secret of success was hard work, discipline and good habits.

Here are two action steps for you. One, write the excuses you are holding on to (such as 'I'm not the right age', 'I don't have the right education', and so on) and reflect on how those excuses are affecting your success. Two, write down five small steps you can take towards the outcome you want, whether it's money, health, or whatever your goal is. For example, if it's money, maybe you can commit to saving fifty dollars a week or reducing your grocery bills by twenty dollars a week. If it's health, perhaps you can make one meal a day just salads or vegetables, or you only have one indulgent (junk food) day a week. The steps don't have to be big. But if you commit to them, you can take your life in a completely new and positive direction.

Now that we've covered the law of compounding development, let's move on to practising extraordinary thankfulness.

Practising extraordinary thankfulness

'Strive for everything you want, while being grateful for everything that you already have.'

It takes vigilance to cultivate an attitude of gratitude because most of us are culturally conditioned to focus on what we don't have rather than what we do have. Sometimes we focus so much on the difficulties and challenges of our climb that we lose sight of being grateful for having a mountain to climb.

Appreciation and gratitude for the big and small things in life is often overlooked, and yet we have so much to be grateful for. If you have a roof over your head, a warm bed, food in your fridge, and clothes and shoes in your closet, you're better off than 75 per cent of the world's population as it stands now. Hard to believe, but it's true. If you eat three meals a day, you're better off than one billion people on earth who have access to one meal a day or none at all. According to a press release issued by the World Bank in 2018, 46 per cent of the world lives on less than $5.50 a day. I'm sharing this to provide some perspective.

When we are not practising gratitude, it's often because of a sense of entitlement. We feel that our health, this job, or our income, is not enough. Now, I understand the paradox here, given that this whole program is about achieving, striving, and aiming for success. I'm telling you to aim higher.

But, you can still maintain *a hunger for success and contentment for what you already have* at the same time.

Many people think dissatisfaction equates to a lack of gratitude. They are not the same. Dissatisfaction is often seen as negative but it can be positive when it is a creative state. When people are dissatisfied with their current situation, they try to improve it. As the proverb goes, 'Necessity is the mother of invention.' A need for improvement is an opportunity to explore, discover, invent, and do things we haven't done before. In other words, tapping into our creativity. Every invention or discovery is a consequence of someone being dissatisfied with the way things were. But, dissatisfaction that makes us strive towards a goal doesn't mean we need to be ungrateful for what we already have.

Gratitude is not something that comes to us naturally. Research shows that we have five times more neuroreceptors to identify the negative, than the positive. If I put a white sheet of paper in front of you and there's a black dot on that white sheet, chances are the black dot is the first thing you will observe. It's how our minds are geared.

Lately there's been a lot of talk about gratitude, especially on social media. But talking about gratitude and practising it are two different things. Practising it means proactively seeking reasons to be grateful and then expressing appreciation.

> *'If the only prayer you ever say is*
> *'Thank you' that will be enough.'*
> **Eckhart Tolle**

For years, Oprah Winfrey has been advocating the power and pleasure of gratitude. She recommends keeping a gratitude journal and writing in it every night before going to sleep. By writing these things down, they don't just slip away. I practise gratitude every day, asking myself, 'What are the five things that I'm grateful for?' The answers don't have to be grand. It could be as simple as spending time with family, going for a walk, tasting good food, having a meaningful conversation with a good friend, relaxation time, sleeping on a comfortable bed, or reading a good book. By making time for a little gratitude every day and seeking out things to be grateful for, I'm reminded how easily I could overlook these little but good things.

From a professional perspective, gratitude has many benefits. Gratitude and appreciation help us to connect better with colleagues, manage staff better, and overall, do our jobs better. A prominent management consulting firm annually surveys two hundred companies about what motivates employees. When given a list of ten possible things that would most motivate employees, the employees always list appreciation as their number one motivator. Another management study once revealed that 46 per cent of employees wanted to leave a company because they felt unappreciated. And 61 per cent said their bosses placed little importance on them as human beings and didn't acknowledge their work.

How do you show appreciation or gratitude to others? Neuro-linguistic programming categorises people as either auditory, visual or kinaesthetic. Auditory people typically feel appreciated when they hear 'Thank you' or a compliment. Visual people feel appreciated when they see evidence of it (kind words or feedback on a sticky note, a card, or gift). Kinaesthetic people often feel appreciated through touch – a hug, handshake, or a pat on the back. When in doubt, I suggest you use a combination of all three types of communication – tell them, show them, give them that pat on the back.

The law of attraction states that the more you express gratitude, the higher your vibrational state. This vibrational state is conducive to attracting what you are grateful for. There's a saying that goes, 'What you appreciate, appreciates.' It's true. The law of attraction states that *like attracts like*, you attract more things to be thankful for when you're constantly expressing gratitude. Think about it – you're more likely to help people if they're grateful for what you do.

Earlier I talked about seeing the negative first. Often we forget about gratitude because we attach faulty interpretations to what happens to us. I've seen it many times: people take what someone has said or done and automatically put a negative spin on it or take things personally. But what if you could form a habit of shifting attention from self-pity and focus on gratitude and seeing the positives in every situation?

> *'The Law of Polarity states that everything*
> *that exists has an equal and exact opposite.*
> *To put it even stronger: for anything to exist,*
> *there has to be an equal and exact opposite.'*
> **Marc de Bruin**

In other words, every situation has a good and bad aspect. But when we are focused on looking at the bad instead of the good, we end up diminishing the sense of gratitude that we need to cultivate. Mindfully practising gratitude helps us concentrate on the positives, and on our strengths, rather than our weaknesses.

This is where it's important to surround yourself with like-minded people. It's difficult to feel bad about yourself when you're surrounded by people who are grateful for life and their relationship with you. If you're surrounded by cynical, negative people who erode your self-esteem you may need to consider who you want to spend time with, (more on this in the next section). Consider seeking out people who nurture your sense of wellbeing and enhance positivity in you by treating you as a worthy friend and equal. You'll find that you go on to treat others in the same way.

Here I want to reinforce how gratitude is linked to giving. Bob Burg and John D. Mann, authors of *The Go-Giver* (it's amazing), say most people laugh when they hear the secret of success is giving. In their book, they maintain there is nothing wrong with making money (and many people associate success with making money) but simply having a goal of making money is not going to make you *feel* successful. Here's a passage:

'The majority of people operate with a mindset that
says to the fireplace, 'First give me some heat, then I'll
throw on some logs.' Or says to the bank, 'Give me
interest on my money, then I'll make a deposit.'
And of course, it just doesn't work that way.'
Bob Burg and John D. Mann, *The Go-Giver*

What do they mean? The mindset, 'Do something for me first and then I'll do something for you' doesn't work when it comes to success. Giving (and gratitude for what you've received) does. If you want to be successful, consider giving before you think about getting.

Seek out opportunities to contribute to others. It doesn't have to be with money. Time, feedback, smiles, and compliments are all worthy contributions (no contribution is too small). At the same time, be open to receiving good things from others. We can't fully give if we are reluctant to receive. Take compliments, for example. I've come across many people who quickly deflect compliments. They say, 'Oh, I don't know, I don't deserve that', 'It's nothing new' or 'It's not a big deal.' If someone gives you a compliment, take it. Just say, 'Thank you.' Be as generous in receiving as you are in giving.

So, how can you bring gratefulness into your life? I mentioned my daily practice of writing down five things I am grateful for. Try to do this. Before you go to sleep, write down the five things that you're grateful for every day. Work hard to cultivate a daily routine of practising extraordinary thankfulness, both by journalling each night and in your daily life. You could carry a physical token of gratitude in your pocket or bag – a little stone, a card or some other item – and every time you touch that item, let it anchor you in a reminder to stop, breathe and experience the emotion of thankfulness. Another suggestion is to replace the words 'I have to' with 'I get to' – instead of 'I have to go to work,' try 'I get to go to work'. When you do this, you're expressing appreciation, something most people take for granted. Show your appreciation for others, but also find reasons to appreciate yourself and what you have accomplished. We all need acknowledgement, so celebrate your successes, big and small.

Before we move on, I'd like you to try this appreciation exercise. Draw up four columns: Who, Why, How, When. In the 'Who' column, write down the names of five people you appreciate. In the 'Why' column write one or two words to indicate why (or what) you appreciate about them. In the third column, write how you can express your appreciation (a phone call, smile, gift, note). And in the fourth column, write when you will do this by.

Now draw up another four columns: What, Why, How and When. It's the same exercise as above but you're replacing the 'Who' with a 'What'(a thing, a place, an achievement).

I'll give you my example: my *What* might be my relationship with my nephew. My *Why* might be that I see the great person he is going to become. My *How* could be as simple as giving him a hug or some words of encouragement. When will I do this? The next time I see him.

Being grateful is simple. But, often what is simple to do is simple *not* to do. It takes vigilance, but gratefulness is a fundamental part of your success practices.

Emotional contagion and success

Are there people in your life who drain you of your confidence and energy? Do some people cause you to doubt yourself? Do they make you feel stressed and anxious? Do you know people who constantly complain, feel sorry for themselves, or blame others? They might be friends, business associates, co-workers, or even family members. We all know people like this – the 'dream stealers'.

While these people do not always operate from negative or malicious intent (and are sometimes quite oblivious), they can have a toxic effect on your self-confidence, self-esteem, and ability to achieve goals. By discouraging us from pursuing our objectives, they can prevent us from achieving excellence in our lives.

Research shows that other people's emotions can rub off on us. This concept, called emotional contagion, is a part of human evolution and helped people understand each other before language was invented. It is facilitated by an interconnected network of cells in the brain that makes up the mirror neuron system (MNS). This system is a natural automated response, much like a high-definition camera, that automatically records details of other people's facial expressions, tone of voice, and body language and then mirrors these details in us. In other words, people who express strong feelings, emotions and beliefs (positive and negative) can be 'contagious'.

Some people are habitually addicted to a toxic way of thinking and living. They don't even realise they have a toxic personality and how they negatively affect others. They will tell you why you can't achieve certain things, and why nobody has become successful doing what you're about to do. They live in a problem zone. Their focus is on the problem, on complaining and blaming, rather than looking for a solution. They'll say, 'Why bother, it's not going to work.' You can ignore remarks like this, especially if you're practising awareness, but sometimes comments like this get through and leave you doubting yourself. You'll ask, 'What if I do fail?' And all of a sudden, you end up adopting their philosophy and fail to go after what you want with complete confidence and conviction. And even if we still go after it, it can be with a 'doubt' energy, which is really not conducive to success.

For this reason, it's important to identify people who are supportive of us, and our journey. People who radiate positive energy, optimism, and encouragement. True, you're going to encounter both positive and negative people in life, and it's impossible to completely avoid negative people. However, when we are conscious of the power negative people can yield through their ability to change our heart and mind, and tendency to crush our self-esteem or dilute our passion, we can put some distance and boundaries in place.

Setting boundaries is easier when that negative person is an acquaintance or someone we don't see on a regular basis. But it can be a hard when it's a family member or a co-worker. In this case, first try to minimise contact with them, even if it's a parent or close relative. Remember, your first responsibility is to yourself and your life. The second thing to try is becoming conscious of their negative attitude towards life or others and deciding not to emotionally engage with their ideas or thoughts. When I'm around a negative person, I say this: 'Cancel, cancel.' This instructs my mind to delete out their negative messages. Our subconscious mind does not have the ability to reject a command that we hear repeatedly.

Saying No is also good. You can let these people know that you respect their view, but respectfully disagree with it and won't be taking it on board. Sometimes they will use guilt as a weapon. Cancel, cancel.

Another way to counteract the effects of negative people is to identify people you admire and make a conscious attempt to spend time with them (if you can). Of course, some people who inspire you aren't around for you to hang out with. Read their autobiographies, books, or blog posts. Watch their videos. Doing this will put your mind in a more positive frame of mind.

Author Tim Ferris (*The Four Day Week*) said he was ten when he recognised that the kids he was hanging out with were not who he wanted to influence his future. He asked his parents to send him to a better private school. They did and that set him on a path that lead him to a junior year in Japan, studying martial arts and meditation, a degree at Princeton University, where he became a wrestler and a national kickboxing champion, and starting his own company at the age of twenty three. Tim knew early on that we become like the people we hang out with.

You can find successful people in many places – professional associations, conferences, clubs, Meetup groups, self-development seminars, or retreats. Driven people with positive outlooks congregate at these places. Positive, like-minded people, who want to develop themselves, like you. People with a solution-orientated approach to life, as opposed to a problem-orientated approach. Don't think that success is reserved for those born into well-to-do families who have inherited advantages in their life. You can build a life of success by being in the company of people who have achieved what you want to achieve, or who are on their own path to success. And the more time you spend with them, the more like them you'll become. Be proactive. A lot of these people want to help. Don't hesitate to make contact and spend time with them.

Here's an exercise W. Clement Stone recommends to identify the positive and negative people in your life. Start by making a list of the people you spend time with on a regular basis (colleagues, friends, neighbours, and family members). Then, put either a minus or a plus sign next to them to indicate whether they're a negative or a positive person in your life. And here's the challenge – make a conscious effort to spend less time with minus sign-people (ideally, avoid them altogether). Make a conscious effort to spend more time with the plus sign-people.

> *'It is absolutely your right and your responsibility to be selective about the types of people that you spend your time with.'*

Surround yourself with possibility-thinkers, visionaries and leaders – people who encourage you to go after your dreams, and applaud your victories. My personal philosophy is to pay any price to be in the presence of extraordinary people. Their positive ambition and energy is the emotional contagion I want to rub off on me.

What we have covered in this chapter

In this chapter we have covered:
- accepting responsibility for success
- the biggest success killer
- the compounding development effect
- practising extraordinary thankfulness
- emotional contagion and success
- the Success Checklist.

What do successful people do? Successful people assume 100 per cent responsibility for their situation and outcomes, without blaming others or themselves. They speak the language of success and avoid the language of mediocrity. Successful people understand that consistency over time results in compounding outcomes in life. They practise gratitude daily and they surround themselves with positive and successful people, avoiding the naysayers and negative people.

In the next chapter I'll show how you make an impact with your personality.

'There isn't a single highly-accomplished, influential or wealthy person who took it easy or squandered their time.'

Ever noticed that only those who push themselves to the limit and face risk, exhaustion, humiliation, rejection & failure become champions in any field? Everyone else who seeks balance becomes a spectator.
Ron Malhotra

CHAPTER 6
Making an impact with our personality

'When you are not clear on who you are, where you're going and what you stand for, this leads to fear, doubt, and confusion. When you know those things, you become more decisive, courageous, and confident.'

Do you sometimes feel like you walk into a room and make a weak impression? Would you like to come across as more authentic and naturally powerful? Would you like people to take interest in you and want to get to know you? Making an impact is all about affecting people positively through your presence. You can only radiate positivity if you're feeling good on the inside. While appearance and grooming definitely helps, a genuine and lasting impact is made by those who feel congruent and good on the inside. This chapter describes how you can make a more positive impact by developing your personality to include an attractive attitude, maintenance of an optimal psychological state, and more.

Aspiring for greatness

> 'Some are born great, some achieve greatness,
> and others have greatness thrust upon them.'
> **William Shakespeare, *Twelfth Night***

Greatness, is achieved by few people, but is not the exclusive domain of a certain kind of person. Once we understand greatness and aspire for it, we engage in thinking and actions far bigger than the day-to-day trivial matters we often get caught up in. We are inspired to dream, think and act bigger than we ever thought possible, which can create outcomes bigger than we ever imagined for ourselves, and those around us.

Who comes to mind when you think of someone who has achieved greatness? I often think of people like Nelson Mandela, Princess Diana, Alexander the Great, Queen Elizabeth II, Abraham Lincoln, Gandhi, or Mother Teresa. All of these people have achieved greatness in different ways, such as risk-taking, rationality, diplomacy, or courageous acts.

Yet, greatness is more a feeling than something to be measured. Consider this: *aspiring* for greatness will make you think bigger than your day-to-day life, job, and paying the bills. Aspiring for greatness means you'll strive for actions and results that will have a far greater impact on other people's lives (and your own personal success). Sadly, most people don't believe greatness is possible for them, because they don't understand what it is and why it's worth aspiring for.

I always wanted to achieve greatness, but because I was programmed to aim small, I didn't entertain the possibility for a long time. My subconscious worldview was that greatness was an inherent quality and certain special people were born with it. But after I turned 31, I realised that greatness had more to do with intent and heart than any other inherent factor.

To find your personal greatness, you need to discover your unique inner voice and then use that voice to add value to others. By voice, I mean the unseen and intangible element of your spirit, which is full of courage, hope and intelligence, is resilient by nature, and desires good for yourself and others. We all have a unique voice that, if inspired and listened to, can think and act big.

'The meaning of life is to find your gift.
The purpose of life is to give it away.'
Pablo Picasso

Life doesn't have to stop when we reach a certain level of personal success. In fact, it's through continual growth that we get to something beyond success – greatness, or as I also call it, significance.

Significance is about finding your unique calling, or what I also call the soul's blueprint. It's about using your talents, skills, and experience to give to others. Significance is not driven by personal interest. Instead, achieving significance allows us to serve ourselves by serving others. It's our heart's calling: 'Yes, I have achieved enough for myself. It's time to consider giving to people and causes that benefit the broader world and I care deeply about.'

We all have a deep desire and inexpressible longing to find our unique voice, but not all of us act on it. It has been said that only 2-5 per cent of people in the world make a difference (or strive to make a difference). The world is full of problems like people trafficking, drugs, violence, crimes against women and children, and wars. If only 2 per cent of the world's population are driven to make a difference, then 98 per cent is either indifferent, or driven by self-interest. Do you want to be one of the difference-makers? What would happen if we doubled that 2 per cent to 4 per cent? We could potentially halve some of these problems. The way I see it, with rights come responsibilities; if you experience a good life, you may also experience a nagging feeling about our responsibility to give to others. But when you use your passion, values, strengths, and talents to give to other people and causes, this is the sweet spot where life becomes meaningful and greatness can be achieved.

Greatness can be a misunderstood concept. Some people think greatness equals self-serving. It's not. Greatness is a consequence of serving others. It's not so much about aiming to *be* great, but to *do* great, valuable, and much-needed work for others that then results in greatness and significance for yourself. Greatness is achieved by people with a mission, people who have a purpose that goes beyond their own needs, one that serves a purpose higher than themselves.

I'll give you an example from my own life. In the past, I suffered because of my own ignorance and lack of understanding of life and success concepts. One day, I took the time to identify my gifts, passion, purpose, strengths, and values. I found that my gifts and skills were in learning, teaching, mentoring, developing, and consulting. I then identified a need to help people develop and evolve into the best version of themselves. Next, I developed and packaged different means of success education, following my belief that professional development and technical education was insufficient for life fulfillment and success. By doing this, I was able to add value and contribute towards causes I deeply cared about.

This might be a good time to revisit Chapter 4, where I talked about discovering yourself. But to recap, all you have to do is to match your passion, strengths, values, and purpose with a need you care about. How do you know what that need is? Think of something you complain about or that frustrates you. An injustice you have experienced or seen, perhaps. This is not a negative exercise rather it will help you discover where you could make a difference. Instead of thinking that someone else should fix it, you could ask, 'Why not me?' Why not you? Why can't you be the person who does something about it? Why can't you use your unique blend of skills, talents, experience, values, strengths, passion, and purpose to contribute to that cause or fix that problem?

I love this quote by Stephen Covey: 'The key is not to prioritise what's on your schedule, but to schedule your priorities.'

What is your core priority in life? Could it be to achieve greatness? It's a fantastic way to contribute to others and leave a legacy. If you look around, you will find that most people, when they die, are usually forgotten within two or three generations. Some even less, maybe forgotten within months or even days. Why? Do you want to be forgotten easily, or would you much rather leave a lasting impact? I'll assume you're reading *Impossible to Fail* because you don't want to live on ordinary terms. If that's the case, start thinking now about how you can achieve greatness.

Start by studying the lives of great people, such as Cleopatra, Winston Churchill, Abraham Lincoln, George Washington, Martin Luther King, Indira Gandhi, Ronald Reagan, Franklin D. Roosevelt, John F. Kennedy, Walt Disney, and Nelson Mandela. Read their autobiographies or biographies to get an understanding of their thought processes. Ask how they found the determination and the drive to do these amazing things despite many having ordinary backgrounds. How were they resilient? How did they find the strength and courage to make a change? How did they find out what they truly cared about? In most cases, the answer is probably frustration. Something bothered them at a very deep level. And they did something about it. Remember, not a single mass movement in the world ever started with the masses. Mass movements start with one or two individuals, and in the beginning, there's always violent opposition.

'All truth passes through three stages.'
Arthur Schopenhauer

German philosopher Arthur Schopenhauer says the stages of truth are ridicule, violent opposition, and acceptance (as inevitable). If all truth has to go through these three stages, a person desiring greatness needs resilience. This resilience is the ability to stand your ground in the face of great opposition. It's knowing in your heart that what you're doing is great work and makes a difference. Remember, this is your world. If you do not consciously shape it for yourself and others around you, someone else will.

'No one has achieved greatness by playing it safe.'

You are stronger, smarter and more resilient than you think. You are capable of achieving far more than you believe. It won't be easy. Just remember, all great work starts off with a big vision, but it also means starting small, and this is what holds back many people. Achieving greatness takes persistence, determination, conscious decision, facing fears, and doing what others don't want to do. The path of least resistance rarely leads to a good place, and where it does, it is not the same as a place of greatness.

Aspiring for greatness will keep your mind focused on the important, big, and great things, away from the cycle of blame and negativity that consumes the minds and energy of most people. It will take time, but you will eventually see results. Your skills and talents, values and strengths will come together to serve the unfulfilled needs of the world and others.

Becoming More Likeable

Why is it important to be more likeable if you want a high level of success?

How much other people know, like, and trust you will elevate your position in life and determine your success. It is possible to have a reasonable level of success without other people's belief and support, but if you want to achieve a high level of success and significance you need the belief and support of others. Getting that is an extremely important part on your journey to success.

Being likeable is not about being fake, pretentious, or opting for superficial behaviours that achieve attention and temporary popularity. It's about understanding the dynamics of social interaction. When you do this, you become a more pleasing, attractive, and desirable person to be around, which will have positive implications for your personal, social, professional, and business life.

In his book *The Science Of Success: Napoleon Hill's Proven Program for Prosperity and Happiness*, Hill showcases US steel magnate Charles M. Schwab as someone who became successful because of his personality and demeanour. In the 19th century, Schwab went from being an average labourer to a highly paid executive who received frequent million-dollar bonuses, astronomical numbers for that era. His boss, the legendary industrialist

Andrew Carnegie, once said Schwab's pleasing personality and ability to get others to do things better were the reasons for his success. One of the benefits of likeability is that once you elevate yourself into the best person that you can be and start to do great work, you will persuade others to work collaboratively towards a common cause, as Schwab did.

Likeability is a vague concept, but let's start by thinking of it as the ability to create a positive attitude in other people. We like to feel positive emotions so we find ourselves drawn to people who create positive emotions in us.

Take a moment to think of someone you like and write down five characteristics that make them likeable. Now think of three emotions this likeable person causes in you. Reverse it. Think of a person you don't like and write down five reasons they make you feel this way. Write down three emotions you feel around them.

I want to make a quick confession here. I don't aim to be likeable. You're probably thinking, 'Ron, why are you preaching the importance of being likeable, when you personally don't care about it?' This is a tricky one to explain. You see, I care more about being trustworthy and respected, which means I end up being liked by most people I develop a relationship with. Do you see? That's *my* way. I work on trust and respect first, then the liking comes. It's a by-product. Whatever your way is, it doesn't change the fact that being likeable is significant contributor towards success.

A Columbia University study, by Melinda Tamkins, showed that success in the workplace was guaranteed not only by what people know or who they knew, but also by their perceived popularity. She found that popular workers were perceived to be trustworthy, more decisive, and hardworking, and were recommended faster for promotions and pay rises. In his book, Likeability Factor, Tim Sanders talks about studies that have shown that children who were likeable, optimistic, and personable, fared better and gained more support than children who were not likeable. Being likeable led to an increased amount of resilience and focus, giving a strong emotional armour that helped the path of success professionally and financially.

The University of Ireland conducted a study run by Brian Hughes in 2017, which showed a positive correlation between likeability and low stress. The report showed that high likeability led to higher self-esteem, which then resulted in overcoming stress-associated physical ailments. It found that men who reported low self-esteem exhibited elevated cardiovascular responses to stress over time. Being likeable can be good for your health.

Let's dig a bit deeper into what makes people likeable. In his book *The Likeability Factor*, Tim Sanders describes four elements of likeability: friendliness, relevance, empathy and authenticity.

The first element, friendliness, is simply communicating a welcome gesture, or expressing a generally positive feeling or attitude towards others. A friendly message conveys without words, 'I'm happy to see you. I enjoy your company. I'm happy to be with you.'

Relevance, the second element, is the extent to which the other person connects to your life interests, wants and needs. For example, you have a health issue and you meet someone at a party who has experience in the medical industry. They understand where you're coming from (and sometimes they can even help). Having a common connection immediately builds likeability.

The third element, empathy, is the ability to identify with and feel someone's emotions. In other words, it's the ability to imagine yourself in the other person's situation and try to understand what they're thinking, feeling, wanting, or doing. It's different to sympathy, which is when you feel compassion – that's about your feeling, not theirs (you're simply feeling bad that the other person feels bad). Empathy is not about feeling sorry for others – it's making an attempt to see things from their vantage point. Think of a time when someone showed empathy to you. How did it feel? Did it make you feel more connected to them?

Lastly, Sanders refers to authenticity or realness. The word 'authentic' is used a lot these days, but it simply means being genuine and true. You can tell when someone's being real and authentic, and when that realness is missing we crave it.

So, what are the habits of people who are exceptionally likeable?

One, they have an optimistic attitude towards life. It radiates from them. A positive mental attitude means less cynicism (a form of negativity) and more relatability.

Two, they tend to be naturally good communicators. They speak confidently and from the heart, with a pleasing tone (how you say something, rather than what you say). You can say the same words but the meaning will change depending on your tone. 'How are you?' means one thing if asked in concern, and another if asked in sarcasm.

Three, exceptionally likeable people are very good listeners. They don't just listen to speak, rather they actively listen by paying close attention.

Four, exceptionally likeable people are usually emotionally stable. They don't overreact to situations (whether the situations are positive or negative) – research has found even positive overreaction can be off-putting.

Five, exceptionally likeable people are open-minded. They are more receptive to other people's ideas, and they try to understand the other person's point of view even where they disagree (this is linked with empathy).

Six, exceptionally likeable people are described as having more pleasant facial expressions. This doesn't necessarily mean they laugh or smile a lot, but that their expressions show up as more pleasing. Maybe they smile a little bit or frown less when they're speaking with others.

Seven, people who are exceptionally likeable seem to find a positive lesson in every setback and challenge. Rather than being pessimistic because of a negative situation, they make a conscious effort to look for the positive.

Eight, exceptionally likeable people tend to have a natural attitude of gratitude. They practise uncommon appreciation and typically do not take things for granted. When they show gratitude, they are specific about what they are thankful for, for example, 'Thank you for being a great listener.'

And nine, exceptionally likeable people are generous with praise. They are sincere, authentic and specific with their compliments, which boosts others' self-esteem. Insincere appreciation causes the reverse effect. Being specific is important – when we compliment someone and tie in a positive word with a specific event, it has more meaning, shows a high level of sincerity, and enhances the likeability factor.

Communicating with impact

Communicating with impact refers to the interpersonal skills we deploy when interacting with others. Good communication is critical for anyone who aspires to a high level of personal success.

Every time we communicate, our words, body language, tone, and listening style forms an impression in the listener's mind. We all want to make a positive impression and impact other people positively and there are a number ways to do that. But it's not all about technique. It's also about how we're feeling emotionally and energetically when we're interacting with others.

When we feel aligned with who we are – our beliefs, values, passion, and strengths – we communicate through our words, actions, tone, and energy. That last one is important. When we combine calm, comforting, harmonious, and trustworthy energies with our aligned selves, we naturally tend to communicate well and create a positive impression on others. Of course, we can strategically position ourselves better for that positive impression; however, strategy is not a substitute for inner alignment, understanding who we are and what we want, an integrity-based philosophy, and a winner's mindset. When this consistently underlies our communication, it naturally creates a positive impact in the mind of the receiver.

What are some skills you can develop to communicate with more impact?

Learning to relax in a social or business setting is one skill for communication that impacts. Remember the discussion of emotional contagion in Chapter 5? High levels of stress and anxiety are contagious, so you need to be mindful. Watch out for those signs and triggers of anxiety or stress. Maybe your breaths are shorter or you feel heaviness in your chest. It's common to feel nervous in a new environment, but I find the best way to get over anxiety and nervousness is by adopting a policy of honesty – acknowledge the feeling and do something about it. Focus on slowing your breathing and taking longer breaths to calm that nervous energy.

How we speak is another important skill. Imagine a person who is talking too much, too fast or too loud. How do you feel in that situation?

When someone's talking in one of these ways, it's often a misdirected attempt to take control of the situation, and this often stems from insecurity. Why do they have this incessant need to dominate the conversation? Do you catch yourself doing that? We all do it inadvertently sometimes, but we also know how frustrating it is to be around a person when you can't get a word in. Watch out for it in yourself. This behaviour will diminish your impact. Instead, try slowing down how you speak. It's an amazingly simple and powerful tool to create impact.

I mentioned empathy earlier in this chapter. Exercising empathy – making a genuine attempt to understand the other person – builds rapport, which builds impact. Rapport is often built unconsciously, but it can also be built by conscious effort by matching verbal behaviours (for example, volume or tone) or reflecting the language (word choice) and speech mannerisms of the person you're speaking with. This is not manipulation – it's a mirroring technique. We tend to gravitate to people who are more like us.

Eye contact is another skill to develop. Physically, when our eyes connect directly with someone, a connection happens at a deep sensory level. The eyes talk to the brain. Eyes are critical for one-on-one and large audience communication. When you make eye contact, look sincerely and steadily at a person, but avoid staring. A note here: there are cultural differences when it comes to eye contact and when you are working with people from other cultural backgrounds, it is worthwhile to make yourself aware of those differences. Your communication will suffer if you don't.

Posture and movement also affects communication impact. How do you position yourself when talking with others? Do you lean back on one hip when you're talking one-on-one or to a small group? Do you cross your legs while standing and chatting informally? Is your upper body posture erect, or do you slouch? When you speak, do you make eye contact, or do your eyes flit around? When it comes to more impactful communication, you need to be aware of how you hold yourself and what your body is doing. Posture-wise, it's helpful to stand tall and avoid slumping in the upper or lower body (imagine your head is dangling from a string that keeps your head up and shoulders back). Next time you're talking to someone, note what you're doing. Observe and change if needed. Try not to be rigid. Imagine talking to someone who adopts a wide stance with hands in their pockets, standing like a statue. It can be intimating, as well as lacking in authenticity. Gesture naturally – don't force it. And be aware of your facial expressions. Pop a smile on your face – it doesn't have to be a big one.

It's a lot to consider, but I'm not expecting you to master this in one go. Just be mindful about how you're coming across when communicating. Are you making a positive or negative impact?

When it comes to masterful communication, listening is a key skill. It's hard work to do it well. Professionally, I'm a great listener but socially I often let my listening skills slip. Listening is something I'm constantly working on.

Good listening has a two-step process. Step one is to ask open and insightful questions. Open-ended questions do not result in a simple yes or no, but invite the person to elaborate. Step two is to actively listen (some leaders use the phrase 'aggressive listening') in a determined and energetic way. It's different to passive listening, which is when you're talking to someone who is thinking about what they want to say next instead of focusing on what you're saying. You know when this is happening because they come up with a response as soon as you finish. Active listeners pay attention to what you're saying, pause, and follow with a well-considered and appropriate response after what you've said. And they also look out for intent and what's not being said, that is, reading between the lines (without overanalysing the speaker and causing discomfort). When you do this well, it's a fantastic way to create impact. Can you remember a time when someone actively listened to you?

Think of it in three steps: pay attention, pause and follow up. First you focus on what the speaker is saying. Then, instead of jumping in with a response, practise waiting two to three seconds – this shows that you have listened and are considering what they've said and how you want to respond. And finally, follow up. You can do this by paraphrasing (restating what the other person has said as you understand it to ensure you are not making assumptions). Research shows paraphrasing creates natural rapport between people. And you can ask more open-ended questions.

'Talk to someone about themselves
and they'll listen for hours.'
Dale Carnegie

Another skill for creating positive impact through communication is expressing gratitude (see Chapter 5). When someone gives us time and listens, thank them. When they are inspired by something we say, thank them. As Gertrude Stein said, 'Silent gratitude isn't much use to anyone.' I firmly believe gratitude is probably the most neglected and least expressed social skill. It's one of my personal weaknesses, and I'm always trying to improve how I express gratitude.

Finally, if you want to communicate with impact you must acknowledge your mistakes. Having the humility to admit mistakes shows others your true character and integrity. And once you've acknowledged your mistake, apologise. Do this when your actions hurt others, even if that was not your intent. Say what you're apologising for. Just saying 'Sorry' is not enough. And then make amends. Take appropriate steps to avoid recurrence of the issue.

Timeless style and fashion

How you present and show up to the world is a big part of how you're perceived by others. This perception will either open or close doors for you.

Some people claim appearance has nothing to do with success and that people should be judged on what they know and who they are. It makes sense, but in reality, most people form an unconscious impression of others within the first seven to sixty seconds of meeting. Every day, people form snap judgements about attractiveness, leadership ability, and personality based on appearance. Whether you're meeting a client or supplier, or going for a job interview, your first impression is caused within seconds. And since it's difficult to communicate character, values or knowledge in such a short time, that impression counts more than you might like.

That first impression comes mainly from what you wear and how you present yourself. It's not about keeping up with fashion or trends – they change from season to season and year to year – although you can if you want to. But it can be easier to adhere to timeless principles of style and fashion, and use those to present yourself in the best light possible.

Before I share what these principles are, let's look at the mistakes people make when it comes to presentation:

1. They don't try, either due to laziness or a belief that outside appearance is irrelevant. By doing this, they fail to see that good presentation can separate them from the pack and strongly increase their chances of professional and social success (as well as improving self-worth and confidence).

2. They wear ill-fitting clothes, instead of finding a happy medium between too loose and too tight (tight doesn't create a positive impression).

3. They overlook the importance of good and well-maintained footwear. Bad footwear choices are reflected in style, colour, quality, and maintenance. Some people hope no one will notice their shoes are falling apart … but people do. Wearing good footwear is part of expressing pride in how you present.

4. They wear clothes that don't align with who they are. There's a fine line between presenting well and trying to be someone you're not, but they haven't quite figured that out. The result is a lack of confidence, which will affect opportunities.

5. They let other people choose or buy their clothes. Doing that means the other person's perceptions and style choices determine how they present.

6. They focus on trends without asking how the 'latest look' suits their personality or body type.

7. They don't dress for their body shape. One outfit does not look the same on two different people.

It takes effort to acquire style, and paradoxically, it takes even more effort to look effortlessly stylish. If you're unsure how, consider hiring an image consultant to guide you through the complex rules about trouser, shirt, skirt, dress, suits, and jacket length, or to help find clothes for your body shape or colouring. A consultant knows different strategies for all body shapes and colouring, and they will show you which ones will help improve your overall image. The return on that investment will be more than the time or money you spend on it. You can also look up free styling tips on the Internet. However you go about it, once you're aware of your right fit and style, and what aligns with your personality, you can make a conscious effort to present your best self. Over time, good presentation will become a habit.

Here are some tips stylish people follow:

1. Confidence: A stylish person understands that their appearance reflects their core values, career, lifestyle, and more. Be confident in what you're wearing and imagine you are the best-dressed person in the room.

2. Appropriateness: Stylish people make sensible clothing choices because they understand what suits their body type and features. They are not dictated by what looks good on someone else, or by saving a few dollars. They also consider the weather and the appropriateness of the outfit for the event.

3. Hair: Stylish people have regular appointments with their hairdresser or barber. They don't wait until their hair looks untidy or unhealthy.

4. Tailoring: A stylish person ensures their clothes fit properly. They find a skilled tailor or seamstress who can alter clothes for the best fit.

5. Maintenance: Stylish people are aware of the maintenance and care instructions for their clothes. They know what needs to be dry-cleaned and what requires a delicate wash. They also keep their shoes in clean, and where appropriate, shiny condition. Some men keep a shoeshine box handy for this.

6. Storage: A stylish person understands the need for appropriate storage for clothes, shoes, and accessories. They know it's easier to have dedicated spaces for different types of items – clothes, ties, jewellery, cufflinks, shoes, and so on – both for accessibility and proper care.

7. Quality: Stylish people choose quality over price. They ask, will this item last? Will it still be in style in a few years?

8. Practicality: A person of style understands that comfort and functionality are as important as aesthetics. They consider how they can perform their duties and still move around.

9. Details: Stylish people consider details like which tie matches which shirt. Which shoes go with this dress? Which blouse goes with that jacket? Where can I put my business cards or phone?

10. Plan: A stylish person plans what they're wearing the night before and has every item ready. It saves them time when they're rushing to conferences or early morning meetings.

11. Suits: Stylish people own at least one well-fitted dark suit. They never go out of style and can be used for many occasions, from work presentations to funerals.

12. Colour: A person of style treats colour like a spice – they use it sparingly, knowing it's the secret ingredient for spicing up an outfit.

13. Fragrance: Stylish people understand the power of smell. They pay attention to the way they smell, maintain daily hygiene (which includes being mindful of foods which affect the body's natural in a negative way), and don't over-apply perfumes.

14. Measurements: A stylish person knows their measurements – collar, sleeve, waist, torso, bust, trouser – and keeps them handy. They don't rely on manufacturers' sizing charts and instead aim for the right fit.

15. Build: Stylish people build wardrobes to suit their lifestyle. They have a 'less is more' approach, valuing quality over quantity. They look for interchangeable classic pieces as a base and change their look with different shirts, blouses, and accessories. They aren't afraid to have duplicate items in different colours if the fit works.

16. Grooming: Part of a stylish person's routine is grooming. They set aside time each week to trim nails, groom body hair, moisturise, and so on. Having a system in place reduces the pain or embarrassment that can result from a lack of self-care.

17. Discard: Stylish people don't hang on to worn-out favourites or stained clothes. Some follow the 'buy one, donate one' formula – for each piece of new clothing they buy, they donate an older item to charity.

Remember, our habits shape our lives. If you are not conscious about the way you present yourself, you will not make a desirable impression. In the end, a lack of effort will diminish your success and undermine your impact.

What we have covered in this chapter

In this chapter we have covered:
- aspiring for greatness
- becoming more likeable
- communicating with impact
- timeless style and fashion principles.

What do successful people do? Successful people aim for more than average or moderately successful – they aim for significance. They understand the importance of being likeable, and make themselves more pleasing and appealing in social interactions. Successful people understand the importance of making an impact through communication (which also involves active listening), and they understand the importance of timeless presentation principles and how to use them to maximise opportunities and impact.

'Talent can be natural, but greatness
has to be developed and earned.'

CHAPTER 7
Build indestructible confidence

'Do not let your temporary excuses, limiting beliefs, and denials become your permanent identity.'

Are your natural talents and abilities hampered by self-doubt? Do you find it hard to say no? Would you like to come across as more confident in social and professional situations?

Confidence is the passport to success in your personal and professional life. When your confidence and self-esteem is high, you have more control of your personal and work circumstances. You can take on new challenges, trust yourself in difficult situations, go beyond your personal limits, tackle things you've never done before, and make full use of your natural talents and capabilities. Without confidence, life's challenges can seem insurmountable. Confidence provides the strength to tackle these challenges.

In this chapter, we are going to focus on what it means to develop confidence. One thing that every successful person has is that they operate from a place of authentic confidence.

The link between confidence and success

What is confidence? Confidence is the feeling that you can trust what you (or others) do. It's about having faith in what you can do, instead of worrying about what you can't, and having the willingness to learn from successes and failures.

There is a preconception that confident people are loud, bold or extroverted, and handle any personal and professional situation with minimum of fuss and a lot of certainty. These behavioural traits, or outward expressions, are not necessarily the same as confidence. Nor is perfection. Perfect people do not exist. Those who try to be perfect are often among the unhappiest in the world. They cannot see that perfection is a race that has no ending.

True confidence is about trust. People with true confidence focus on their strengths and have a keen sense of what they want, so they have less doubt and know they can succeed. They also have a hunger to succeed, leading others to mistake confidence with arrogance. However, arrogant people believe they're entitled to success without actually working for it. Arrogance means undervaluing other people's capabilities. An arrogant self-view happens when someone is so caught up in their own self-importance and success that they're unable to make space in their life for anyone or anything else. Ultimately, this kind of egotistical behaviour repels people.

How do you build true confidence?

The first thing is to minimise self-doubt, by focusing on what can go right (positive outcomes) rather than what can go wrong (negative outcomes) – even if in the past there has been a negative outcome. Much of self-doubt comes from past situations where performance or outcomes were not as good as hoped. When this comes up, ask 'Did I really fail? Did I do the best I could with the experience, knowledge and skills I had at the time?' Then ask, 'What can I learn from that experience? What can I do better next time?' Conquering the fear of failure is an important step in confidence building.

Read about people like mountaineer Edmund Hillary, former British Prime Minister Winston Churchill, or American businessman Colonel Sanders to see how they overcame fear of failure by focusing on strengths.

Secondly, accept yourself. If you fear rejection and seek acceptance from others, you're like most people on the planet, because one of the greatest human needs is to be accepted. But before others accept you, you need to accept yourself. It's a choice. By choosing to think, behave, and believe differently about yourself (self-acceptance), you are choosing confidence. By choosing not to agree with others' perceptions or rejections of you (in order to accept yourself), you are choosing confidence.

Next, remember these words: commit and deliver. Confident people do not commit to something they cannot deliver. Every time you make promises or commitments and don't deliver, not only do you let others down, but your subconscious mind gets the message that you are not aligned with what you say and do. In the long term, this affects self-esteem. It undermines your trust in yourself. Focus on committing to things you trust you can deliver, and then make every attempt to follow through.

Now, notice how confident people speak. They don't say things like 'I can't', 'It's too difficult', 'Hopefully …', 'I wish', or 'One day'. That's the language of people who lack confidence, of words and phrases embedded in the subconscious. It's self-limiting. Words mirror our thoughts and feelings, and the way we use them makes a profound difference to the way we think, feel, act, and ultimately, our success. Confident people often practise the three R's: rename, reframe, and redirect. How? When you notice a worrying thought, just say to yourself, 'Stop' and understand that a thought is not necessarily a reality. Then reframe – focus on positive thoughts, or distract yourself. For example, pay attention to your breathing, or start counting backwards from a hundred. Force yourself to change negative thoughts to positive ones. Redirect to do something uplifting, fun, and engaging: just changing your physiology by getting up, bending forwards, hanging like a rag doll, or just doing a few jumping jacks will switch off the worry button. Even if it's just brief, sometimes it's important to do that to break that negative pattern.

How do you reframe negative and self-defeating thoughts that diminish confidence? Here are some examples to give you an idea:

- 'I will never have my own business' becomes 'With enough work and diligence, I'm capable of having a successful business.'
- 'I don't have the skills to go to the next step' becomes 'If I put my mind to it, I can learn those skills and I get ahead.'
- 'I'm not financially savvy' becomes 'Being financially savvy is a skill that can be developed and I can do that.'
- 'I can't survive without my other half' becomes 'I feel lost inside without them, but I will heal and find inner peace again.'
- 'I should have done it yesterday' becomes 'Today's another day. I'll get it done.'
- 'I can't possibly do that' becomes 'I won't know the extent of my powers until I give it everything I have.'
- 'I wish things could change' becomes 'I can make things change.'
- 'I wish I could succeed like that person' becomes 'I create my own success.'
- 'I wish I was rich' becomes 'I create my own wealth.'
- 'I'm not very lucky' becomes 'I'm alive. I live in a free society not a war-torn country. All my needs are met, and I have a lot of opportunities at my disposal.'

You get the idea? See how reframing helps develop confidence? Watch the words you say to yourself. Be aware of when you're putting yourself down, and don't put yourself down when you've made a mistake. Everyone makes mistakes. But try this: reframe a mistake as 'a learning opportunity'.

Finding what you love and doing it well also increases confidence and happiness. Make time to do things that inspire you, whether it's listening to Luciano Pavarotti sing, watching your favourite V8 race car driver win the cup, or whatever it is that inspires you. Inspiration emerges during those moments when we see excellence. Remember, if you spend more time on things you hate, it will negatively impact your confidence.

Lastly, go for diversity of experience. Always opting for safety and security, or sticking to the comfort zone, will end up killing your confidence. But the more you get out of the comfort zone to experience varied situations and environments, the better you will handle diverse situations. I cannot stress this enough.

Confidence is a key ingredient to success, but there are no shortcuts to building it. Over time, if you are consistent, aligned, and show integrity, your self-concept will strengthen and your confidence will increase. The more confident you are the more people will trust and rely on you. And because people's trust is a vital ingredient of leadership and influence, this will elevate your success in life.

Combating negative influences

We are all born with a degree of natural confidence. This gives us the ability to do 'automatic' things, such as breathing, smiling, walking, talking, laughing, and crying. Only when we fear losing one of those abilities, do we realise how important they are to us. The confidence we have, whether it's natural or built over time, can be adversely affected by external negative influences.

The first negative influence is blame and criticism. This can come from many different sources, such as parents, partners, or work colleagues, and the reasons can be unexpected. Maybe you were born male and your parents had their hearts set on having a girl, or vice versa. Maybe as a child you were constantly berated for being clumsy. Maybe they have high expectations and express disappointment if you don't (or haven't) lived up to them. Or perhaps someone finds fault with everything you do. All of these examples affect confidence and self-esteem by creating an atmosphere of uncertainty and fear. If all you hear is blame and criticism, your confidence will suffer.

The top five symptoms of blame and criticism are:

1. You think everything is your fault
2. You are highly sensitive to criticism
3. You expect to be told off for whatever you do
4. You blame yourself when things do not work out
5. You fear failure so you don't take risks.

The second negative influence is conformity. Have you ever been in a room full of people and known the answer to a question asked by a presenter, but kept quiet in case you were wrong? Perhaps in your childhood you gave a wrong answer and you felt ridiculed or laughed at. Sometimes the pain of that experience embeds in the memory and affects the desire to stand out.

When we don't want to be excluded from certain social or professional situations, we often give in to the pressure to conform. Sometimes we want to speak up for something we believe in, but fear keeps us silent. And sometimes we conform to societal standards and expectations about whether we should do a course, learn an instrument, sail around the world, leave an unhappy relationship, or start a new career or business. But every time we go against our authentic self it leads to an inner state of contradiction. We stop trusting ourselves, and second guess. We ignore our instincts because they go against what everyone else is saying, feeling, or thinking. Our decision-making is increasingly influenced by what others do rather than our gut feeling and instinct. All of this affects our confidence at a deep level, triggering a cycle of regret and remorse.

The top five symptoms of conformity are:

1. You put off making decisions in case you're wrong
2. You're timid and do not accept opportunities when they arise
3. You judge yourself excessively
4. You try too hard to please others
5. You make decisions on what you think you *should* do, rather than on what you want to do.

The third negative influence is exclusion, which is when we feel, or are, overlooked. Examples include missing out on a promotion at work or not being invited to a social network gathering. Feeling excluded impacts our confidence because it leads to loneliness or the sense that we're not good enough. We decide there must be something wrong with us, especially when exclusion comes without explanation or reason, which can lead to self-sabotaging decision-making.

The top five symptoms of exclusion are:
1. You suck up to the decision-maker to ensure inclusion
2. You are uncertain because you don't know where you stand with others
3. You constantly feel that you're not good enough
4. You feel resentment and jealousy when others get opportunities you don't
5. You compare yourself with those who are included.

The fourth negative influence is competition. We're introduced to this from an early age via competitive sports or academic performance, and it's reinforced later in work and business environments. When competition regularly has no reward, it's tempting to develop a mindset that says, 'What's the point in trying? I'll never achieve what I want. Someone always gets there first.' But if you accept this mindset, you become accustomed to disappointment, which affects confidence levels.

The top five symptoms of competition are:
1. You compare yourself with others
2. You doubt your own ability
3. You put yourself under stress and pressure, when you're already trying as hard as you can
4. You seek approval and confirmation from others
5. In extreme examples, you may even steal, lie, or cheat to achieve the desired result.

The fifth negative influence is disappointment, which can erode self-confidence in a major way. Imagine expecting the next work promotion was yours, and dreaming of benefits such as an increased salary. Imagine hoping to date someone, and dreaming of spending time with them. When things we hope for don't come our way – we get overlooked, or someone else gets that opportunity – all of that built-up expectancy turns to disappointment. And the more disappointment is experienced, the less trusting we become of ourselves and others, and the more fearful we are of commitment or trying. We become cynical. We don't believe what people tell us. Our confidence wanes.

The top five symptoms of disappointment are:
1. You expect things to go wrong, so you don't bother trying
2. You don't think you deserve good things
3. You don't hope in case you're let down
4. You're suspicious when things go well, fearing that something is bound to go wrong
5. You don't commit to relationships for fear of being let down.

The last negative influence is dominance, which is often experienced through bullying. Being bullied at school, home, or in the workplace has devastating and long-lasting effects on our confidence. Bullying includes being treated differently, undermined, singled out, ridiculed, or subjected to excessive monitoring or supervision, all of which diminishes self-confidence. The moment bullies sense our vulnerabilities – such as a physical imperfection, an accent, background, age, or gender – we become a target. We start to attack ourselves and perceive that it's okay for people to take from us at will. We don't have the mental muscle to resist, so we become a compulsive giver, before people even ask. Giving becomes a safety measure. For example, people who undercharge for their professional services and have been on the receiving end of bullying are often too scared to charge the going rate.

The top five symptoms of dominance are:

1. You take on the role of the victim and accept the blame for everything that goes wrong
2. You give too much of yourself to others, because you think they expect it
3. You let others walk all over you at great emotional cost to yourself
4. You find it difficult to say no
5. You give more importance to what other people think of you and how they value you.

What other negative influences are affecting your confidence? Having an awareness of this means you can take steps to remove behaviours and symptomatic thinking that erodes your confidence.

Conquering self-sabotage

Many people metaphorically shoot themselves in the foot when they're on the verge of success or something good is about to happen in their life. Whenever they have the opportunity to succeed, they unconsciously find ways to sabotage that opportunity. We call this behaviour self-sabotage.

For example, a person who believes they do not deserve to make money may self-sabotage by making a bad investment decision. A person who believes they do not deserve a relationship may self-sabotage by making their relationship untenable. Someone who believes they are not 'a person of good character' may self-sabotage by engaging in behaviour that is not morally or legally right. I know many people who do these things.

Self-sabotage is not something we do deliberately. It's an influence in our subconscious mind that stems from certain disappointing or negative experiences, such as being stood up on a date, making an error that negatively impacts others, being mocked or put down, or being regularly overlooked for opportunities or promotions. These experiences shape how we evaluate ourselves at a deep mental level. When we self-sabotage, we are often helplessly acting in ways that repel successful outcomes.

Over time, some people become comfortable with not succeeding. They develop an identity or persona of someone who does not succeed, and when success doesn't come their way, it confirms this view of themselves. In turn, their actions align with this expectation, creating a self-fulfilling prophecy.

The good news is that self-sabotage can be conquered in five steps: mindset, positivity messaging, completion, attraction, and willpower.

Step one is to develop a mindset that enables diffusion or dilution of negative experiences. For example, let's say you've been stood up by a date. You could respond in one of these ways:

- Say, 'It wasn't meant to be.'
- Go to a bar and meet someone else
- Acknowledge your miserable, annoyed, and disappointed feelings and move on
- Say 'I'm unattractive and I don't blame them for standing me up.'

Which of these approaches is conducive to self-sabotage programming? It's the last one – taking the blame for something going wrong that was completely out of your control. In contrast, the first three approaches all act to diffuse the negative experience. By telling yourself it wasn't meant to be, you're taking a philosophical, no-blame approach; going to a bar to meet someone else is a proactive approach; and acknowledging your feelings means they are less likely to fester and create resentment.

Step two is receiving positive messages about ourselves (from ourselves and others), which in turn helps build and sustain confidence. What do you need to hear in moments of self-doubt or challenge? Seven-time Wimbledon champion Pete Sampras carried a letter from his wife onto the tennis court to help him through moments of self-doubt and uncertainty. The letter reminded him of his accomplishments and encouraged him to look at himself as the best tennis player in the world. Is there someone who could give you a positive or inspirational message like that? Why not ask them to write you a motivational message? Don't assume they would have done so if they wanted to. Often the people closest to us don't know what we need until we ask them. Or write your own motivational message that's a reminder of your best qualities. These messages can provide the emotional support and strength to get us through the difficult, self-sabotage times so we are able to reach our goals.

Step three is to 'complete your messes'. Most people with self-sabotage programming have a habit of not completing things. Rather than developing discipline, they get bored easily and collect a lot of loose ends or get seduced by something new (a.k.a. Shiny Object Syndrome). This causes them to fall short of success. Examples of incomplete messes include giving up on a course or professional certification only a few weeks in, a piece of art left unfinished, home repairs left undone, not using the gym membership you paid for, and so on.

We all do this at times – get excited or inspired about a new project or thing, and then get distracted or bored. But some do this more than others. They develop an internal programming of never finishing things. They find reasons to confirm the project is not a good idea, or use rationalising excuses such as 'It's not working for me anyway' or 'It won't benefit my career.' Self-sabotage supersedes their original motivation. And they don't even know they're doing it. Try this: Don't start another project, until you've completed all the outstanding ones. Trust yourself to develop the mental muscle required to finish what you started. Let yourself cross the finish line.

Step four is to become a success magnet. Get used to attracting success. Why shouldn't you be successful? Some people are almost embarrassed at the thought of having great success, while at a deep level they desperately crave it, and they self-sabotage because they expect success for others and not themselves.

So how do you get on good terms with success? The key to becoming successful is to develop success habits (see Chapter 5), but if you tend to self-sabotage, you need to start small. Attract success a little bit at a time so you can get used to it. Reduce your goals into simple, manageable chunks you can achieve effortlessly. Don't try to set impossible targets or put pressure on yourself too early. For example, if you want to lose weight but you self-sabotage by not following through with gym programs, try five minutes exercise a day for thirty days to create a new habit. Notice the weight this takes off your shoulders as you move bit by bit towards your goal. You can add more challenge eventually, but for those who need to reprogram their thinking, giving birth to a new pattern is more important at the start. Small achievements often lead to bigger ones, because success attracts success.

Developing willpower is the final step to conquering self-sabotage behaviour. Willpower is the refusal to accept the limitations of a given situation and the desire to change it. It's a critical step for achieving an outcome or facilitating change. For example, imagine waking up in the middle of the night to hear rain, then remembering that you forgot to put your gardening tools away. What would you do? Would you go back to sleep and deal with them in the morning? Or would you go outside and put the tools away? What action you will take depends on the value you place on your equipment; the greater the value of an outcome, the stronger the desire to make it happen. We all have a degree of willpower, but it can be superseded by self-sabotage behaviour. How do you change this? It comes down to choice. Choose to persevere in the face of adversity. Choose not to accept 'No' for an answer. Choose to believe in your own capability. And choose your dream. Give yourself the opportunity to do things you didn't know you could achieve.

Here are some extra ways you can develop willpower:
- Do a sponsored walk or run that takes you out of your comfort zone – surprise yourself
- Read books about people who never gave up, despite adversity, such as Helen Keller
- Don't leave the dishes in the sink overnight – start fresh in the morning
- At the gym, do a few extra repetitions once you've passed your targets – go the extra mile.

Self-saboteurs are addicted to struggle because they listen to negative messages about themselves and do not finish what they started. Successful people complete what they set out to do, learn from their mistakes, under-promise and over-deliver, do not punish themselves if they don't succeed, and celebrate success.

Developing inner self-belief

Self-belief is a quiet self-assurance that comes from within. It's confidence in your own abilities and judgement. It's a feeling of authenticity that says, 'I'll make something of my life because I know what I'm good at.' But, as discussed earlier in this chapter, it's not the same as arrogance.

When we are born we are preloaded with natural self-belief. You only have to look at toddlers to see evidence of that. Very young children don't have a critical voice inside that berates them every time they make a mistake. When they spill their food, they don't think they're an idiot; when they wet themselves, they don't think they're an embarrassment. The critical voice and negative beliefs come later. Most of us spend years of our adult lives trying to reclaim this childlike self-belief, without really knowing how.

It starts with recognising any negative beliefs and habits you have developed and understanding the power of your mind (see Chapters 2 and 3). By now, you understand how beliefs, even when they're false, act as our truth and form a lens through which we see ourselves, and the world. And by now you have some tools to replace limiting beliefs that affect confidence with self-supportive beliefs that lead to success. You know that negative thoughts create anxiety, tension, increased blood pressure and heart rates, and impact self-esteem. This is a good time to remind you that thoughts affect feelings, feelings affect behaviours, and behaviours and actions produce results. Our beliefs become our reality. So, to reclaim positive self-belief, don't feed thoughts that lead to negativity or self-doubt.

'The most important words you will ever hear are the words you say to yourself.'

A positive attitude contributes to developing inner self-belief. If you believe you're attractive and that people like you, you will act in a confident way. If you believe you are unattractive and that people are not drawn to you, you will act with less confidence. In order to feel good about yourself, you need to learn to forgive the past, feel great about the present, and look forward to the future with excitement and positivity. Respect yourself. Don't put yourself down when you make mistakes (it's how you learn). Silence your inner critic and use praise instead of criticism for your actions. Be aware of the language and the words you use to describe yourself and other situations. Remember, whatever we tell ourselves with repetition, our mind absorbs and accepts.

Earlier in this chapter, I talked about how confident people talk to themselves. One of the quickest ways to develop inner belief is to speak the way confident people do. Changing your language is relatively easy (and there are steps earlier in the chapter) and the results can be significant. Here are some examples:

- Instead of 'I'm terrified' try 'I'm excited.'
- Instead of 'I can't stand it' try 'I have the ability to deal with it.'
- Instead of 'I'm freaked out' try 'I'm calm and in control.'
- Instead of 'They won't like me' try 'I like myself and so do others.'
- Instead of 'I'm falling apart' try 'I'm doing very well.'

If you copy the language of confident people, you will elevate your own self-belief. When we take on someone else's emotional vocabulary, we also take on their emotional state – that's the emotional contagion effect I talked about in Chapter 5.

Visualisation is another way to develop inner belief. In Chapter 3, I discussed visualisation in terms of mindset. But at this stage, it's important to know that visualisation is a useful technique to see yourself as confident and certain. You can 'see' your posture as self-assured. You can 'hear' people telling you how great you are and how much they enjoy being with you. You can picture the job you want or the date you're going on. By using visualisation to create positive mental images, you can develop unshakeable confidence in yourself. On the other hand, visualising possible negative outcomes simply keeps confidence low. Rather than thinking about what you don't want when you visualise, focus on what you do want.

'Whatever you focus on, you move towards.'

Sometimes people think that to have inner self-belief they should exhibit signs of success. You are not:

- your current situation
- your past
- your bank account
- your body
- your weight
- your age
- your job.

These things are part of the package that is you, the part that others see (to greater or lesser extent). Your inner self-belief does not depend on this outside package. You can have everything on the outside in order, but still lack self-belief. But as long as you feel inadequate, you will never achieve the success you truly desire. So, say things like, 'I'm enough, I'm always enough, I will always be enough.' Language like this helps you feel better about yourself – it encourages you to expect success and aim high. It is more important to believe in yourself before aiming for success. Remember, success is a by-product of self-belief, not a determiner.

Finding what you're good at (see Chapter 4) is another way to develop self-belief. The more time we spend on things we're good at, the more confident and happier we feel (it's hard to feel successful doing what we hate). When you know your talents and passion and you're living your purpose, you believe in yourself. You don't feel the need to impress anyone, or to be liked or acknowledged. Every human being has the ability to achieve excellence. Everyone is here for a purpose with something valuable to contribute. It's up to each of us to find our talent and be outstanding at it.

'It is neither wealth nor splendour; but tranquillity
and occupation which give you happiness.'
Thomas Jefferson

When you are doing something you're good at and striving towards excellence, you feel good and then you start to like yourself. In turn, you like other people and they like you. It becomes an amazing cycle. How much you like yourself often determines how well you do in life, because it influences our energy, creativity, and stress responses. Here's the paradox: we can't truly like ourselves unless we know our areas of excellence and learn to trust them; but we can't find out who we are unless we like ourselves enough to try.

Finally, self-belief is propelled by your state of expectation. If you expect to fail, that's exactly what's going to happen. Try this: instead of expecting to fail, expect to succeed. Expect to feel confident and assured of success. Expectation produces a higher vibrational frequency than wishing, hoping or wanting. The subconscious mind will act on whatever mental image of expectation you engage with. If you worry about taking on something new, and expect it will be too hard, that's what your subconscious mind will engage with. If you expect it will be a challenge, but that you can cope, you're acting from a place of positive self-belief. When you combine an intense desire with relaxed expectation, meaning you're not worried about the outcome, you will find that your desires will manifest faster because you're operating from a higher vibration.

Earlier in this chapter I talked about the difference between confidence and arrogance. I want to be clear here, people don't dislike confidence, or confident people, rather they admire them. If you rang up Gordon Ramsay and said, 'I want to have dinner at your restaurant. How do I know the food will be good?' what do you think Gordon Ramsay would say? Something like, 'Listen, I'm the best f#@king chef in the world. The food won't just be good, it'll be bloody marvellous!' His passion makes him believe in himself and what he does, and as a result, most people, including his staff, like and respect him.

How are you going to believe in yourself today?

What we have covered in this chapter

In this chapter we have covered:
- self-confidence and success
- combatting negative influences
- conquering self-sabotage
- developing unshakeable confidence.

What do successful people do? Successful people understand the link between confidence and success, and know how to deal with negative influences that affect their confidence. They are aware of self-sabotaging behaviours and know how to overcome them. They have authentic and unshakeable confidence in themselves and their abilities.

'The victim has a story why they can't.
The victor has a story why they must.'

CHAPTER 8

Lead your way to success

'Acquisition and accumulation without contribution will never result in a positive legacy.'

Do you want to be the best version of yourself? Do you have a vision that goes beyond your own needs? Do you dream of making a difference? If you want your actions to inspire others to be more, do more, and have more you need to become a leader. Not a leader with positional power, but one people willingly follow. Leadership, is not about position, it is about passion. It is not about impressing, it is about making an impact.

How to become a person considered valuable by others

How do you become a person of value? And what does leadership have to do with being valuable and successful?

One of the things that will determine your success is how valuable you are perceived to be. Now, don't misunderstand this. Every woman, man, and child is valuable – to their families, communities, and so on. However, I am referring specifically to the context of perceived value within the marketplace and industry. For others to consider you valuable to them, you must have something to offer. You must build your worth with the people around you.

The amount of remuneration we receive is based on how valuable we are perceived to be in the marketplace or industry. When someone says to me 'I don't have money,' or 'I'm not making enough money,' I usually respond by saying, 'Perhaps you don't have enough money (or you're not making enough money) because you are not adding enough value to enough people.' Our remuneration is directly proportionate to the amount of value we add in the marketplace (people outside your family), and how many people we add value to. When we are paid, we are not paid for an hour of *time* – we are paid for the *value* we bring to the hour. If someone is knocked back for a pay rise, it's usually because the market determines that the value they're providing per hour is insufficient for their desired level of remuneration.

Leadership is one way to become more valuable within the marketplace. Later in this chapter, I will clarify and demystify some of the myths and misconceptions about leadership – what it is, what it isn't. But for now, let's look at why leadership is important and why everyone should consider it as a means of adding value.

John C. Maxwell said, 'Everything rises and falls on leadership.' And it does – from families to communities, from industries to nations. Imagine a country run without leaders, a police force without leadership, a school without a principal. What would happen to children if they didn't have a parent or guardian to guide them? Leadership is part of our everyday lives, and is vital to effective functioning of organisations, groups, communities, and families.

Leadership is not only for the select few. We can all aspire to leadership and incorporate leadership characteristics in our lives. When we do this, we not only make a difference, but we also attract more value in the marketplace (and often, a higher level of remuneration). By consciously deciding to become a leader, we open ourselves to more possibilities.

Surveys show that many people today are not interested in leadership because of the way they perceive leadership. Globally, we're currently experiencing a leadership crisis. We have witnessed many leaders – whether in organisations, corporations, or politics – who have not done the right thing by those they are leading. This exposure to bad leadership has influenced perceptions of what constitutes leadership, of what makes it valuable, and puts off people who might aspire to leadership. Yet, there are many fantastic examples of leaders and leadership in the world, past and present – people who served as inspirational role models, who went above and beyond their personal needs to serve the needs of broader humanity. People like Martin Luther King, Nelson Mandela, Gandhi, and Mother Teresa.

Leadership is something you must invite yourself into – something you consciously and decisively step into. It will not be imposed upon you. People often think they need to be a manager or decision-maker to be perceived as a leader, but leadership is really about initiative. It's about driving change. It's about influence. Instead of, 'I'll become a leader first and then I'll learn about leadership' it is, 'I'll learn about leadership and cultivate leadership qualities and then I'll attract leadership opportunities and higher levels of remuneration.' Any person at any level in an organisation can step up and drive positive change by using initiative and consciously building influence. A person who does that will, in time, be elevated to leadership positions.

> *'Before you are a leader, success is all about growing yourself. When you become a leader, success is all about growing others.'*
> **Jack Welch**

I mentioned earlier that leadership is not a title or position but a function. It is a service to render for the betterment of others. Some people become leaders through contacts and unfair influences. But it's difficult to keep people following you willingly if you are not perceived to be adding value. When you become a leader, you have a real opportunity to add value, go beyond your personal needs, create positive change, and influence decision-making, as well as create a great lifestyle for yourself.

Defining proper leadership

There are thousands of books written on leadership. It is talked about in every business, yet few people understand it. Few people achieve the privilege of influencing a cause or organisation, but the traits and qualities of leaders can be acquired by anyone.

Before going further, I want to distinguish between a leader and a manager. Many people believe there is no distinction. Consider it this way: A worker does their job, a supervisor shows others how the job is done, and a manager makes sure the job is done. In contrast, a leader inspires others to add value or work *better*. Management is a form of leadership, but leadership is not only about management. No one wants to be managed, but everyone wants to be led. And there are no world-class managers, only world-class leaders.

In his book *Good Leaders Ask Great Questions*, John C. Maxwell shares a story told by British author Leonard Ravenhill about a group of tourists visiting a picturesque village where they saw an old man sitting by a fence. In a rather patronising way one of the visitors asked, 'Were any great men born in this village?' Without looking up the old man replied, 'No, only babies.' The point is that leadership is developed over time. Even those born with natural leadership characteristics have to further develop these characteristics to become great leaders.

So what makes a leader?

> *'Leadership is influence. Just because someone has a title, doesn't mean that person is a leader.'*
> **John C. Maxwell**

I love that quote. After four decades observing leadership within his family, community, and other organisations, and many years developing his leadership potential, John C. Maxwell concluded that leadership is ultimately about influence. Many people don't understand this. They aspire for leadership because they want a position or a title, and believe they will become a leader after that happens. But if they don't have leadership skills, such as influence, others will not be willing to follow them (unless their salaries depend on it). Interestingly, sometimes people who don't have senior or high-ranking positions have more influence than those who do, but because they do not perceive themselves as leaders, they do not develop their leadership traits further.

Leaders need followers who believe in their vision, mission, and cause. If people don't follow you, then you are not a leader. This is where influence comes in. Leaders influence and inspire people to work with (and for) them without obligation. If you have no influence, people won't want to follow you, or work for you, or believe in your cause.

'People don't care how much you know
until they know how much you care.'
Theodore Roosevelt

As a speaker, I often share that quote. Roosevelt means that to be a leader you must capture people's hearts before you capture their minds. Many aspiring leaders believe that knowledge plus authority equals leadership. In reality, if they lack influence and have failed to win the hearts of people, they will not retain their role as leader. Winning influence can be quite challenging, but I will cover this more in Chapter 9.

Character development is another key quality of effective leaders. When leaders fail, more often than not it is due to a character flaw than a lack of competence. Character development is important for leaders, but it is overlooked by a need to develop skills and competencies. But leadership is a process of growth. It's not a platform to rest on. Leaders who stand the test of time never stop growing – personally, professionally, mentally, emotionally, and spiritually. We cannot take people further than we've been ourselves because leadership starts with self-leadership. Leaders do this by raising the standards by which they judge themselves and by which they're willing to be judged.

There is no definitive list of character traits for leaders because what is needed varies according to situation. But one that all leaders need is courage. Leaders have to get out in front of others. They need to have the mental and moral strength to stay in front despite the difficulty of the challenge.

Another leadership requirement is knowledge of human nature. When we understand our emotional biases, limitations, and personal potential, we naturally understand other people's biases, limitations, and potential. Leaders who do this are more empathetic – they consider why people do the things that they do.

'I am only one, but I am one. I cannot do everything, but I can do something. And I will not let what I cannot do interfere with what I can do.'
Edward Everett Hale

Leaders also have vision, or foresight. They see things – opportunities, possibilities, problems, and solutions – before others do. Vision also allows leaders to be proactive rather than reactive. They don't wait for change to happen – they create change. People who innovate, discover, and invent, all start with a vision. Apple was perceived to be a conventional computer company until Steve Jobs had a vision for the iPod music player. Vision is the energy behind a leader's effort; it is the force that pushes through all the problems.

What comes first, a leader or a vision? A leader must have vision. Without vision, leaders lose their influence and their power to lead. John C. Maxwell says, 'People do what people see.' According to a Stanford study, 89 per cent of what we learn and follow comes from what we see in others. People depend on visual stimulation for growth. But, even though vision creates a leader, people will not follow the vision unless they follow the leader. Leaders need to win hearts first and then get people to embrace their vision.

Becoming a trustworthy person of authority

Education is usually focused on technical skill, qualifications, and experience, rather than character development. However, possessing certain character traits – such as honesty, integrity, trustworthiness, and kindness – contribute to your success more than you might realise. Such traits cannot be measured in a tangible way, but they can be seen and felt.

Character should not be confused with reputation. Look at how William Hersey Davis makes the difference:

>Reputation is what you are supposed to be; character is what you are.
>
>Reputation is the photograph; character is the face.
>
>Reputation comes over one from without; character grows up from within.
>
>Reputation is what you have when you come to a new community; character is what you have when you go away.
>
>Your reputation is learnt in an hour; your character does not come to light for a year
>
>Reputation is made in a moment; character is built in a lifetime. Reputation grows like a mushroom; character grows like the oak.
>
>A single newspaper report gives you your reputation; a life of toil gives you your character.
>
>Reputation makes you rich or makes you poor; character makes you happy or makes you miserable
>
>Reputation is what men say about you on your tombstone; character is what angels say about you before the throne of God.

People of good, strong character make you feel comfortable. You trust them to handle your affairs and help you make decisions. On the other hand, we feel little to no trust for people with perceived negative character traits, whether in a personal, professional, or social context. When there is trust, there is a greater focus on working together. There is mutual tolerance and more forgiveness of mistakes. There is more forgiveness of mistakes, acceptance, commitment, and positive communication and less worry, misunderstandings, energy-draining conflicts, hidden agendas, confrontation, hostile behaviours, doubt, and defensiveness.

> *'The moment there is suspicion about a person's motives, everything he does becomes tainted.'*
> **Mahatma Gandhi**

For a leader, when trust is low, the cost to their leadership is high. On the other hand, when trust is high, the spirit of decision-making goes up and the cost lowers. As Ralph Waldo Emerson said, 'Our distrust is very expensive.' For example, airport security measures are much more time-consuming in the current global political climate. Your bags are checked and you are screened multiple times. It's a protective, necessary response to low trust.

To me, in a world where trust is already very low between people and corporations, customers and staff, and shareholders and companies, the need for integrity (honesty and strong moral principles) is as great as it has ever been. And it's not a now-and-then thing. Anyone who desires to be seen as successful and trustworthy must embrace integrity as a principle to live by.

> *'There is no such thing as a minor lapse of integrity.'*
> **Tom Peters**

How do you measure integrity? Ask yourself the following questions:
- How well do you treat people who can give you nothing?
- Are you transparent with others, or do you deliberately hold information?

- Are you the same person in the spotlight as you are with your family or by yourself?
- Are you quick to admit faults and mistakes?
- Do you put your personal agenda or selfish interests ahead of people?
- Do you make difficult decisions even when there is a personal cost?
- When you have something to say about people, do you say it to their face or behind their backs?

'Many succeed momentarily by what they know.
Some succeed temporarily by what they do.
Few succeed permanently by what they are.'
Anonymous

Character is not determined by our credentials, it is not determined by how skilled we are, how many degrees and titles we have, or our social or professional positions. Credentials are about adding value to ourselves; character is all about adding value to other people. Credentials are what we've achieved in the past; character decides what we'll accomplish in the future. Credentials may get the opportunity, but character continually attracts more opportunities.

How do you become more trustworthy as a leader? I've talked about the importance of good character and integrity already. Competence is also important – doing a good job, and delivering on the deliverables and promised results. You might have good character and intentions, but if you are incompetent, people's trust in you will suffer. If you don't deliver, you will lose trust. It may sound harsh, but it's true. Most people will judge you on what you do, not on your capabilities and potential. So, you need to know what is expected of you. You need to clarify the results you can produce and commit to what you can deliver.

Here are some other ways:

- Talk straight – tell the truth, don't sugar-coat, and don't withhold information. This is different to being outspoken and talking too much. Talking straight means stating your intentions, sticking to the point, and being transparent.
- Be transparent – build trust fast by being transparent about your intentions, struggles, and mistakes.
- Demonstrate respect – when you respect other people and their opinions, you are perceived as more trustworthy.
- Do the right thing – as human beings, we have an innate sense of what it means to do the right thing. As Confucius said, 'To see what is right and not to do it is cowardice.' Make this your personal philosophy.
- Confront reality - when you're hit with a situation or problem, be real about it. Be honest and transparent. When you sweep things under the carpet, people eventually find out. It can take years to build a reputation, and moments to lose it.
- Be loyal – give credit where credit is due. When you do this, you're not only validating the value of that person's contribution, but you're also creating an environment where people feel encouraged to collaborate and freely share ideas. And only talk about people as if they're in front of you.
- Apologise – people stay angry when they're owed an apology and they don't get one. They are more likely to act against you in that case. If you've made a mistake, give a heart-felt apology and get that weapon out of people's hands.

During my twenties, I was a person of weak character. I've worked on developing good character traits for more than fifteen years. It doesn't mean my selfish instincts don't kick in once in a while, but I have become better at detecting my intent and considering others' interest as I do mine. Like me, you must strive to become a person of good character, integrity, and competence. If you don't make this an intention, it won't happen.

Sometimes the hardest thing to do is to look at yourself directly in the mirror and address your own conscience. But you have to address the tough stuff directly. Acknowledge what's not being said. Be courageous and have the conversations that need to be had. Don't beat around the bush with the real issues or bury your head in the sand.

Becoming a successful leader

'Ultimate leadership is helping others achieve personal success.'

A successful leader must first strive to become successful themselves because credibility begins with personal success. But as I've mentioned, great leaders also grow and develop people – that is their intention. Good leadership is about making an effort to care for people, to love and understand them, and to bring out the best in them. If we are continually indifferent or frustrated with people, it is difficult to be a good leader.

There is a reason I talked about the power of the mind, discovering yourself, and defining success before leadership. It's because the toughest person to lead is always yourself. We cannot lead people further than we've led ourselves, so we must discover where we need self-development before we can truly embrace leadership.

Leadership has been personally challenging for me. I am good at leading myself but I have experienced many setbacks when leading others. I am continually learning how to become a better leader. Why? If you want to lead, you must learn. If you want to continue to lead, you must continue to learn.

John F. Kennedy once said, 'Leadership and learning are indispensable to each other.' When you take the time to develop yourself, you start to build an advanced perception of how you think and how others think, greatly enhancing your ability to deal with people and situations. So, educate yourself on anything to do with human psychology, philosophy, sociology, human behaviour, and organisational behaviour – this will help you become a more effective leader than technical skills.

What else do successful leaders do? Successful leaders:

- Motivate and inspire – they understand that successful leadership is about people performing together and supporting each other. They do not mislead and exploit people.
- Create rather than compete – they understand that operating from a place of ego or competition is not conducive to influence. They are creative visionaries who allow their experience and inner voice to guide them.
- Observe – they rarely miss anything that is going on around their world and they're active listeners.
- Show courage – they understand that courage is contagious. Think of Martin Luther King's 'I have a dream' speech and how that inspired others.
- Communicate – they understand the need to clearly articulate their vision and how it can be achieved so people will support them.
- Solve problems – they don't fear problems, because they know there will always be opposition, challenges and issues, so they develop a habit of solving problems, rather than avoiding them. The more you avoid problems, the harder it is to deal with them. Leaders see the bigger picture and deal with one issue or challenge at a time.
- Give and serve – they have a spirit of generosity, a desire to serve, guide, and help others. They don't bark orders and focus on self-interest. They know they are working for a cause that's bigger than them.
- Invest – they are generous with time when it comes to coaching, informing, developing, and training. They understand there is no such thing as a one-minute manager, instead focusing on leadership that is open-ended and based on quality.

- Stay positive – they know attitude contributes to communication and actions.
- Lead by example – they don't say one thing and do another. They walk the talk.
- Respect – they know that trust and respect are earned, in the same way that reputation, loyalty, and friendships are built.

If you want to be a successful leader, spend time answering these questions:
- What example do you set on a daily basis?
- Are you likeable?
- How much and how do you take responsibility? Are you accountable to others? Or do you blame?
- Do you collaborate?
- Are you generous with praise?
- Do you invest in others?
- Do you give objective feedback that focuses on the issue rather than the person?
- Do you earn respect and trust, or do you expect it?
- Do you currently have influence?
- Do enough people know, like, trust, and follow you willingly?

What we have covered in this chapter

In this chapter we have covered:
- becoming a valuable person
- proper leadership
- becoming more trustworthy
- becoming a successful leader.

What do successful people do? Successful people understand that leadership is the highest human function and one of the scarcest resources in the world. They understand that leadership is not just about position, but also about vision and influence. They understand the characteristics of building trust and relationship when it comes to successful leadership, and they understand what contributes to the ongoing success of a leader.

'Our personal achievements serve to raise, advance, and benefit ourselves. Our greatest achievements serve to raise, advance, and benefit others.'

CHAPTER 9
Becoming a successful influencer

'The more influence you have, the less competition you will have to deal with.'

As a child, what did you want to be when you grew up? Rich? Famous? A President or Prime Minister? An Olympic athlete? A charity founder? We all have dreams and ambitions, some accomplished, others not. But most of us still have unfulfilled dreams and goals, no matter how successful we are. Often, we need influence to achieve them. Can a business leader run a company without being able to influence their employees, teams, and other stakeholders? Can someone lead a country or movement without influence?

How much influence you have will exponentially magnify your success. With the right type of influence, you will accomplish things way beyond your capabilities. Without it, you're likely to severely limit your progress.

Understanding influence

Much of your success depends on how much influence you have with others – or, the ability you have to sway, modify, or affect others' opinions. Money may come our way via talent or skill, but these alone are not sufficient for building influence. A salesperson after more sales needs influence with customers. A manager's success comes from building influence with employees. A coach can't build a winning team without influencing players. And if you want to raise a strong, healthy family, you need to positively influence your children. No matter what your life goals are, you can achieve them faster and contribute more effectively by becoming a person of influence.

> *'You can get everything in life you want if you*
> *will just help enough other people get what they want.'*
> **Zig Ziglar**

Influencers are people others come to for advice. They have a genuine and loyal following because they add real value to their industries or communities. They usually have insights and actionable information, which attracts the eye of major brands. In short, influencers have power.

Influence isn't built in a day. Becoming influential grows in stages over time. But as you start to increase your influence, your name will come up in conversations more often (for the right reasons). You will attract more opportunities, increase your earnings, build your following, and add value to others.

Many people feel they've hit peak professional success when they have been trained or skilled in a particular area (or have developed a particular expertise). In other words, they are a professional in their field. To me, becoming a professional is the foundational category of career success. A professional provides specialised services in exchange for a fee. They are paid for what they do. The next level is expert. An expert is considered by others to have deep-level understanding of their subject matter, and they are paid more than a professional for the same level of work. The third level of professional influence is authority. An authority is perceived to be the go-to person in any organisation, association, or industry. They consistently get results. And while professionals and experts are paid for what they do, an authority is also paid for who they are.

Let's say you decide to be a life coach. You have some coaching experience, and that puts you at the professional level. As you develop deep expertise in your area, people perceive you as an expert. But once you cause transformation for people and consistently get results, you will be perceived as an authority. At this point, your remuneration is based on who you are, not what you do, and more opportunities come your way.

If you want to create influence and become successful, becoming a professional is the first step. But once you become an authority, you will see a significant difference in remuneration and influence.

Applying the fundamentals of influence

Some people seem like they're born to succeed. They come across as being gifted physically, intellectually, and artistically, and they seem to have the Midas touch when it comes to quickly connecting with others. Don't be fooled. Even the most gifted people have worked hard to develop these skills. Through hard work, we too can propel ourselves into positions of influence.

Connecting with others – a.k.a. building rapport – is a fundamental part of building influence. Knowing how to build rapport, and quickly gain trust and respect, is a skill that, once learnt, can bring many opportunities. So, how do you do it? What strategies can you employ to help you relate to others better? As you work through the following strategies, consider how you can immediately apply each one into your interactions with others. Keep in mind that the more rapport you build, the more influence you will have.

Strategies for building rapport include:
- Admitting mistakes – many people believe admitting mistakes labels them incompetent and unworthy, yet mistakes are the seeds of evolution and change. It's about

putting things into perspective. What can others learn from your mistake? Remember, people generally have little respect for those who cannot admit their mistakes, and when there is no respect, there is no room for influence.

- Admitting errors in thinking – sometimes we form assumptions and draw conclusions, based on thinking later proven to be incorrect (or incongruent with our values). When we can admit that we are not computerised machines incapable of making errors, we accept three things: we are not perfect, we admit imperfections when they arise, and we have emotional and human qualities. Doing this helps build emotional connections and rapport with others, leading to influence.

- Ignoring people's minor and social mishaps – we're not perfect and neither is anyone else. If you want to build rapport, the worst thing you can do is judge someone for something minor they have done wrong, especially in front of others. Give a bit of leeway where needed. And consider protecting them from social embarrassment by providing a quick escape route that keeps their dignity intact.

- Considering others' viewpoints – our opinions are only one side of the coin. It's easy to become lost in our own thoughts and perspectives, yet a simple shift in perspective and some clever questioning will enable you to unlock another person's thoughts, emotions and outlook on a situation. You don't have to agree with them, just acknowledge their viewpoint with a respectful and open mind.

- Arousing the ego – whether we admit it or not, everyone wants something. When you show someone how you can help them to get what they want, with as little inconvenience as possible, you will develop an energy of intrigue and curiosity that results in greater influence over the other person's decisions and actions. Just ensure that the way wants are fulfilled fits in with their values.

- Showing genuine interest in people – most people like to talk about their interests. Screenwriter and Forbes blogger Mark Hughes described former US President Bill Clinton as follows: 'When you are talking to him, you feel like he doesn't care about anything or anybody else around but you. He makes you feel like the most important person in the room … He made people feel special. He made them feel like he understood them and that he cared deeply about what they wanted, and he made them feel that what he wanted and what they wanted were the same thing.' Wow!

- Giving honest and sincere appreciation – everyone likes to be appreciated. When you give people honest and sincere appreciation, it shows them you care and enables you to develop deeper levels of rapport and influence.

This is by no means an exhaustive list, rather a starting point. Think about how you can immediately apply this knowledge in your daily interactions with others. By incorporating these behaviours into your habitual thinking and acting patterns, you will create deep and long-lasting rapport with those who, at times, appear closed off or distant.

While rapport takes time and effort to build (and develop as a skill), it is easy to break down, thus damaging influence levels. How can you avoid demolishing rapport?

- Don't make promises you can't keep. Nothing will break rapport faster. Promises create an invisible bond between people, and a set of expectations. However, the bond is only as strong as your word, and if you don't meet the expectations, doubt forms, rapport is lost, and the power of influence decreases. If something genuinely prevents you keeping your promise, acknowledge that expectations were unmet and apologise.

- Don't flatter people. Most people can discern the difference between flattery and authentic praise, and the moment they perceive insincerity all trust, rapport, and influence is lost.

- Don't play favourites. People already compare themselves with others. When you do the comparing for them, and favour one person over another, it might work for a while. However, when the cat is let out of the bag, the rapport you worked so hard to maintain will disappear as quickly as the mouse.

- Don't play the victim. It may gain attention in the short term, but in the long term it's an ineffective way of building rapport and gaining influence. Most people do not like being around those who manipulate situations to gain sympathy.

- Don't argue unnecessarily. Some people argue because they have a deep conviction of what is right or wrong, some enjoy the emotional rush of arguing, and others simply have to be right. If you are working to build a long-term relationship that will aid your success, what is more important – being right or maintaining the relationship?

Remember, the greater the rapport you establish with people, the more powerful influence you will exert in their lives.

How to influence people

Establishing rapport is a fundamental step for building influence. But there are many other things you can do. By incorporating the following strategies, your influence, leadership, and success will benefit.

- Integrity: I talked about this in Chapter 8, but to recap, being a person of integrity is not only about avoiding unethical choices and situations, but also about proactively becoming a person who adopts values of service, character, and commitment. Zig Ziglar said, 'If you do what you need to do when you need to do it, then the day will come when you can do what you want to do when you want to do it.'

- Invest: All influencers invest in themselves. They grow their expertise, get certified, and cross-train. Why? The more you know, the more you can help. People will respect the efforts you have made to learn in order to help others.

- Get to know people: Influencers make a point of finding out people's hobbies, kids' names, strengths, goals, motivations, fears, and concerns. When you demonstrate genuine interest in others, you're showing you care and a stronger relationship will build.

- Praise liberally: When someone does a great job, tell or show them. Whether it's by email, in a meeting, or with a gift card or bonus, make sure you show sincere appreciation.

- Coach and advocate: Be a resource and sounding board for others. Provide a safe place to talk. People need to know that you're on their side and you'll help them, even if it means leveraging your own influence to help them achieve their goals.

- Align: Self-aware influencers understand the folly of trying to be all things to all people. It is impossible to be an expert in everything. Instead, surround yourself with people who are like-minded and possess expertise in an area you're less skilled in. For example, if you lack detail-orientation, bring in someone with strong organisational skills.

- Listen: There's a saying often attributed to former US President Lyndon B. Johnson that goes, 'You ain't learnin' nothin' when you're talkin.' Influencers listen to learn. They wait to hear what others say and they observe body language, rather than jumping in with their own opinions, forming conclusions, or making assumptions. See Chapter 6 for a recap of effective listening.

- Expect greatness: Influencers never settle for average. Instead, they have a steadfast belief that the best is ahead, and they make constant progress towards greatness. See Chapter 6 for a recap of greatness.

- Believe in others: Influencers don't only see people for who they are today, but for who they can be tomorrow. They believe in them *before* they succeed. When people sense that you truly have faith in them, they want to live up to it, to go the extra mile. But if they sense scepticism or doubt, they will return your lack of confidence with mediocrity.

- Encourage: Influencers know that success is a journey of process and progress, not a destination, and they demonstrate belief in others through encouragement. They emphasise strengths and instil confidence, while acknowledging that everyone has setbacks and challenges, flops, failures, and fumbles. When you are open about your failures and successes, it encourages people to go on despite their own setbacks.

'Those who believe in our ability do more than stimulate us. They create for us an atmosphere in which it becomes easier to succeed.'
John Lancaster Spalding

I want to dig a little deeper into the skill of effective listening and why it is so crucial as a means of building influence (refer to Chapter 6 for more about communicating with impact).

E. W. Howe once joked, 'No man would listen to you talk if he did not know it was his turn next.' Unfortunately, that accurately describes how many people approach communication. They're too busy waiting for their turn to speak to really listen to others. But people of influence understand the incredible value of becoming a good listener.

Effective listening shows respect. It builds relationships, increases knowledge, generates ideas, creates loyalty, and it's a great way to help yourself and others. Common barriers to effective listening are talking too much, lack of focus, mental fatigue, excess emotional baggage, and self-preoccupation (probably the most formidable barrier to listening).

If you don't care about anyone but yourself, you're not going to listen to others. But when you don't listen, the damage to yourself is greater than what you do to other people.

To be an effective listener:
- look at the person who is speaking
- do not interrupt
- focus on understanding
- pay attention to the pauses
- listen with good heart and head intention
- consider the message behind the message
- look for words and emotions
- watch body language (this will reveal more than their words)
- listen to discover their interest, not just their position
- listen for what's being said and what's not being said
- show empathy and acceptance
- listen as you would like to be listened to.

When you listen effectively, you will unlock unexpected insights, motivations, and motives that drive deeper levels of meaning into the message, and enable a better understanding of people's needs and wants.

'The ear of the influencer must
ring with the voices of the people.'
Woodrow Wilson

You need to aim for connection if you want to influence. Don't take people for granted - you can only connect with people, and influence or lead them if you genuinely value them. Have a 'making-a-difference' mindset, like former US President Ronald Reagan who said, 'We can't help everyone, but everyone can help someone.' Show conviction, because if you don't believe what you're saying, no one else will. And while it's good to find common ground, it's also good to recognise and respect personality differences (they'll appreciate your sensitivity and understanding). Finally, try to discover what people need and what's important to them – think of it as a key. Kahlil Gibran said, 'To understand the heart and mind of a person, look not at what he has already achieved, but at what he aspires to.' Doing this will help you find their key. And once you find it, use it with integrity: turn the key only with their permission and for their benefit.

'Natural talent, intelligence, wonderful education
– none of these guarantee success. Something else
is needed: the sensitivity to understand what other
people want, and a willingness to give it to them.'
John Luther

Creating and developing your own personal brand

Your personal brand is your reputation. It's what people think about you when your name comes up.

Personal branding may sound like something that's only relevant to consultants, experts, celebrities, and authors. But ultimately, your reputation is one of the most important assets you own.

Is your reputation what you want it to be? Do people think you have integrity? Is your image seen as professional? Do people describe your work and abilities as high quality? As influencers, we want people to think of us in these ways. But we have to be strategic about the messages we send to others. How you show up and present yourself in all ways (not just appearance, but the content you share), and the consistency with which you do this, is an important factor in the way others perceive you.

You don't need to create a unique and personal brand, especially if you're already aligned with an organisation, movement, or vision that has a brand. But if you want to influence, you do need to be conscious about how you present to others. You can still stand out even if you're working for someone else, by creating a powerful impact through your personal presentation and communication, and developing deep expertise in your work.

If you want to develop a personal brand, remember that it's about standing out. It's about intentionally being visible and memorable. To do this, it's helpful to identify your niche. What sets your business or passion apart from others? Your niche must be something you strongly align with but also be something other people need or want. You need to be absolutely clear about what sets you apart and makes you remarkable and memorable, so your expertise speaks for itself.

Here are some tips for personal branding:
- Be great at what you do. If you lack confidence and don't develop expertise, it's hard to stand out.
- Improve your presentation and communication skills. How you speak, interact, and connect with people makes a difference.
- Be visible and accessible. You can't hide in your office or behind a computer and expect to build a brand. You need to show yourself – attend conferences or networking events, share content consistently on social media, and put yourself forward as an expert. If you use social media (and you don't have to use it as your only marketing platform), be authentic. If you come across as robotic or fake it will have the reverse effect.
- Understand your industry inside and out. Your personal brand is only as good as your understanding of your industry, so stay up-to-date with trends to maintain your competitive advantage.
- Practise two-way networking. This means both people have an opportunity to benefit from the relationship, which results in more connections and opportunities, and a stronger personal brand.
- Maintain a detailed database of contacts. As your expertise and influence grows, so will your list of contacts. You never know when you might need them. Note who the person is, where you connected, potential opportunities, and how you can help them.

- Become a trusted source of relevant information. Strive to be the person who shares expert advice or insights that promote thinking. Share this on social media or to your email lists. As you gain trust, you'll attract more people and increase your influence.

- Know your value proposition. What is your innovation, speciality, service, or feature that makes you attractive to clients? Once you clearly establish your value proposition – who you are, and why you do what you do – tell people at every opportunity.

- Build your online platform. Your website and social media accounts form a virtual representation of your personal brand and allow you to share your voice.

- Be clear about your uniqueness and strengths. Use your personal story to share not only what you do but why you do it. People want to know why you have this vision (or why you're part of an organisation), as well as your failures, struggles, and success.

- Invest in yourself. You can never stop learning.

- Know your values and priorities. Have a clear picture of your short and long-term personal and professional goals. This helps personal branding by giving clarity to where and how time should be spent.

- Be authentic. Authentic passion energises you (and your followers). When you feel passion, you can't help but take action.

- Use high-quality content. Your content represents you. Don't take shortcuts with poor-quality material.

- Use LinkedIn – it's currently the best professional platform for growing your personal and professional influence. By using this platform effectively, you will build a referral network, position yourself as an expert, and attract your ideal clients.

- Form connections with influencers and thought leaders, and leverage the trust, respect, and the audience they have to extend your reach.

I have used the above strategies to expand my sphere of influence, which has attracted many clients, collaborative, and business opportunities. Remember, your reputation (or personal brand) is your ticket to realising your personal and professional objectives. This means marketing yourself in combination with marketing your business.

If you still think you have nothing remarkable to build a personal brand on, don't worry. For now, align yourself with a brand that matches your beliefs, thought leadership, and vision and leverage off that. It's a fantastic way to start.

What we have covered in this chapter

In this chapter we have covered:
- understanding influence
- applying the fundamentals of influence
- how to influence people
- creating and developing your own personal brand.

What do successful people do? Successful people understand the importance, fundamentals, and application of influence, and its connection to success. They intentionally expand their influence and understand the importance of developing their personal brand alongside the organisational brand.

'If you network and connect with the sole intention of adding value to yourself, you can never become an influencer.'

CHAPTER 10
Achieving goals that will accelerate your success

'If you play for safety and security, you can survive.
If you play for growth and impact, you can thrive.'

Most people don't set goals. Of those who do, few write them down, and of those who write them down, few set the right goals the right way. Goal setting and its importance is nothing new, but most people do not understand why it works and how to set goals that trigger high levels of energy, creativity, and inspiration.

In this chapter, I'm going to dive deep into the science of goal setting and show you how to set amazing goals for the life you truly want.

What are goals and why set them?

'Without goals, we simply drift and flow in the
currents of life. With goals, we're like an arrow
– straight and true to our target.'

Goals give your life direction and unlock your mind's potential. If you don't know where you're going, and you've set no specific objectives, how will you achieve success? You can't fulfill your purpose and reach your potential without knowing your direction and setting goals to get you there. Instead, you'll drift about like a boat with no captain and compass. Even a state-of-the-art ship will drift with the wind if it lacks direction.

By now, you should have identified your life's purpose (see Chapter 4) and the vision that speaks to your heart. You should have an idea of what you were born to do. If so, now is a good time to dig deeper into goal setting that leads you along your success journey. And the potential for success seems to be unlimited. Look around. How many records have been broken in sports, music, business, and the arts within your lifetime? No matter where we look, the human race keeps progressing more and more. Things thought to be impossible fifty years ago are being done. On TV shows such as *X Factor*, *Masterchef* or *America's Got Talent*, people seem to be increasingly talented at younger ages. They're getting better and faster. Could it be that what the human race has accomplished until now is only a small fraction of what is truly possible?

'It doesn't matter where you are coming from.
All that matters is where you are going.'
Brian Tracy

175

Goals help us concentrate our focus and energy towards a single cause (or even multiple causes). Brian Tracy also said, 'Goals are the fuel in the furnace of achievement.' Rather than allowing circumstances to dictate what happens, goals allow us to take control. Having goals also improves confidence, develops competence, and boosts motivation levels.

All successful people are intensely goal-orientated. One of the greatest teachings behind old religions, philosophies, metaphysics, psychology, and the science of success, is that you become what you think about most of the time. Successful people know what they want, and focus single-mindedly on achieving it. Being able to set purpose-aligned goals is one of the master skills of success. But if goal setting is so important, why don't most people do it?

Firstly, most people don't fully comprehend the importance of goals. How many people do you know – friends, family members and co-workers – who are clear about their goals and committed to them?

Secondly, most people confuse goals with hopes, wishes, and dreams, so they don't know how to set them. Things like, 'I want to be happy/wealthy/peaceful/successful/healthy,' are not goals. They are vague and can't easily be measured. Goals are clear and specific, easily described to others; they are in writing and easily measurable.

Thirdly, most people don't set goals because they fear failure. They don't want to experience the emotional pain of setting a goal and not achieving it. In his book *What They Don't Teach You at Harvard Business School*, Mark McCormack describes a Harvard study conducted over ten years. In 1979, graduates of the Harvard MBA program were asked, 'Have you set clear written goals for the future and made plans to accomplish them?' Only 3 per cent of graduates had written goals, 13 per cent had goals that were not in writing, and 84 per cent had no specific goals aside from finishing school and enjoying life. In 1989, the researchers re-interviewed the graduates with surprising results. The graduates who did not write their goals down earned, on average, twice as much as the ones who had no goals. The graduates who wrote their goals down were earning, on average, ten times as much as all of the other graduates in their class. Having clear goals, not talent or skill, is what made the difference.

'Happiness is the progressive
realisation of a worthy ideal, or goal.'
Earl Nightingale

In *Man's Search for Meaning*, Viktor Frankl wrote that the greatest need for human beings is a sense of meaning and purpose in life. Setting goals will give you that sense of meaning and purpose.

What kind of goal should you set for massive results?

Unless goals lead to a higher level of success, not even writing them down guarantees completion.

Bob Proctor, co-founder of the Proctor Gallagher Institute and featured teacher in *The Secret*, believes most people do not set goals correctly. Instead of aiming higher, they keep their goals at the same level. He uses an A-B-C framework to explain effective goal setting.

A-Type goals are those you know how to achieve because you've already accomplished them in the past. For example, if you set a goal to get a 5 per cent bonus and achieve it, then aim for the same the next year, that's an A-Type goal. You've done it before and you can do it again.

B-Type goals are those you haven't yet done, but wouldn't be too hard to achieve. For example, if you set a goal to get a 5 per cent bonus two years in a row and achieve it, then aim for 10 per cent. You do some maths and think, 'If I work slightly longer hours, maybe do some training, make a few more sales calls, I can do it.' It's not a real stretch.

C-Type goals take you out of your comfort zone. They're based on something you want badly, and they excite you and scare you at the same time because you have no idea how you're going to achieve them. Think of them as fantasies you want more than anything to come true.

Most people set A or B-Type goals. But the problem is, they don't excite or inspire. They're not exponential by nature and don't drag you out of bed. They don't change your life much because they are based on what you know or believe you can already do. The most successful people choose C-Type goals that fill their lives with passion and inspiration. And even though they have no idea how they'll achieve these goals when they set them, they don't give up. I want to encourage you to set a C-Type goal. I want you to write one down. Something you truly want, something that excites and scares you, and you have no idea how to accomplish.

You might be hesitating now. It's natural to resist doing something you don't know how to do. Don't worry about that for now. The how is not as important in the beginning (I'll come to that later). To start, your C-Type simply needs to meet the criteria mentioned before: something you truly want, something that excites and scares you, and you have no idea how to accomplish.

So, write down that goal in the present tense. Write, 'I am happy and grateful [fill in the blank with your C-Type goal in the present tense]. For example, 'I am happy and grateful to be driving around in my $100,000 blue Porsche.' Read what you have written. Do you truly want it? Does it excite and scare you at the same time? Do you have no idea how you'll make it happen? If you have some idea how to make your goal happen, it's probably an A or B-Type goal (based on existing tools, ideas, and assumptions). If so, try again. Get out of the comfort zone and create an assumption or expectation that the goal has already been accomplished.

C-Type goal setting can be transformational. Most people are satisfied to accept small incremental improvements in their life. Maybe they want to grow their business, confidence or money a little. They don't want to play a big game. But C-Type goals are the big game. They are exponential – they address huge problems, propose radical solutions, or engage breakthrough creativity. They make your heart race and sweat drip down the middle of your back. You'll feel crazy for aiming so high (and others might think you are too).

'The hard part of standing on an exponential
curve is: when you look backwards, it looks flat,
and when you look forward, it looks vertical.'
Sam Altman

An exponential goal-setting mindset requires a mentality that radically shifts thinking, decision-making, connections, and actions. It takes courage and creativity, and has an immediate impact on us internally, because we're deeply engaged and walking a fine line between fear and excitement.

I'm a living, breathing example of someone who's achieved many C-Type goals. Since watching a YouTube video about the concept, I have built and scaled businesses, written multiple books, and spoken on numerous international stages. If I didn't watch that video when I did, I'd probably still be aiming too low.

The Reticular Activating System (RAS)

Why don't we need to know *how* we're going to achieve our C-Type goals when we first set them?

Many of us are conditioned to believe solutions only come from conscious faculties. In Chapter 3, I discussed the distinction between the conscious and sub-conscious mind: the conscious mind is responsible for reasoning and thinking; the subconscious mind contains our beliefs, habits, values, and self-image, which determine most of our results. By now, you know your subconscious mind is like a 24/7 memory bank that stores every piece of information, and every word, emotion, and image we've ever seen. Nothing is forgotten, but in reality, we can't extract all that information because of our limited memory recall capabilities. What this means is that we don't consciously need to know *how* we're going to accomplish a C-Type goal when we set it, as long as it's effectively handed over to the subconscious mind. This is where the solution will come from.

It's a difficult concept to grasp for people conditioned through traditional academia who are heavily reliant upon their conscious faculties of willpower, perception, analysis, memory, and reasoning to drive their personal and professional decisions. This conditioning is often why people settle for A and B-Type goals (something they believe they can have) because they don't trust the *how* to come to them later. They fail to acknowledge and understand the power of the subconscious mind.

As soon as a C-Type goal is impressed in your subconscious (the more emotion and repetition associated with the goal, the faster this will happen), a mechanism called the Reticular Activating system (RAS) is triggered. The RAS is defined is a bundle of nerves at our brainstem that filters out unnecessary information, like a gatekeeper, so the relevant information gets through to the conscious mind. Most people don't understand how it works, so they don't trust the process, and stick to goals they already know how to achieve.

The RAS has two basic functions:

- Dismissing irrelevant information: the RAS makes sure your brain doesn't take on more than it can handle. It keeps you sane by blocking out unnecessary sensory information and filtering through the information your conscious mind needs. The brain can't pay attention to everything. Have you ever noticed that when you buy a new car, you notice the same kind of car everywhere for a while? The cars were always around but you didn't notice because the RAS filter dismissed that information as irrelevant. However, once you buy that car, the RAS is triggered to share that information. If you stop reading this for ten seconds, you will notice sounds (the hum of the fridge), sensations (air going in and out of your nose), and information (the item you have to add to the grocery list) that the RAS blocked while you were focusing on words.
- Selecting information: The RAS constantly searches the subconscious for information you need for the task at hand, or to reinforce a belief or value (which can sometimes lead to self-fulfilling prophecies). It acts as a filter, but it doesn't have a filter. It doesn't interpret the type or quality of the information coming in – whether it's true or not – it just decides whether you need to know it right now. It reinforces what you already believe, but doesn't interpret whether it supports you or not. For example, if you believe you can do well in a depressed economy, the RAS will identify ways and

opportunities to reinforce this belief. If you believe that the economy is bad, the RAS will bounce information through that proves how people are struggling.

When you program a C-Type goal in your mind, the RAS will start to think about the *how* and alert you to people, events, opportunities, and situations that, until now, have been in your blind spot. It's like a radio searching for a frequency and broadcasting when it's found. The key to getting it to find the right frequency, is believing that anything is possible, and the way you do that is by reprogramming your subconscious mind (which we've talked about in earlier chapters). You want the RAS to bounce through the opportunities, information, and beliefs that will help you become successful. You can't capitalise on opportunities you don't or can't see.

For many years, I found it difficult to grow wealth. My RAS was showing me examples of people who were not moving up the corporate ladder, who were stuck at a certain level of income, or who missed out on opportunities in life. Once we get beliefs in our head, we tend to prove them right, for better or worse. Things changed once I made the decision to set C-Type goals.

One of my C-Type goals was to speak on an international stage in front of more than a thousand people. I really wanted it, had never done it before, and I was emotionally charged and scared at the same time (the criteria for a C-Type goal). At the time of setting the goal, I had no idea how to achieve it. However, because I had programmed that goal into my subconscious mind through repetitive visualisation, affirmation, and emotional association, my RAS was triggered to look out for speaking opportunities and people I could connect with in the industry. That's when I started to attract the opportunities I needed to achieve my goal.

I set another C-Type goal to be featured regularly on mainstream financial media. I haven't accomplished this yet, but I've accomplished many other C-Type goals through the activation of my RAS.

The 'power of your mind' is a phrase that gets thrown around a lot, but I hope you're starting to appreciate that it's not just the power of your conscious mind, but this combined with the subconscious mind, *and* the RAS, that can make things happen beyond what you think is possible.

How to achieve goals faster

How can you achieve goals faster?

Firstly, set your goal in the present tense. I mentioned this earlier when I asked you to write down a C-Type goal. Your subconscious mind does not have a concept of time and doesn't distinguish between real and imagined events. It responds best to *right now* messages, such as 'I am travelling around the world', rather than future or past. Writing a goal as if it has already been accomplished produces images and related emotions that give the goal a higher probability of impressing in your subconscious mind.

Secondly, write down the reasons you must achieve that goal. Not all goals have to be big, bold C-Type goals, but for any goal you set, try to write between five to twenty reasons why you must achieve that goal. For example, when I set a goal for financial security, I wrote down fifty reasons why it was important to become financially secure. The reasons ranged from material things like the type of house I wanted to live in and the car I wanted to drive, to being able to afford high quality organic food, invest in my business, supporting my family, providing my daughter with world-class education, travelling the world, and so on. When you write down the reasons, it gives you ammunition for the days when you're full of doubt and you need inspiration and motivation. We all have those days. I do too, but because I have trained myself to live from my zone of genius and operate from a highly inspired worldview, they don't happen often. When I feel down-and-out and I want to give up, I review my reasons, and that's enough to re-motivate, reenergise, and re-inspire me to do what I need to do.

Thirdly, understand the difference between results-based and process-based goals. Results-based goals are the result you want (for example, achieving a certain body weight in a certain time) and process-based goals are the processes you need to follow to get the result (getting up every morning at 5 a.m. to go for a run).

Next, to achieve goals faster you must put some measures around it, such as how much and by when. The more specific the measures are, the faster you will achieve the goal. For example, 'I want to be financially secure,' is a non-specific results-based goal, and 'I want to save a million dollars by the time I am forty,' is a specific results-based goal. You can do the same with a process-based goal too. For example 'I'm going to save 10 per cent of my income every week,' is less specific than 'I'm saving $400 a week until the end of the year.'

Make sure your goals have emotional value. Goals that don't involve any kind of emotion will not arouse the burning desire you need for success.

Finally, set goals that can be clearly validated by a third party. For example, if I set a goal to lose twenty kilos by a certain time, how does anyone know I really achieved it in that time frame? However, if I tell a third party I want to weigh eighty-five kilos by a certain date, they can validate the goal. It will hold me accountable, give the goal credibility and clarity, and help me stay focused.

Setting your goals correctly and clearly will help you achieve them faster. But sometimes they need to be reviewed, or even rewritten. I do this regularly so my RAS remains tuned into my goals; the more I keep them front of mind, the more my mind will activate what I need to move closer to my goals.

What we have covered in this chapter

In this chapter we have covered:
- goals and why we should set them?
- types of goals
- the RAS
- how to set goals effectively and achieve them faster.

What do successful people do? Successful people understand the importance of goal setting and what kinds of goals to set. They know how to activate their mind to identify people, events, opportunities, strategies, and situations to assist in faster and more effective goal success.

'As risky as it may be, I prefer to pay the price of success, instead of the price of struggle or mediocrity.'

CHAPTER 11
Money mastery

'Pursuing wealth does not have to be about materialism.
It can also be about contribution.'

While success is not all about financial security and materialism, it is hard to feel successful without certainty around money and your financial future. If you're working and have expenses, bills, and taxes to pay, and you're seeking financial security, you are already in the game of money. Unfortunately, most people don't know the rules of the game. What are the chances of winning a game when you don't know (or understand) the rules?

Money may not be the only indicator of success, but it does afford us more options, control, and ability, to contribute to causes and people we care about.

Money consciousness

Money consciousness simply refers to how we see money. How you perceive money has a tremendous effect on the money you make and wealth you create. In fact, it's probably one of the most vital prerequisites for your wealth attraction and creation capabilities.

Do you know someone who seems to have the Midas touch and makes money no matter what? Do you know someone who always loses money, no matter where they invest? In my experience, most people are money repellant. Most people, due to their conscious and subconscious conditioning, have programmed themselves to be poor or middle class, which is not the best place for financial security. I was in this category for probably the first twenty-five years of my life. For most people, the associations with money and rich people are disempowering and based upon a scarcity mindset.

Take a minute to write down what you were taught about money, wealth, and rich people when you were growing up. What did you learn about money from your family? What did you learn about wealth and money from your friends, school, or religious institutions? Were the associations good or bad? Were your ideas about money associated with scarcity or abundance? Do you, at a deep level, resent rich people and their success? Do you believe there is a limited supply of money and opportunity to go around (which reflects in behaviors like hoarding and always feeling fearful of letting go of money)?

Which of the following statements or clichés ring true (or sound familiar)?

- 'Money is the root of all evil.'
- 'Rich people are greedy.'
- 'Money doesn't grow on trees.'
- 'Rich people are selfish.'
- 'Rich people hoard money.'
- 'To be rich, you have to be a crook, a liar, or you have to get lucky.'
- 'Money won't make you happy.'

- 'Money isn't that important anyway.'
- 'There are more important things than money.'
- 'We don't have a lot of money because we care about people.'
- 'If God wanted us to have money, He would have given it to us.'
- 'You have to work hard and lose life balance in order to make a lot of money.'
- 'Having a lot of money makes you a bad person.'
- 'If you have a lot of money, expect a lot of problems.'
- 'If you have a lot of money, your friends and family won't like you anymore.'
- 'Having a lot of money is a hassle.'
- 'Having a lot of money means you will spend time watching and protecting it.'
- 'Save your pennies for a rainy day.'
- 'A good job is the only way to become wealthy.'
- 'Clean your plate and eat everything on it – there are children starving in Africa.'

I bet you have heard a lot of these statements in your life, especially as part of your childhood conditioning. In reality, most people are money repellant because their brains are full of these negative attitudes towards money and wealth, and they use statements like these to justify their own financial predicament. A lot of people genuinely believe their lack of money is not a consequence of how they think and what they do. They live in denial and have false belief systems in regard to money. Charles Baudouin puts it like this: 'To be ambitious for wealth, and yet always expecting to be poor, to be always doubting your ability to get what you long for, is like trying to reach east by travelling west.'

If you're anything like me, the people who taught you about money were people you loved and respected. They were well-meaning and wanted you to succeed in all ways, but unfortunately, they probably transferred their own limited knowledge, beliefs, and scarcity thinking about money onto you. In most cases, that's what they grew up with – a poverty-based consciousness based on scarcity thinking, not prosperity thinking. Perhaps they lived in a state of constant insecurity that led to their negative views and justifications about their lack of money.

The world has changed radically since our grandparents' (and parents') day, and the pace of change is accelerating. To have financial success, we need to adopt conscious prosperity-based beliefs. We need to rethink our views and attitudes in regard to money. Think about it: if you hate, dislike, or resent wealth or wealthy people, how can you ever become wealthy?

Imagine you have been introduced to two people at a party: one person is the wealthy billionaire; the other is Mr Average Nice Guy. Who would you choose to spend time with at the party? If you've grown up with a poverty-based consciousness, chances are you will feel more comfortable with Mr Average Nice Guy. You might make a snap judgement about the billionaire that they are arrogant, egotistical, or maybe just not nice, because of their wealth. You might assume that the person who represents the average financial situation will not look down on you, unlike the person with the abundant financial situation. Here's the dilemma: if you think that wealthy people are intimidating or 'not nice', your subconscious mind will never let you become wealthy, because that would make you a not-nice, intimidating person. It's a catch twenty-two.

Many people live their entire lives pretending money is unimportant to them. They believe wealthy people worship money for its own sake and would do anything to get it and keep it. But the reality is, people without money think about money more than wealthy people do. People without wealth work day after day, year after year at jobs they hate, just for the money. They wish for a little bit more money; they worry, stress, and talk about it all the time. Many sacrifice time with their families to have more money. Yet most millionaires and billionaires do what they love to do. To them, the way they earn money is not work, and even though they could retire, they choose not to. They make their money work for them.

'I have nothing but contempt for the people who despise money. They are hypocrites and fools. Money is like a sixth sense without which you cannot make a complete use of the other five. Without an adequate income, half the possibilities of life are shut off.'
W. Somerset Maugham

How does that quote make you feel? Like I said, most people are money repellant. Their negative wealth mindset becomes their reality. What about you? Would you like to have more money and feel good about it? Would you like to provide your family with all the good and beautiful things in the world? Would you like more time to do the things you're passionate about rather than be a slave to money? Would you like to contribute to causes and help people? Of course, you would – that's why you have committed to reading *Impossible to Fail*.

There are three basic steps towards changing your money consciousness:

1. **Awareness:** Understand how your money consciousness is not working for you (especially if you find yourself constantly struggling with money). By becoming aware of outdated and limiting beliefs about money, you will unlock unlimited financial resources for you and your family. Review your financials and money habits regularly to prevent the damaging effects of complacency or ignorance.

2. **Beliefs:** Adopt a prosperity mindset about abundance and success (more on this later in the chapter). When you adopt the attitudes of a financially successful person, your conscious mind tells your subconscious that *you* are a financially successful person. This doesn't mean being extravagant and buying things you can't afford – that's not how prosperity conscious people act.

3. **Action:** You're responsible for your finances, so pay as little attention as possible to any limiting beliefs that will hold

you back from becoming financially successful. We're all exactly where we deserve to be financially. If things are not working out the way you want, you must take action, instead of blaming parents, partners, employers, the government, economy, taxes, education, corruption, or God for your financial situation. Stop justifying and do something about it.

You are in your current financial situation based on how you think and what you believe. If this upsets you, try not to be upset at me, but at what is now your past. Use your emotions to motivate positive change.

Vow to make the necessary changes to change your future forever.

Money principles

There are some winning and losing attitudes when it comes to money and wealth, and if wealth building is not in your top five values, you'll find it difficult to attain wealth. What a lot of people don't realise is that money is an energy – wealth flows from those who value wealth building the least, to those who value wealth building the most. Understanding the fundamental principles of money will help you create more abundance and lead to better choices around money management.

Have you ever heard someone say, 'Wealthy people are always crooks?' Some people assume that those who achieve wealth must be up to something wrong. Why? Maybe their financial difficulties have led to envy or bitterness. Maybe their friends became rich and successful while they remained poor. Their distorted second-hand view of money tells them you have to be a bad person to have a lot of money, and they say, 'I don't want to be wealthy, I'm a good, honest person.' They justify their poverty by attaching honour to it, implying that there are no honest wealthy people. In reality, some dishonest people are poor and some are wealthy, and vice versa. This twisted logic suppresses their ability to attain wealth.

Condemning those who have achieved financial freedom blocks your financial energy. It's self-defeating, especially if your goal is to be wealthy.

If you think being wealthy is bad, your attitude must change to release your money-attracting potential. Do you want to be a financially successful person of good character? Here are some money thoughts to consider before I move on:

- Money is energy. The person who values money more will typically end up with more money.
- Money is neutral. It's not good or bad – it's the people, and what they do with it that's good or bad. If it's in the hands of someone devoid of social conscience, it can be used for bad. But when it's in the hands of those who want to make a difference, it's a fantastic resource.
- Money is a tool. It helps people to make a difference (like build schools), or to do terrible things. Money simply magnifies by making good people better and bad people worse.
- Poverty consciousness is a disease of the mind. There is nothing virtuous about being poor – it's crippling. But there are no financial hospitals for those who are financially sick. Instead, self-education is the treatment. As Andrew Matthew said in *Being Happy!*, 'The best thing you can do for the poor is … not be one of them.'

As I said, it's important to rid yourself of the conflicted attitudes you have towards money and wealth. If you don't, you will struggle to attract it. By loving the way wealth can be used in wise and constructive ways, you will be able to create positive associations in your mind that will attract money and wealth to you. You will have plenty of money to do what you want, when you want, and to have what you want, and this money will flow in and out of your life continuously, creating a state of equilibrium. Money on its own may not make you happy, but it gives options, and it makes more people happy than poverty does.

There are many ways to become wealthy, but these four time-tested principles, strategies, and fundamentals of money with universal applications will underpin your financial success:

1. Spend less than you earn: if you spend all (or more) than you earn, you will never get ahead. This is Financial Planning 101 and unfortunately a lot of people skip this crucial step on their path to creating sustainable wealth. If you're like that, perhaps the seeds of financial greatness are not in you.

2. Pay yourself first: no matter how much money you make, put aside a small percentage for your future. The first bill you pay is to yourself. Do this before you pay your bills, mortgage, buy petrol or groceries. Why? If you pay everyone else first, you will never have any money left for yourself. But by paying yourself first, you're prioritising saving, developing sound financial habits, you're prepared for emergencies, and you're showing you value yourself. In my own experience as a wealth advisor, I've seen so many people fail to do this.

3. Protect yourself: as you make more money, ensure that you have appropriate risk management structures in place. Things happen, so while you create wealth, you need to protect it. It can take years to create wealth, but it can be lost in an instant.

4. Make your money work for you: if you are working for money, you will never be wealthy. Struggling in life is a consequence of not having a plan, and if growing wealth is your aim, at some point you need a plan to save, eliminate debts, and invest.

I will revisit these principles more in Chapter 12 – for now I just want you to have a basic understanding.

Money mindset

Do certain mindsets increase a person's probability of becoming financially successful?

Yes, I believe so. From my own observations derived from having thousands of money conversations over the last two decades, I have never seen anyone who acquired wealth and kept it, unless they placed a high value on wealth creation. Those who placed a high value on wealth creation prioritised savings, insurances and investing. Those who didn't placed a high value on spending. Those who placed value on wealth creation made money work for them. Those who like to spend all, or most, of their money, only worked for money, with no plans to make money work for them.

As Francis Bacon said, 'Money makes a great servant but bad master.' In the same survey, most self-made millionaires said the foundational stones of financial success were:

- integrity
- discipline
- social skills
- a supportive spouse
- working harder than most people.

You may think these observations are nothing new. What I'm trying to do is reinforce the concepts into your mind, so you become highly aware of them.

'What's simple to do is also simple not to do.'
Jim Rohn

Interestingly the survey also observed that most of the respondents were not intellectually gifted, or law or medical school-calibre students. Most were not qualified to pursue MBA degrees, but they all talked about the quality of fighting for gold because they didn't want to be labelled as average or of less ability.

At Harvard University, Dr Edward C. Banfield studied the mindset of financially successful people. He wanted to know why some people became financially independent and improved their social status, while the majority did not. He found that people became financially successful because of a certain mindset, rather than education, race, family background, influential contacts, or intelligence. He called this attitude (or mindset) long-term perspective, and concluded that it was the most accurate predictor of upward financial mobility.

Long-term perspective means how far you look into the future when deciding what you will and won't do with your present financial decisions. People with long-term perspectives consider what their choices *now* will mean in ten or twenty years. Dr Banfield found that people who took their long-term future into consideration when making decisions in the present were more likely to experience financial success than those driven by short-term results or instant gratification. In other words, people who made sacrifices in the short term were more likely to get better results in the long term.

In contrast, financially unsuccessful people have short-term perspectives. They typically give little thought to the long-term consequences of their financial decisions, only thinking a week, a month, maybe a year or two ahead. And those who use the shortest timeframe – instant gratification – are often the least well-off in any society. Early school leavers are at much greater risk for remaining unemployed in the longer term, earning considerably lower wages when they are employed, and are likely to struggle to accumulate wealth over their life span (Deloitte Access Economics, 2012). Overall, short-term thinking leads to negative financial consequences in the long term.

'Your income can only grow to the extent you do.'
T. Harv Eker

What will help you achieve your twenty-year vision for your financial goals? What can you do today? To answer this question, you need to use long-term perspective. It is this mindset that will help you make the most effective day-to-day decisions to secure your financial future.

T. Harv Eker (*Secrets of the Millionaire Mind*) puts it like this: 'Money is a result, wealth is a result, health is a result, illness is a result, your weight is a result. We live in a world of cause and effect.' He also said, 'If your motivation for acquiring money or success comes from a non-supportive root such as fear, anger, or the need to prove yourself, your money will never bring you happiness.'

Eker believes the only way to change your level of financial success permanently is to reset your financial thermostat. Remember in Chapter 4, I compared the cybernetics mechanism to ducted heating systems in homes? If you're about to take on a challenge, risk or action that's inconsistent with your self-concept, your mind triggers the cybernetics mechanism and gets you to engage in self-sabotaging behaviours. The same thing happens here – if your financial mindset isn't reset, then your finances will stay at a fixed level because the mindset works against success. When you complain, you become a living, breathing crap magnet. People, who complain too much, very rarely (if ever), become wealthy and keep their wealth. And if you're not totally committed to creating wealth, chances are you won't. If your goal is simply to be comfortable, chances are you'll never be rich, but if your goal is to be rich, chances are you'll end up quite comfortable.

> **'You will be paid in direct proportion to the value you deliver in the marketplace.'**
> **T. Harv Eker**

In Chapter 8, we also looked at the difference in being valuable to others as a person and valuable in terms of what you *give* others in the marketplace, and how that affects income. Eker's statement above reminds us that if you're not making enough money, it's because you haven't found a way to add enough value to enough people in the marketplace.

The true measure of wealth is net worth, not income. Many self-made millionaires are entrepreneurs who have moved away from having a steady pay cheque (there's nothing wrong with a steady pay cheque, unless it interferes with your ability to earn more than you're truly worth). They reset their financial thermostat and it led to success. It was not their income that made them wealthy, but what they did with it.

Understanding money

Money is probably one of the most misunderstood subjects in the world. The vast majority of people do not have a proper understanding of money, even though they are playing the money game by having an income and expenses. But like all games, you need to understand the rules if you want to win the game.

Most people think of currency when you ask them to define money. But money is not currency – it is purchasing power. If you have $10,000, it is what that money buys (the purchasing power) that makes it worth anything. What that $10,000 buys now is different to what it would have bought a century ago (that was a lot of money back then). It's not the face value or currency value, but the purchasing power of money that is most important to understand.

Lack of basic money-management skills is one of the major causes of stress and relationship break-ups worldwide. I have seen a lot of destruction and stress come to individuals and families in my work, and we've all heard about the economic devastation faced by organisations and countries due to improper handling and use of money.

> *'Economic disaster begins with a personal*
> *philosophy of doing less and wanting more.'*
> **Jim Rohn**

Once you have developed money consciousness and a money mindset, and you understand the basic principles, it's important to develop money-management skills. As author George S. Clason said, 'Our acts can be no wiser than our thoughts.' In his modern-day classic *The Richest Man in Babylon*, Clason maintains the laws of money have not changed since its early use in ancient Babylon. Fads and trends change, but the fundamentals remain the same. The sooner you learn money-management skills, the better off financially you'll be.

When it comes to money management, seek assistance from qualified and trustworthy financial professionals, rather than family members and friends. Would you ask a taxi driver about the stock market? Check the track record and credentials of financial advisors (some simply sell financial products or take your money in return for poor advice). And remember, seeking help doesn't excuse you from obtaining basic knowledge about money and wealth creation.

Learning results in earning. Mental and physical labour has always been, and still is, the foundation of building a fortune, but when combined with insightful knowledge and leverage, the opportunity to exponentially increase our earnings arises. It's worthwhile studying financially successful people to see how they became wealthy (I will talk about wealth creation principles in greater detail in Chapter 12), but the basics of money-management are:

- saving vs investing
- debt management
- budgeting.

Saving is connected to goal setting (see Chapter 9). You set a specific dollar amount as a personal money goal with an action-by date. The goal is then turned into a concrete plan, with actions and milestones that align with the set timeframe. To achieve this goal, you need to have a burning desire and that's where many people go wrong with saving. They either don't set savings goals at all, or if they do, the goals are non-specific and based on wishy-washy want or hope. A burning desire is a prerequisite to success. In Chapter 10, we learnt how to set and achieve goals – use this knowledge to set your savings and money goals. Write them down (be specific), and make sure you have a burning desire to follow through with positive associations around amassing a personal fortune.

There is a difference between saving and investing. Saving is short-term – putting aside money to achieve a set goal or for emergencies. Savings need to be easily accessible. Investing is long-term, such as buying real estate or stocks with the expectation of creating long-term wealth. Saving is like starting school; investing is like graduation.

Saving long term is for pessimists, while investing is for optimists. There is no point in saving just for the sake of it. Savings accounts provide a good parking spot for your short-term money goals and for emergencies (everyone should have at least three to six months' income in emergency funds, but anything over that amount should be invested). As a general rule, if you're going to need to access money within three to five years, it should generally not be invested. And if you're young, and have more than fifteen to twenty years until retirement (or gaining financial independence), save with the purpose of investing.

Debt is another aspect of money that is often misunderstood. Debt can be good or bad, depending on its use. Consumer debt – where money is borrowed in order to buy items such as TVs, cars, or other lifestyle item that depreciate in value – is often called bad debt. The cost of borrowing money to buy these items is often quite high, so consumer debt can be detrimental to your finances by severely impeding your ability to create wealth. It's best to avoid or minimise bad debt.

Good debt is money borrowed to buy high-quality assets that are expected to appreciate in value over time. If you're not retiring in the short to medium-term (within ten to fifteen years) it's not a bad idea to consider good debt as means of buying assets to create wealth (I will talk about this more in Chapter 12). Depending on which country you live in, good debt can attract government incentives and tax benefits as a means of generating economic wealth or growth. Rules vary from country to country so specific advice should be sought from a financial professional in your country.

Borrowing money, whether for good or bad debt, is a double-edged sword; it must be approached with caution because whenever you borrow money, you are open to risks like interest rate changes and market volatility, which can threaten your ability to create wealth. However, debt avoidance is not the answer. Instead, debt needs discipline management, which means ensuring you only borrow the amount you're comfortable with and you allow for interest rate rises that would increase your liability. Debt can be a powerful tool for growth but it can also be a weapon that destroys if the risks are not understood. When looking at how to manage debt, it's useful to get assistance from a financial professional who can help you maximise the use of debt and, at the same time, help you minimise the risks associated with taking out debt.

The last thing to understand about money is budgeting. As boring as it is, unless you set a budget and follow it religiously, you will not achieve your money goals. It's easy to skip this step but remember, you need money to make money. Budgeting means allocating your money into specific pools for recurring basic expenses, discretionary spending, and future savings and investments. Remember the 'pay yourself first principle': if you don't regularly save at least 10 per cent of your income for your future, you will never have the money to make money. You don't need a lot of money to make money, but you need some.

It's hard to resist the urge to dip into other pools and spend money foolishly. The odds are against the average person, which is why successful money management requires high-level money discipline. But when it comes to wealth creation, time is more important than money. You need a long-term perspective. Think back to Chapter 5 where I talked about the compounding effect. Small amounts of money, saved over a long period of time (and invested properly), will create wealth.

Attracting money

Love and appreciation are powerful magnetic energies. If you don't proactively find reasons to love and appreciate money (and what it can do for you, your family and others), and you unconsciously resist or mistrust its true nature, it will not be drawn to you. Unfortunately, most people are unconsciously focused on the negative aspects of money, rather than the positive aspects so attracting money eludes them.

Recently, I was approached by a student doing a thesis on why motivational speakers charge so much money. We talked about former US President Bill Clinton and the fees he charges for keynote speeches. Her perspective was, 'If people have this amazing gift that can improve and transform people's lives, why do they charge for it, especially when the gift is given to them by God?' It's a fair question, but what I heard behind the question was her confusion about the purpose and value of money. So, I asked her, 'Where did you get the idea that services are better given freely?' She couldn't answer, which further confirmed that she had probably long ago accepted this worldview as truth without question.

I explained that many people have a misguided, idealistic view about giving. Giving and receiving are two sides of the same coin. When there is imbalance on one side, the other side becomes unbalanced – it breaks the universal law of equilibrium. Those who don't understand the importance of receiving send the universe a message about their lack of self-worth and gratitude. Many people misinterpret spiritual messages and resign themselves to a life of poverty and struggle. But the universe's natural state is abundance, not scarcity. I further explained that people are compensated in accordance with the value they add to the marketplace. No one is born skilled, and some of these motivational speakers, like Bill Clinton, have worked very hard to develop their skills. Why shouldn't they charge for the value they bring?

Mastering your financial beliefs will help you master your financial destiny. As we know, people who have a negative or scarcity money mindset will never attract large amounts of money. They ask, 'How can I afford to do this?' and accept that they can't. On the other hand, a resourceful mind asks, 'How can I wonderfully and generously be paid for adding value to others by doing what I really love?' People will invest in you to the extent you invest in yourself.

'A man should make all he can and give all he can.'
Nelson Rockefeller

Giving is no more honourable than receiving. To think it is more honourable to give than receive puts things off balance. Whenever we try to receive something for nothing or give something for nothing, the universe will intervene to fix the imbalance. In the same way, imbalance occurs when people with a narcissistic wealth complex believe someone else must lose so they can get ahead, and those with an altruistic wealth complex believe they must lose, so others can get ahead. In the long term, these outlooks do not work individually because the powerful wealth attraction mechanism is triggered through a balance of self-interest and interest in others.

Your financial *deserve* level is determined by your *serve* level. Zig Ziglar said, 'You will get all you want in life, if you help enough other people get what they want.' How can you give others what they love while simultaneously receiving what you love? To make lots of money, shift your mind and touch hearts. Proactively find ways to serve, help, empower, develop, or provide for others, and your wealth will increase as a result.

When it comes to attracting money, remember, money is an inside job; prosperity needs to be developed in your consciousness before it will show up in your outside world. Wealth is created, built, and grown. It doesn't happen by itself. When you consciously observe your money beliefs and adopt a prosperity-based mindset, you go from becoming an unconscious observer of your financial results to becoming a conscious architect of your financial results.

To help you develop a prosperity consciousness, following is a list of positive affirmations. I suggest you say these several times a day every day to replace your old poverty mindset with a prosperity mindset. If affirmations are hard for you, start by saying they work whether you believe them or not. With consistent use, especially if you combine your affirmations with emotion, conviction and a state of expectation, you will start to become highly aware of the money opportunities around you. I practice these affirmations regularly and can vouch for their effectiveness.

- Day and night I attract money and prosperity
- I am open to receiving abundance
- It is Ok for me to have a lot of money
- I feel good about making money
- Money comes to me in increasing quantities on a continuous basis
- I am becoming more and more financially savvy each day
- I make lots of money by adding lots of value to other people

- I am ready to deal with the responsibilities that come with great wealth.

Another way I developed a prosperity mindset was to write a 'Why I must become wealthy so I can …' list. I use the word 'must' because it's a lot more powerful than should. Write down fifty reasons to help you stay motivated and inspired on your journey to wealth – and read them when you feel doubt.

- My 'Why I must become wealthy so I can …' list includes:
- help my family
- have a great lifestyle
- travel the world
- continue writing books
- afford good quality food
- invest in my companies
- buy generous gifts for everyone.

Someone asked me once, 'Why do you write books? You don't make a lot of money writing books, do you?' I said, 'I don't write books to make money. I make money, so I can write books.' My list keeps me highly motivated and focused and I highly recommend that you have your own list.

What's on your 'Why I must become wealthy so I can …' list?

What we have covered in this chapter

In this chapter we have covered:
- money consciousness
- money principles
- money mindset
- understanding money
- attracting money.

What do successful people do? Successful people develop positive beliefs about money, and understand and abide by the irrefutable principles of money. They understand that simply engaging in actions without developing money consciousness will not grow wealth, so they engage in wealth-building thinking and actions.

'You can't be wealthy if you unconsciously dislike wealthy people and automatically presume the worse about them.'

CHAPTER 12
Wealth creation fundamentals

'Survival requires little planning; success requires a lot.'

Wealth is one of the most misunderstood concepts in the world. Most people equate wealth with a high level of materialism (such as owning a Ferrari or a mansion); to me, wealth means financial freedom and choice, not acquiring possessions. If you're responsible for managing your financial future and you want to contribute to causes you care about, wealth building is essential for your success.

This chapter is designed to help you understand the game of wealth creation; however, none of this information should act as a substitute for professional financial advice. Nor is it designed to make you a financial expert. Financial professionals go through years and years of training, and you can delegate financial matters to them when your money understanding is limited. This doesn't mean that you give up control of planning your financial future, rather that you are empowered to make the right financial decisions and form a collaborative relationship with an advisor when it is the right time for you.

Mastering wealth concepts

Globally, wealth is concentrated in very few hands. It's estimated that about 15 million, 6 hundred thousand people in the world, currently have a net worth of a million dollars outside their family home. This represents approximately 2% of the world's population. Living in a wealthy country doesn't necessarily mean you have a better chance of creating wealth.

In 2016, the Census Bureau reported that more than 45 million people, or 14.5 percent of all Americans, lived below the poverty line. Even in Australia, which is considered to be one of the wealthiest countries in the world based on income and lifestyle, it's estimated that 85% of people retire with less than 150 thousand dollars, after spending 30 or 40 years in the work force. This was based on a study done by the University of Canberra, by their National Centre for Social and Economic modelling.

To me, wealth is the ability to fund your chosen lifestyle without having to work. In other words, to do what you enjoy without worrying about having enough money. Unless you want to work for the rest of your life, it makes sense to have created wealth (financial freedom), at least by retirement age.

However, most people are unable to create wealth. The reasons are partly psychological (see the discussion of money consciousness in Chapter 11), and partly strategic (a lack of understanding, planning, and commitment). As I've mentioned before, anyone can make money, but no one can create wealth without planning. It doesn't happen naturally. So, by the time they get to retirement age, many people turn to government welfare or families for financial support.

Perhaps you're thinking retirement is a long way off and wondering how relevant this is. Try replacing the word retirement with financial independence. The aim of creating wealth is the ability to fund your chosen lifestyle without *having* to work, whatever your age.

Assets are a big part of wealth creation, but not everyone fully understands what assets are. If you've ever applied for a bank loan, mortgage, or a credit card, you'll recall being asked to list your assets and liabilities. In this context, assets are things we own (things worth money if we sold them), and liabilities are things we owe money on. But, assets can be categorised in three ways: lifestyle, investment, and operating.

Lifestyle assets include your home and contents, cars, jewellery, boats, golf sets, and so on. They are worth money if you sell them, but not if you hold on to them. Do they help create wealth? No. Lifestyle assets may create the illusion of wealth, but they don't help you become financially independent.

Investment assets are items acquired with the expectation of creating income or value appreciation, such as stocks, bonds, and dividends, managed funds, and real estate (income is generated when rent is higher than the mortgage payment). Investment assets can be sold, but they generally take time to appreciate in value, so getting actual money in your pocket takes longer. It's like planting a seed: if you plant a seed today, it could take fifteen to twenty years to grow a tree that provides shade. When you acquire an investment asset, it won't provide money or a return of investment for a long time, but eventually, it will. The earlier you acquire investment assets, the better.

Operating assets include a business that produces an income (and the assets needed to generate revenue such as cash and inventory), as well as active endeavors such as renovating real estate, buying and selling shares, finding depressed assets and creating value in them, or real estate sub-division projects. They can be sold, and they can also produce income. However, these assets require a lot of mental and physical exertion to create income.

To me, operating assets are like the superhighway to wealth (with high risk and possible high reward), and investment assets are like the slow road to wealth (passive and eventual reward). Where do you think more people have crashes? On the superhighway because they're going faster. It's riskier. But when operating assets work, they are probably one of the fastest ways to create wealth. However, not everyone wants to take that kind of risk or put in that level of mental and physical exertion.

So, this is where you can make a conscious decision about how you want to use assets to achieve financial independence and where you need to concentrate your efforts and resources. Remember, lifestyle assets only create the illusion of wealth, so you need to either have money working for you, or people and systems working for you. If you want money to work for you, focus on investment assets; if you want people and systems working for you, focus on operating assets. What do you want to do? Focus on investment assets, operating assets, or a combination of both?

Every time you open your wallet, ask, 'Is this money going towards a lifestyle asset, an investment asset, or an operating asset?' It's important to understand the pros and cons of each and be conscious about how you're spending, so you don't mistake having lots of lifestyle assets for wealth. By not understanding the implications of how you spend on assets, it can lead to ending up in a financial space you don't want to be. What do I do? My financial independence plan includes having finds invested in investment and operating assets, and I minimise expenditure on lifestyle assets.

Creating wealth involves asset acquisition. More importantly, it involves acquiring the right assets. By now, hopefully you're starting to see why it is so important to have a plan in place.

Creating financial wealth

The main determinant of wealth is your net worth, not your income. Research shows financial success is not determined by how much you make, but what you do with your income. In Chapter 11, I referred to a survey of self-made millionaires, which revealed that prudent saving and investing – not income – resulted in their financial success. Rather than focusing on earning more income, your focus should be on also acquiring the disciplines and acquiring the right types of assets, so you can make sensible financial decisions over the long term.

Net worth is what you own, minus what you owe. My aim is to see my net worth increase every year, so every August I do a net worth calculation. I highly recommend you do the same at a set time every year. In this calculation I suggest you do *not* include your lifestyle assets (your primary place of residence, contents, jewellery, or electronics). Instead, include your investment assets (if you have any), and operating assets (where you are certain the operating assets can be sold at a particular price, a.k.a. as a going concern). The net worth calculation is a reality check for most people. Many avoid it because it makes them feel bad about their money situation. But if you want a true indicator of your financial health, you must do the calculation. After that, set the intention to increase your net worth by a minimum of 10 or 20 per cent every year. Until you set that intention, and trigger the RAS (Chapter 10), you won't focus on what you need to do to achieve that goal.

Most ways to create wealth fall into one of two categories: people and systems working for you (a business where people work for you, or an entrepreneurial venture where you leverage off other people's time and expertise); or money working for you (investing). In this section, I will focus on making money work for you.

When we invest, money comes in the form of a return, whether in income (or cash flow), or in growth (appreciation in value). Before going further, I want to distinguish between speculating and investing:

- Speculating has the intention of creating a quick profit, while investing aims to generate a medium to long-term return.
- Speculating puts less emphasis on the underlying quality of the asset, and more on price movement (buying something cheap and trying to sell it for more than cost to make a short-term profit). Quality is considered when it comes to investing, because the expectation is for the asset to grow in value.

One of the best ways to make money is to avoid losing money. With speculation it is possible to make money, but also highly improbable. However, when investing is done correctly, you have a high probability of making money (although nothing can ever be guaranteed). The game of wealth creation is about maximising your probability. Many people lose money because they speculate, rather than invest – they don't know the difference. Just because someone has made money on something doesn't necessarily mean you will. It's possible to win money at the casino, but for most people, it's highly improbable. Possibility does not always mean probability.

In Chapter 11, I also made the distinction between saving and investing. Saving is more like a short-term activity to reach a set money goal (such as three to six months' income as an emergency fund), rather than a long-term wealth creation endeavor.

With investing, there is always an element of risk. Whenever you acquire investment or operating assets, you take on a level of financial risk. Financial risk can never be completely eliminated, but it can be minimised and managed through understanding financial concepts and working with the right financial experts. It's like driving a car; we can never guarantee we won't have a car accident, but we minimise the risk of a collision through skill improvement, awareness of road conditions and other drivers, regular car maintenance, and taking precautions where necessary. No one wants to lose money, but since risk is part of the game, we have to take steps to minimise and manage the level of risk.

So, what are these risks? When it comes to wealth creation, the four main risk types, are:

1. **Capital loss** – this is the loss that happens when a capital investment decreases in value. Sometimes people concentrate all their money in a particular place or asset, and then end up losing all their money because the assets are bad quality or they do not have a long-term track record. They speculate and lose. Many years ago, I learnt that money was very similar to golf – winning is less about hitting lots of good shots, and more about avoiding the bad ones. By minimising the bad shots in the game of money, you increase and maximise your probability of winning the game.

2. **Markets** – economic conditions and developments affect the entire financial market (where financial instruments a.k.a. financial securities such as bonds, stocks and shares are bought and sold). The market also affects real estate investments by creating a temporary

fluctuation in the value of your asset or investments (known as volatility risk). History shows that any good quality asset will go up and down in value, rather than performing in a straight line. Generally speaking, in the long term, the markets tend to go up (and most assets appreciate in value if they're quality assets), but in the short to medium term, there can be quite a bit of fluctuation or volatility. Understand that this is a normal part of the game; try not to give into fear and react when the markets are down. At the same time, try not to succumb to greed when those assets go up in value.

3. **Inflation** – if the value of your investments does not keep up with inflation, you risk a loss in your purchasing power. In general, the cost of goods and services increases with inflation over the long term. If you look back twenty, thirty, forty or fifty years, it's unlikely that a loaf of bread, car, clothes, or any other essential items cost the same back then. Many people never make the connection that over a long period of time their money will buy less and less, because they measure their money based on face value as opposed to purchasing power. If you don't actively grow your money, the purchasing power of your money will erode.

4. **Longevity** – simply put, it's the risk that you'll outlive your savings. People are living longer and longer. Once upon a time, the life expectancy of an average human being was about thirty years; now populations are ageing and life expectancy is anywhere between seventies and nineties. This means people need to consciously plan how they will support themselves financially, when their linear income (what they receive from work) stops.

When it comes to financial risk and wealth creation, there is not just one type of risk to be mindful of, but several. One of the chief challenges for investors is to find the right balance between the different types of risks. For example, if a person is too conservative with their money, they will inadvertently take on inflation and longevity risks. At the same time, someone who does not understand market volatility might make bad decisions and blow their money. People often tell me they do not want to take financial risk, but as I said, to make money, risk is inevitable. Rather than avoiding risk altogether, I suggest you consider which type of risk you are more comfortable with, based on your life stage and your net worth objectives.

I hope this has shed more light on what it takes to create wealth, as well as the key considerations and challenges. It's important that you take the time to understand these concepts – I call them the rules of the wealth creation game. If you don't understand the rules, you're likely to make the same mistakes most people make, and end up with financial struggles not financial independence.

Ten steps to financial freedom

You can achieve financial freedom in ten steps. The steps are simple, but not easy (there are no quick fixes). These time-tested steps require commitment, discipline, and planning. But, if you stick to these steps, you'll take massive leaps towards an independent financial future.

1. **Commit** – everyone is interested in having money but very few people commit to making it. Set a strong and clear intention to create wealth (which will trigger the RAS – see Chapter 10), even if it means giving up time and money to make it happen. The best way to demonstrate commitment is to start the planning process. Wealth won't happen by itself.

2. **Pay yourself first** – you can only pay yourself first if you spend less than you earn. I discussed this briefly in Chapter 11, but it's worth a reminder. Set the intention to live on 90 per cent of your income and use 10 per cent for wealth creation. Get into the habit of spending less than you earn, and pay yourself (your financial future), first.

3. **Emergency fund** – take steps to save the equivalent of three to six months' income in an interest-bearing, hard-to-access bank account. In most cases, three months' income in a buffer will give you comfort and confidence, but if the industry is highly seasonal or volatile, or if there is risk of redundancies, save up to six months' income. Having that buffer will not only provide a sense of security, but will empower

us to act from a prosperity mindset.

4. **Invest the rest** – once you have three to six months' income in reserve, look at investing for growth. Understand the importance of time and compound interest (see Chapter 5). A mistake many people make is to invest when they have large amounts of money, but it is often more beneficial to start investing early with small amounts and adopt a long-term perspective.

5. **Understand investment options** – the four main options are real estate (commercial, tourism, or residential, or real estate trusts where an organisation invites investors to invest in a group or package of properties), business (shares and stocks), money market investments (bonds, cash-based investments, or bank accounts that earn interest), and 'everything else' (hedge funds, private equity funds, or collections of art, wine, stamps, coins, vintage cars, and so on). I will add more information about these four investment types after the steps, but remember to stick with something that is proven.

6. **Minimise financial risk** – diversify your investments (try not to hedge your bets on any one investment strategy or type) and obtain appropriate insurance. Generally speaking, diversification provides the benefit of reducing investment risk. But, it doesn't mean having a random collection of investments. For diversification to be effective, the investments you hold must perform differently to each other. When it comes to insurance, a competent finance professional can recommend appropriate insurance amounts and products, such as income protection, death and disability, and so on. If you're highly reliant on your continued ability to make an income and you have debt, insurance is critical because things can and do go wrong in life. Get into the habit of budgeting a small percentage of your income for insurance-related costs (I allow 5 to 10 per cent of my income for this).

7. **Minimise costs and taxes** – make sure you're getting value for what you're paying. The investment world is prone to vested interest in certain products and strategies, and it is good practice to compare alternatives to see if you can get the same benefit for a lower cost. A

finance professional can help with this, and while that costs money, it will often save you even more money, time, and consolidation costs. Taxes are a big cost and unavoidable, but a good tax professional can help you minimise tax. What you save, you can put towards creating wealth.

8. **Delegate** – all financially successful people have teams, so seek out competent finance professionals for advice where necessary. While there is nothing wrong with talking to a salesperson about a financial solution you already know is right for you, it's best to get advice from someone qualified to suggest investment and wealth strategies to suit your needs. Check their credentials and make sure they specialise in the financial area you're seeking advice in. Have they dealt with clients with a similar situation to yours? Can they share case studies showing outcomes they have produced for clients? There's no point going to a home loan broker if your need is retirement planning.

9. **Debt awareness** – getting this wrong can mean the difference between creating wealth or destroying wealth. In Chapter 11, I talked about the difference between good and bad debt: when used wisely, good debt can help create investment or operating assets (and may have tax incentives); bad debt can put tremendous pressure on our cash flow (and the items purchased lose value). I highly recommend you seek professional advice when it comes to debt.

10. **Behaviour** – your behaviours and reactions will impact your wealth creation more than anything else. Most people react through fear and greed, but that does not lead to financial success, so be conscious of your behaviours and biases (more on this later) around money.

Remember, it won't be easy but, if you stay committed and disciplined, you will be on the way to creating financial wealth.

Before I go on, I want to add a bit more on investment types (see step 5). Real estate has potential for growth if selected well, and it can provide rental income and sometimes, depending on your country, significant tax benefits. If you are interested in purchasing property, be clear about your goal. Is it growth, income, tax benefits, or a combination? Seek advice where necessary (see step 8). Consider the location (research the infrastructure such as medical, transport, educational, and lifestyle facilities), demand (if supply exceeds demand, growth opportunities will be limited), street appeal, design, and number of owner-occupiers versus investors in an area.

Business investments can provide growth and income (in the form of dividends), and in some countries stocks and shares have significant tax benefits. If you invest well, the stock or share market can be a fantastic way to create wealth. Just remember the difference between investing and speculating, and consider the goal. The primary objective should be to create growth and make an income, and legal tax minimisation should be secondary. Constructing a good quality stock portfolio is something best left to financial professionals (see step 8).

Investing in money markets, offers high security and stability because they're less volatile than real estate and shares. However, they typically do not offer great growth potential, and are often not very tax effective, so growth may be less, and longevity and inflation risks are often higher. As for the 'everything else' investments, these are higher risk because they generally have a smaller market (not everyone might be as enthusiastic about your rare stamp collection as you). Limited markets limit growth. Also, unless someone desperately desires your collection, these types of investments have a speculative element and may not provide income or tax benefits. As always, seek advice from financial professionals if these types of investments interest you.

Financial market investments have, in the long term (this spans a couple of hundred years), done very well. But in that same period, most investors have *not* done very well, because investors don't always do what investments do. DALBAR research has repeatedly found that over any twenty-year period, there is a difference of up to 6 or 7 per cent in returns (what investments return and what investors receive). Why? When financial markets are up, most investors feel highly confident and invest more, but when the markets are down, most investors succumb to fear and start selling. The share and stock markets are one of the only markets in the world where people sell when the prices are slashed.

You now know the ten steps to financial freedom, but there are four common biases that can affect you from making good financial decisions and creating wealth:

1. **Loss aversion bias** – a fear of losing money. Mark Twain said, 'If a cat sits on a hot stove, that cat won't sit on a hot stove again. That cat won't sit on a cold stove either.' Hearing about people losing money, or hearing bad news stories about money losses, can paralyse people with fear and distort their thinking so they'd rather make less money than lose any at all. Fear destroys wealth just like greed does.

2. **Recency bias** – people tend to make decisions based on what has happened recently rather than in the long-term past. Unfortunately, most people are myopic and only look at recent trends to drive their financial decisions. If the trends are good, they feel overly optimistic; if the trends are bad, they feel overly pessimistic. In Chapter 11, I mentioned a study by Dr Edward C. Banfield of Harvard University, who found that a long-term perspective was the most accurate predictor of upward financial mobility.

3. **Familiarity bias** – we have a tendency to stick to our comfort zone and avoid new things. Doing this affects our ability to create financial freedom because we resist learning new skills or taking new advice.

4. **Overconfidence bias** – the assumption that you have a higher level of intelligence compared to the general population (or finance professionals and experienced fund managers). Many men suffer from this bias and assume their ability to make good financial decisions is better than it actually is.

Following the ten steps to financial freedom and understanding the psychological biases that can hold you back, will make you the architect of your financial future. Why not set the intention to take control and make more empowered decisions today?

What we have covered in this chapter

In this chapter we have covered:
- mastering wealth concepts
- creating wealth
- the ten steps to financial freedom.

What do successful people do? Successful people take time to understand the basics, fundamentals, and principles of wealth. They know why it's important to create wealth, and they take proactive steps to create, grow, and protect their financial position.

'Don't chase income to buy liabilities.
Chase income to invest in assets.'

CHAPTER 13
Productivity and performance

'Your approach to productivity determines your level of achievement and performance.'

In business and personal life, how you perform is not only a great source of satisfaction, but also greatly lifts your self-esteem. As the general saying goes, 'Success breeds success.'

Managing your time well

To become highly successful, it is important to become skilled at time management. You need to get as much return as you can for your investment of time and energy. Why? Because time is finite – once it's lost, it's lost forever.

Being productive and performing to your capacity is about maximising what you can do with the time you have. In other words, maximising efficiency. Personal productivity is all about maximising output and minimising input in a world that's increasingly ambiguous about time.

Productivity and performance are not taught in school. We are not taught how to process information or focus on outcomes, or what actions to take to make things happen. However, many highly successful people have a demonstrated ability to deal with crises and take advantage of opportunities. They focus their energy strategically and tactically, without letting anything significant fall through the cracks. We need to know how to maximise our own productivity and performance so, we too, can take advantage of opportunities and add value to ourselves and others.

As the world gets busier and busier, more and more people are experiencing anxiety. Much of this is caused by feelings of lacking control, organisation, preparation, and action. Most people I come across say they have too much to handle and not enough time to get it all done. It's a strange paradox – people work hard to enhance their quality of life, while at the same time adding to their stress levels by taking on more than they can handle. As the lines between work and life become blurred, we need better tools to manage the infinite quantity of information available and tasks required.

The good news is that it's possible for people to have an overwhelming to-do list and still function productively. When we adapt how we work and achieve optimum levels of productivity and performance, we feel a sense of being in control. Our stress levels are reduced and our focus is sharper. We feel like we're making noticeable progress towards meaningful outcomes. It's a great way to live, work, and achieve high levels of effectiveness and efficiency.

The major issue is how to make appropriate choices about what to do at any point in time. It's about task-management more than time-management. So, how can you better manage your productivity and performance and achieve more than most people? How can you fit in as much as highly successful people do? I designed a tool to help me with this, in which I start by compartmentalising my life into five areas:

1. health
2. peace of mind
3. relationships
4. business and career
5. finances and money.

I believe these five areas are pivotal to success, and most people would agree they are critical components of their lives. But how many people neglect some of these areas, if not all of them? How many do you neglect?

Now, imagine these five areas as five balls. Imagine juggling all five balls. Occasionally you're going to drop a ball. That's okay. It's not the dropping of the ball that causes major cracks in your life. It's how long the ball sits on the floor, and how long it takes you to pick it up.

On the first day of every month, I reflect back on the previous thirty days and ask, 'Which area did I neglect the most?' Health? Did I eat too many unhealthy meals? Did I take enough time to exercise and look after my health? How's my peace of mind? Have I neglected my mental and emotional state? Have I taken enough time to relax and meditate? Have I spent time in solitude or silence? Have I walked in nature or had a massage? Was it relationships? Did I neglect some of my important relationships? Did I spend enough time with my family and friends? How's my career and business faring? Did I put off some of the tasks I've been meaning to do? Perhaps it was to do with catching up on filing, business development, or following up with a client. Did I work diligently? Are some business and career issues still outstanding? Or was it money? Did I pay attention to my bank accounts and resolve outstanding expenses? Have I reviewed my assets and liabilities? Did I calculate my net worth for business and home?

Let's assume I neglected health the most. If in the last thirty days health was the area I neglected, then for the next thirty days I make health my biggest focus. I become extremely conscious about what I'm eating, how much I'm drinking, my exercise levels, and so on. Of course, it's not a few bad meals or a few junk food lunches that cause serious health issues. It's not missing a workout every now and then, or overspending once in a while. But if we repeatedly engage in bad behavior or neglect an area over a long period of time, massive cracks will appear. When I continually neglect areas of my life, I start to lose balance. Like I said, I can't avoid dropping the ball completely because life's not perfect. But if I don't pick it up, a loss of balance and control results. It's how quickly I pick up that ball that determines my future productivity and efficiency. So I make a point of doing this activity every month, so I can reflect on where balance needs correction, and keep those balls in the air.

Why not try it? Draw a line across a piece of paper and create five columns, one for each life area: health, peace of mind, relationships, business and career, finances and money. Carefully consider which areas need attention, and then set an intention to pick up that ball for the next month. If you do this every month, you will be able to spot the cracks and fill them in.

Eliminating timewasters

Do you sometimes feel like you spend all your time managing trivial stuff or reacting to crises? Do you feel like you're constantly putting out one proverbial fire after another? Do you feel completely drained of energy because you're always busy and working? Do you ever feel like you haven't accomplished anything of real significance or importance despite being busy all the time? If that's the case, you might be confusing urgency and importance.

'What is important is seldom urgent,
and what is urgent is seldom important.'
Dwight. D. Eisenhower

Dwight D. Eisenhower was the 34th US President. Before this, he was a five-star general in the US Army, the first supreme commander of the new NATO forces assembled in 1951, and president of Columbia University. He had an incredible ability to sustain his productivity, not just for weeks or months, but for years on end. But despite his busy schedule, he always made time for leisure, golfing, and painting. How did he do all this? He developed the Eisenhower Matrix, a simple decision-making tool to help him be more productive and efficient. To begin to see how this works, consider the difference between urgent and important tasks:

- Urgent tasks demand your immediate attention (such as, emails from your boss), kind of like they're shouting, 'Do this! Read this!' We tend to these reactively (stopping what we're doing) and the result is feeling rushed, negative, narrowly focused, and even defensive, especially when we're juggling too many urgent tasks.

- Important tasks contribute to your long-term goals (such as studying to advance your career) and overall fulfillment. We tend to respond to these with planning and organisation, which helps us remain calm, rational, and more calculated in going about the task.

Unfortunately, because most people do not make a conscious distinction between urgent and important, they fall into the trap of believing that urgency equates importance. And yes, sometimes important tasks can be urgent as well, which can be confusing, but in many cases, they aren't. With the daily bombardment of tasks and information through social media and the internet, we rarely take time to ask, 'Is this important or urgent?'

Stephen Covey made Eisenhower's Matrix popular in his book *The 7 Habits of Highly Effective People* and it's now seen as a mainstream way to define tasks. Covey called it the Urgent Important Matrix, which separates tasks into four quadrants: Crises, Goals and Planning, Interruptions, and Distractions. The idea is to help people distinguish between what's important and not important, and what's urgent and not urgent. Using this matrix to organise your tasks makes acting relatively simple.

So, using this matrix, you separate your tasks into the four quadrants as follows:

- **Quadrant 1** – Crises (urgent and important). These tasks need immediate attention such as emergencies, things left to the last minute, deadlines, and complaints. They have to be managed straight away. Spending too much time here can lead to burnout and stress, but with planning, delegating, and organisation, many Quadrant 1 tasks can be made more efficient.

- **Quadrant 2** – Goals and Planning (important and non-urgent). These activities or tasks don't have a pressing deadline, such as financial planning, exercising, personal development, meditation, and car maintenance, but they help you achieve your important personal and professional goals. It's the big picture quadrant. Writing a book is a personal example of a Quadrant 2 task. It's not urgent, but it's very important, because it allows me to increase my impact and influence, and live according to my life's purpose of teaching, mentoring, guiding, and enabling.

- **Quadrant 3** – Interruptions (urgent but not important). These tasks demand attention now but don't contribute to your long-term goals, such as meetings, phone calls or text messages, and people dropping in announced. These tasks keep you busy (or *doing*), without really getting anywhere. According to Covey, many people spend most of their time on Quadrant 3 because they're stuck in *doing* mode without thinking about whether what they are doing is important or not. And, often Quadrant 3 tasks help others achieve their goals while holding you back. It's a recipe for frustration and resentment, unless you learn to say 'no' and be assertive about the way your time is used.

- **Quadrant 4** – Distractions (not urgent and not important). These tasks distract you from doing what matters to help you achieve your long-term goals, such as reading irrelevant emails, playing video games, gambling, shopping, scrolling through social media, or mindlessly watching TV. There's nothing wrong with relaxing and taking time out for entertainment (that can be energising), but when you're unconsciously engaging in distractions, it can impact productivity physically and mentally. I suggest spending less than 5 per cent of your waking hours in this quadrant four.

This matrix pushes you to question whether an action is really necessary and identify which tasks you need to focus on as a priority (or ignore). It challenges habits (like mindlessly repeating things because you're in the pattern of being busy), and helps you regain control of your time. Working with this model requires you to make hard decisions and say 'no' to things that don't help achieve your mission, goals, or values. I personally love using the matrix because it provides a clear framework for making decisions again and again. So, my challenge is for you to apply the Urgent Important Matrix to as many aspects of your life as you can. When faced with a decision, ask, 'Am I doing this because it's important, or am I doing this because it's urgent?' I promise that as you spend more time working on not just urgent but *important* tasks, you will feel a renewed sense of control and confidence in your life.

However, while separating tasks into the four quadrants is relatively easy to do, implementing this principle on a consistent basis can be challenging. You need to develop the habit. When you do, you'll feel like you're achieving something and making real progress towards your goals. Remember that by investing time in Quadrant 2, you can prevent and eliminate many of the crises and problems that happen in Quadrant 1. Balance the requests of Quadrant 3 with your own needs, so you can enjoy chill-out time in Quadrant 4, knowing you've earned it.

Software development consultant Kevlin Henney once said, 'There is no code faster than no code.' If I apply this to time-management, it means the fastest way to get something done is to eliminate that task entirely. There is no faster way to do something than not doing it at all. Now this doesn't mean being lazy. Just think hard about whether what you're about to do is important. Will it add value to your life, business, health, relationships, or your peace of mind?

> '*Being busy is a form of laziness – lazy thinking*
> *and indiscriminate action.*'
> **Tim Ferriss, *The Four Hour Work Week***

Follow the Pareto Principle

Have you heard of the Pareto Principle? If you've studied business or economics, you would be aware of the 80/20 rule: 80 per cent of results come from just 20 per cent of the action. Applying this rule is an extremely smart way to increase your productivity and stay organised.

The Pareto Principle was named after Italian economist Vilfredo Pareto who found that 80 per cent of Italy's land was owned only by 20 per cent of Italians. He then observed this same imbalance in other areas of life, such as production (80 per cent of production came from 20 per cent of the companies in that industry). These observations led to the generalisation also known as the 80/20 rule. It's been observed in many areas such as:

- 20 per cent of people make 80 per cent of income in any industry
- 20 per cent of clients account for 80 per cent of revenue
- 20 per cent of workers generate 80 per cent of results
- 20 per cent of technology problems cost 80 per cent of lost time
- 80 per cent of sales volume comes from 20 per cent of products.

How does this apply to time management? What it means is that 80 per cent of your output potentially comes from just 20 per cent of your time and input. Taking it further, the 80/20 rule is another option for time management, and with some adjustments, it could be used as an ideal solution for you and your organisation.

So, how do you apply the Pareto Principle?

Firstly, frequently evaluate your tasks. If 80 per cent of your results potentially come from 20 per cent of your effort, then it stands to reason that 80 per cent of impact will come from 20 per cent of your tasks. So, identify which tasks form the 20 per cent. Ask, 'Is every task on my list urgent? Are the tasks on my list within my expertise, or should they be delegated? Am I spending too much time on certain types of tasks? Which tasks are necessary to achieve the overall outcome?'

Secondly, continually assess your goals. Your goals and tasks may be intertwined, but not always. Think about your professional goals and the activities that are needed to accomplish them, remembering that 80 per cent of those goals will be achieved with potentially just 20 per cent of the necessary activities. Take an inventory: which activities form the 20 per cent that will get you closer to your objectives? For example, if you decide to work late so you can take the day off tomorrow, what are the vital few activities (the 20 per cent) you can do to finish the task you've been set and make your boss happy? Ask, 'Is this task in the top 20 per cent or in the bottom 80 per cent of what I have to do?'

Thirdly, know your prime time – the time you're most productive. You may do your best work between 9 a.m. and 11 a.m., or you may get more done between 3 p.m. and 5 p.m. I'm most productive between 5 a.m. and 7 a.m. I spend an hour or two writing and coming up with new ideas and content because as an author, speaker, writer, trainer, and coach, it is important for me to be consistently researching and producing new content. That's an 80 per cent goal for me. When do you feel the most energetic, focused, and productive? Determine this, then use that time to tackle the 20 per cent of tasks and goals you have identified as most important for your goals. Invest the most productive time of your day on the tasks and activities that will yield the best result. Build your perfect workday around your energy levels.

Finally, identify and eliminate distractions. They are everywhere and cause loss of focus, delayed task completion, and an overall reduction in your productivity. Emails, incoming phone calls, unplanned visitors, thirst or hunger, making coffee, and social media notifications are some examples. According to the Pareto Principle, 80 per cent of your distractions will come from 20 per cent of sources. Write a list of distractions. Which ones happen the most? You're likely to find two or three form the 20 per cent causing 80 per cent of your distraction. Now find ways to eliminate those interruptions. Four things I do are:

- I block out specific times to work on emails
- If I'm going to be working on a task that requires a lot of time, I bring drinks and snacks with me, so I don't have to constantly leave my desk and interrupt my work pattern
- I try not to check my social media regularly when I'm working
- I let non-urgent calls go to my voicemail.

How can you eliminate the worst distraction offenders?

The Pareto Principle can bring a lot of success through consistent use. The trick is for you to identify 20 per cent of your efforts which result in 80 per cent of your outcomes. What 20 per cent of choices can you make relating to your clients and tasks, that would contribute to 80 per cent of your results? Instead of juggling your time to accomplish a large number of tasks, identify the ones with the highest value, and proactively and consciously spend more time on them.

Doing this will improve your productivity, increase your income (which could allow you to pay someone to do tasks that are of lesser value), and use the limited time you have for the best results.

Adopt the philosophy of productivity

Productivity is about freeing up time for yourself, so you can engage in leisure activities, spend time with family, work on your health, and so on. To do this, you will need the power of decisiveness more than any other single quality or attribute. Your ability to decide when to take time off, and then make it happen, is the key to improving the quality of your life.

Many people believe they have too much to do to take time off. They feel they have to sacrifice their personal life for work. This is not necessarily true. In many cases, it is not an exaggeration to suggest that a big percentage of a person's time at work is spent on distractions or activities that contribute very little to the actual work the person is being paid to do (or their professional development). Half of an individual's work time can be wasted on idle socialising with co-workers, personal phone calls, social media, and daydreaming. If this rings true, and you're aware of wasting time at work, remember that the work will not go away. At some point it will need doing, and the longer it is left undone, the more other work piles up, creating stress.

Many years ago, I heard a speaker at an event share the following story, which demonstrates this point well:

> LITTLE GIRL: 'Why does Dad bring home a briefcase full of work every night and work all evening?'
>
> MOTHER: 'Honey, you have to understand that Dad can't get all of his work done at the office and that's why he has to bring it home and work in the evenings.'
>
> LITTLE GIRL: 'Why don't they just put him in a slow class?'
>
> It's fair to say most people are not organised enough to take enough time for their families and personal activities. I've been guilty of this myself. I have fallen into the bad habit of working inefficiently and ineffectively, which is why I turned to performance and productivity models to enhance my results.

So, how can you organise yourself so you can take time off?

Firstly, identify the tasks that contribute the greatest value to your work (the 80/20 rule). Be certain that the tasks you do will make the greatest contribution to your profitability, revenue, or career growth.

Secondly, drop or delegate tasks that contribute little or nothing to your long-term goals (the Urgent Important Matrix). For me to do what I do, I had to learn to delegate many tasks to others. At first this was difficult, however, when I experienced the payoff of being able to spend more time in my zone of genius, I was convinced of the benefits of delegation. People often ask me, 'How do you delegate when you're working on your own?' My response is, 'Develop your natural skills and talents so you can make enough income or revenue to afford to hire help.'

Thirdly, leverage ways that help get a better return on your time, such as other people's knowledge. One key piece of knowledge applied to your situation can make an extraordinary difference in results, as well as save money and time. Successful people are constantly looking out, and searching for, people with the right ideas and insights that will help them achieve their goal faster.

Next, aim to take at least one full day off each month in which you have nothing to do with work – no business calls, emails, nothing work-related. Let your brain completely recharge: go for a walk, meditate, get a massage, and spend time with loved ones. You will feel reinvigorated and be more productive when you return to work. Once you're comfortable taking one day off each month, expand your time to two or three days a month. Then, schedule a three-day holiday every three months, and eventually every two months, building up to two to four weeks' holidays every year. Reorganise your life so that your time off becomes a major priority. You won't feel guilty doing this if you're highly productive in work times.

It's not uncommon to feel guilty taking holidays, or time off, because we know that our productivity levels drop at this time. Think of it like this: the more relaxed and rested you are, the more alert and productive you'll be at work. And the more productive you are, because you're using your time well, the more you'll enjoy your work.

I use a to-do list every day and I usually prepare this list the night before. It helps me to sleep well, knowing that there is no unattended business that I'm forgetting, and in the morning I'm primed to tick items off my list. I mark the items as 'important, not urgent' and so on, as per Urgent Important Matrix, and as I tick them off, I get a strong feeling of satisfaction and accomplishment. On my list, I ensure there is one major item that's highly important to achieving my goals and I invest time each day on that goal.

You can start being more productive now. Pay close attention to what you do. Think about tasks carefully before you begin. Identify your most important tasks and concentrate on them single-mindedly. Doing this, will result in new habits that will lead to greater levels of productivity and performance.

You will be amazed at the improvements in every part of your life. They will happen faster than you imagine. And by the end of the year, you will feel as though you have accomplished something substantial.

The secret of sustainable performance

I want to share some less-known secrets about sustainable performance from people who have dedicated their lives to understanding how it works.

'Growth comes at the point of resistance. We learn by pushing ourselves and finding what really lies at the outer reaches of our abilities.'
Josh Waitzkin, *The Art of Learning*

The first secret is having a positive attitude towards struggle. Struggle can be good when it comes to performance (or developing expertise), because it builds skills. We develop our craft to peak performance by pushing ourselves to the outer reach of our abilities. The journey of elite performer Josh Waitzkin (*The Art of Learning*), who was recognised as an international chess prodigy as a child and later turned into a martial arts world champion, provides us with some interesting insights into this concept. His mind was stressed to the point of complete exhaustion during his chess years. Much of this was necessary for growth in expertise – when he was meticulously studying chess patterns and the deep structures underlying them, he had to push himself to the point of resistance for growth to happen. Later, he took the training philosophy that turned him into a world champion in chess, and used it to become a world champion in martial arts.

In the 'Art Of Learning,' Josh Waitzkin discusses how students who were forced to grapple with complex problems before receiving help from teachers, outperformed students who received early assistance. In fact, the most effective skills development came when assistance was delayed until they reached the point of failure. The authors summarised their findings in a simple yet elegant statement: skills come from struggle. Or as Waitzkin said,

'Growth comes at the point of resistance.'

People who dare to push the envelope will, in most cases, keep getting better. The key is in the attitude towards struggle. It's not so much the struggle that causes burnout or giving up, but the perception of struggle as failure, rather than a setback. People with this perception of struggle cannot see that it's an opportunity for growth. Developing a new skill takes effort and it's okay to fail productively. But don't ask for help or give up too early – allow yourself to grapple with the task so you get maximum growth.

> *'The most effective (improvement) method of all:*
> *deliberate practice. It is the gold standard, the ideal*
> *to which anyone learning a skill should aspire.'*
> **Anders Ericsson**

The second secret to sustained performance is deliberate practice. In the early 1990s, Swedish psychologist Anders Ericsson and his colleagues set out to investigate how some people became experts in their field. They discovered that the number of years' experience bore no correlation to how successful a professional was at their task. In every field that was studied, from wine tasting to financial investing, when it came to differentiating top performance, experience was actually not the critical variable. Ericsson wondered, 'If it wasn't experience, then what made someone an expert in their field?' He concluded that experts engaged in what he termed 'deliberate practice'. This doesn't mean practising the same thing over and over until it's mastered, but stepping out of their comfort zone and trying activities that test them. In other words, it's the type of practice that determines expertise and sustainable performance.

In *Peak* by Ericsson and Robert Pool, a formula called S.P.I.C.E was shared to demonstrate how to turn practice sessions into deliberate practice sessions. S.P.I.C.E has helped me improve my skills in writing, speaking, and creating programs and I highly recommend it.

- The **S** stands for 'specific performance target'. Ericsson and Pool cautioned against having vague performance targets like 'get better'. To improve your performance, you need specific and measurable performance goals such as, 'I will increase my net profit by 15 per cent in twelve months.'

- The **P** stands for 'periods of intense, undistracted focus'. As Ericsson said, 'Deliberate practice is deliberate, that is, it requires a person's full attention and conscious actions.' Going through the motions without the intention of becoming better will not improve your performance. Simply following directions without evaluating your experience isn't enough.

- The **I** stands for 'immediate feedback'. You need accurate and immediate feedback if you want to improve, and the quicker the feedback, the faster you will improve.

- The **C** stands for 'cycling between comfort and discomfort'. You need to approach skill development the same way you would approach bodybuilding. There is a period of discomfort when you lift weights slightly heavier than usual, and then that period is followed by a recovery phase (which helps grow stronger muscles and the ability to lift larger weights). The same applies to deliberate practice. You must go out of your comfort zone and accept that discomfort is essential to improvement. In my business, my team knows the ability to thrive under pressure is essential to success. We don't avoid pressure. We welcome it. After all, diamonds are made under pressure.

- The **E** stands for 'expert coaching from proven performers.' Expert coaches keep you on the right path, add social pressures to hold you accountable, raise the intensity of practice, provide accurate and immediate feedback, and give that push when you need it most.

Remember, it's not the quantity of experience or training, it's the quality that determines how quickly you will achieve expertise and top performance in your chosen field.

The next secret to sustainable performance is taking on challenges that make you feel a little out of control (but not too anxious). When we take on challenges beyond our skills, it stimulates growth. Maybe not very, very big challenges immediately, but big enough so they are not easy. It's a bit of a balancing act where you can ask, 'Is this going to challenge me and take me to the outer edge of my comfort zone?' What you choose should test you, but it should not discourage you from even attempting it.

Performance coach, author and lecturer Steve Magness has researched peak performance and designed workouts for world-class distance runners, such as Sara Hall, Mark English, Natosha Rogers, Jackie Areson, and Brian Barraza. The workouts were designed to stretch their limits and push the athletes beyond their current abilities. According to Steve, it's not uncommon for his athletes to show up to practice a little uncertain. However, he believes uncertainty is a great thing when it comes to performance because it signals that a growth opportunity is emerging. The mind is trying to pull us back to the familiar path that represents our comfort zone, but if you are prepared to venture down an unknown path, that is where peak performance will happen.

Consider the activities you engage in on an everyday basis. Where do they fall in the zone of challenge? Are you pursuing growth in a healthy sustainable way, or is your habit to take the path of least resistance? Remember, if you fully feel in control, make the next challenge a bit harder; if you feel so anxious that you can't focus, you may need to dial things down a notch.

So, seek out challenges that exceed your ability, and constantly think of new skills you want to develop and stretch. That little voice that says, 'I can't possibly do this' is a sign you're on the right track.

What we have covered in this chapter

In this chapter, we have covered:

- managing productivity and performance
- eliminating time wasters
- the Pareto Principle
- the philosophy of productivity
- and the secrets of sustainable performance.

What do successful people do? Successful people understand the importance of time management. They differentiate important tasks from urgent tasks and prioritise accordingly. Successful people know that being intentional and strategic about performance gives them an edge, personally and professionally. By understanding the key areas of their life, they ensure that no key area is neglected over the long term.

'Who you become tomorrow is determined
by what you do today.'

CHAPTER 14
Enhance your spiritual awareness and intelligence

Many people believe humans simply comprise of a mind and body. They don't consider that we have an intelligence that goes beyond the mind – thinking like this is for a select few, they believe. However, spiritual awareness is far from being an esoteric concept, and understanding more about it can have profound implications for the quality, performance, and perception of your personal and professional life.

What is spiritual awareness?

Through the ages, humans have believed in an invisible power through which, and by which, all things have been created, and are continually being recreated. Some call this power God. Some call it the universe or universal intelligence, and others call it Spirit. Whatever way humans personalise or connect with this power, it certainly seems possible an invisible intelligence operates beneath the visible surface of life, and that the mystery of life is an expression not of random accidents. Is such an intelligence believable, or should we continue to only believe in science, random events, chances, and coincidences?

I'm bringing this up to show how many of us simply follow a set of beliefs and habits, going about our daily lives, living myopically and disregarding the mysteries of life. Sure, there is a material world and it's full of things, events, and people. I'm one of those people in the material world. So are you.

My purpose is no different to yours – it's to find out who I am.
To do this, I'm called to explore the material world and my place in it, just like you are. However, extraordinary people don't simply focus on what is obvious – what can be sensed through sight, smell, touch, hear, and taste. They're interested in going beyond, going deeper. They find and follow their purpose through feelings, thoughts, actions, and the sense of being.

Think about it. How much we experience is based on our level of awareness or consciousness. Consciousness is with us at all times. It permeates everything – it records everything that has occurred, existed, or evolved in our lives from any time or space within the past, including every passing thought. Consciousness also turns *things* in the material world into *experiences* in the internal world. When we live only through our five senses, we live a life more limited because we fail to recognise the energy and power that goes beyond our physical state of being.

Consciousness is full of potential. One of life's paradoxes is that the most crucial secrets to success cannot be found within the conventional education system. One secret is this: to become highly successful you must deliberately adopt a conscious lifestyle. That's what leaders do (Chapter 8). A leader has to be more aware than other people (and quite often, be aware for other people). Consciousness produces a realistic self-assessment by making us ask fundamentally important questions: Who am I? What am I? Why am I here? What do I want?

Living consciously will make you more dynamic, flexible, and resilient in a crisis, because awareness leads to better understanding, which then leads to better decisions. And better decisions carve out the higher paths to success. By being conscious, you tap into your sixth sense of intuition. You live from the inside out, not the outside in. But when you live in an egotistical world, purely through your five senses, you block out awareness, and invite in selfishness, ruthlessness, competitiveness, and clouded judgement.

Henry Ford is a great example of someone who lived from inside out, rather than the outside in. His whole life was based on a rock-solid self-evaluation. He knew he was special and had something big to contribute. He wanted to make advances in machinery and automobiles (he was twenty when this became his focus), and he wanted to change the lives of common people (his own factory workers were given the highest wages in the industry at the time). Eventually, Ford's vision extended to build utopian communities in places like Brazil, so his ideal American worker model could be used worldwide. Ford's rise to greatness looks as if it occurred with incredible speed. But did you know that after he turned sixteen he worked for ten years in the machine shops of Detroit, and that his first order venture, was shut down by his investors after three years? What sustained him during this time was self-awareness as much as education.

Awareness is like an antenna, constantly assessing feedback sent inside and out. When you're self-aware, you know where you stand in relation to your environment and yourself.

Deepak Chopra said, 'Awareness is the birthplace of possibility.' Everything you want to *do*, everything you want to *be*, starts with awareness. To be a successful visionary, like Ford, you must be as aware as possible. Many paths lead in many different directions, but awareness tells you the right one to take. When you're acting from awareness, there's no limit to what you can change because awareness brings light to every aspect of your life. If you're in a constant state of expanded awareness, everything else will expand. But if your consciousness is constricted, everything in your reality and circumstances will be constricted.

Awareness is more than just knowledge. Do you ever think about what you think about? Consciousness has a unique and important link to the pursuit of advancement, enlightenment, self-improvement, and spiritual growth. All the knowledge you need to attain everything you want is already out there. The question is, are you aware of that knowledge?

Let's try something – write down your phone number. Now ask, 'Was I thinking of my phone number before I was asked to write it down?' It wasn't really at the top of your mind, was it? You knew the number, but it wasn't at the forefront of your mind until I prompted you to think of it. How much more is in your mind's background?

As I've discussed earlier in *Impossible to Fail*, we all carry around a plethora of ideas that are outside of our conscious awareness at any given point in time. By now, you understand how these ideas accumulate and form belief systems, which express themselves in habitual ways of thinking and acting. Unless the cycle is interrupted, these habits recreate the same results over and over again.

Awareness is the common denominator of every result on your path to success and journey through life. Most people live quite unconsciously on autopilot, so they're being driven by some of the unconscious ideas and beliefs they've inherited. One way to determine a person's level of awareness in any aspect of their life is by looking at their results in that area. If the results haven't changed a lot, there's a high probability this person lives and acts from a place of very limited consciousness or autopilot. And you already know you can't change what you're unaware of. But when you switch off autopilot, you become the creator of your outcomes, the controller and manager of your success. There is no greater power of transformation.

Connecting with your heart's intelligence

Most people equate intelligence, learning, understanding, and reasoning with the brain. However, in 1991, neuro-cardiologist Dr J. Andrew Armour found that the heart has its own intrinsic nervous system, which he called the 'heart brain'. Since then, scientists at the HeartMath Institute have learnt more about how the heart's intelligence system independently senses and processes information, and then communicates with the brain. I encourage you to visit the HeartMath Institute website to gain more insight into their findings.

'Researchers began showing in the 1980s and '90s that success in life depended more on an individual's ability to effectively manage emotions than on the intellectual ability of the brain in the head.'
Doc Childre and Howard Martin, *The HeartMath Solution*

Childre and Martin concluded that intelligence and intuition were heightened when people learnt to decipher the messages received from their heart's rhythms. In other words, tapping into the heart's intelligence results in making better decisions and a higher level of success. It makes us more aware of what's going on inside ourselves and in our environment.

American consciousness author Gregg Braden is internationally renowned as a pioneer in bridging science, spirituality, and human potential to create real-world solutions. His work has provided real insights into how we can strengthen what he calls the intuitive 'heart-brain connection' and tap into our heart intelligence. Braden described this connection as an ongoing silent (and often subconscious) conversation that takes place inside us. This never-ending conversation of emotion-based signals is vital because the quality of the emotional signal that our heart sends to our brains, determines which chemicals our brain releases into our bodies.

The HeartMath Institute discovered the connection between negative emotions and heart rhythms in its early research. When we feel negative emotions like anger, jealousy, or hatred, our heart sends a signal to our brain that mirrors our feelings. If you looked at these negative emotions on a heart monitor you would see a chaotic display of jagged, unbalanced signals. Think of it like the volatile up-and-down stock market, subject to negative and positive influences. So, the brain interprets these negative emotions as signs of stress, and in response, it increases the levels of stress hormones called cortisol and adrenaline, and prepares the body for a 'flight or fight' response. Spending a lot of time in 'flight or fight' mode' is extremely detrimental to our physical heart and immune system.

In contrast, positive emotions like appreciation, care, gratitude, and compassion produce smoother, harmonious heart rhythms. This reduces the impact of the 'flight or fight' response on the nervous system.

> **'But these harmonious and coherent rhythms did more than reduce stress: they actually enhanced people's ability to clearly perceive the world around them.'**
> **Doc Childre and Howard Martin,** *The HeartMath*
> *Solution*

This is one of those areas where science and spirituality meet. Science focuses on the electrical relationship and connection between the heart and the brain, while spiritual practices have long helped people apply this relationship in their lives without the need for scientific explanations. It is no coincidence that some of the scientific findings developed by researchers and scientists now, are very similar to the techniques advocated by ancient and spiritual traditions a long time ago.

There are many ways to create better harmony between the heart and the brain, but the simplest is to become aware of energy building up in your chest region when you experience emotions, and observe those physical and mental responses. This simple technique has helped me to monitor my reactions and become calmer and feel more in control.

Try it. Next time you feel a strong emotion, note the energy in your chest. Is it pounding? Is it calm? Observe the way your emotions feel in your heart space. If you practice this regularly, your heart intelligence will start to communicate with you through emotions, leading to more clarity, better decision-making and responses to difficult situations, and increased emotional intelligence over time. It's a gift we all can tap into, regardless of religious or spiritual beliefs.

Just remember, heart intelligence is not a substitute for intellect. However, when we apply different forms of intelligence (such as intellectual, heart, intuitive, emotional, social, financial, and commercial intelligence), we give ourselves the highest chance for success.

Tapping into your creativity

Creativity – what people use to solve big challenges.

Most people associate creativity with artistic pursuits such as painting, music, poetry, or theatre. However, creativity is more than artistic expression. It's about (and incorporates) problem solving. Scientists use creativity when they are researching new ways to combat disease. Engineers use creativity to design infrastructure. Teachers use creativity to help students apply their learning. Any innovation, discovery, or exploration is a consequence of someone's creativity. Creativity is a way of thinking that allows people to move beyond tried-and-tested methods to new and innovative expressions and problem-solving methods. It's a form of free thinking.

> *'Many highly intelligent people are poor thinkers. Many people of average intelligence are skilled thinkers. The power of the car is separate from the way the car is driven.'*
> **Edward De Bono**

Many people know *what* to think (and what they think is usually a consequence of a highly developed intellect), but they don't always know *how* to think. These people opt for existing jobs because they can work with systems that have already been created for them. Very few people can create new systems, jobs, ideas, businesses, and innovations because that requires thinking outside the square. That's what leaders and highly successful people do. They think outside the square. They have creative vision, even when the way forward is unclear. Of course, creativity is about more than perceiving possibilities before they become reality. But when it comes to solving personal and professional problems, creativity determines how successful you'll be.

At its heart, creativity is a method of reaching your goals. It's a tool you can use to overcome obstacles by helping you rethink. Tapping into creativity will define what is most important to you, so your energies are directed properly and usefully. And when it's unleashed, creativity will completely transform your life and clear the path for an exciting future. So, why is it that despite creativity being the foundation for human progress, very few people tap into it?

Unfortunately, many people have false beliefs about creativity, such as:
- 'People are born creative.'
- 'Creativity is exclusively for people with artistic ability.'

These beliefs stifle their ability to tap into their creative potential. Do you think that way? Tell yourself this: 'Creative thinking is as much my domain as anyone's.'

Habits are another barrier to reaching creative potential. As you know, the mind is wired to feel comfortable with information consistent with what we already believe. Often, new ideas make us feel uncomfortable or unbalanced because they challenge the status quo. This discomfort is called cognitive dissonance, and when we experience it, we want to shut the ideas down before they take shape. This stifles success because true creativity requires being open to seeing things differently and reserving judgement until ideas are fully formed.

> *'You cannot dig a hole in a different*
> *place by digging the same hole deeper.'*
> **Edward de Bono**

Ultimately, you can change these habits and form new ones. Conscious effort is required to change a lifetime of viewing the world the way you do. One way to do this is by practising metacognition, which is the ability to observe (or think about) your thinking. What is the thinking behind your belief, habit, or perception? You have to become conscious if you want to do something different. But when you think about your thinking, you will become increasingly aware of how you're stifling creativity. And when you make the conscious effort required for more creative thinking, and when you catch the curveball thrown at you, your outcomes will be massively enhanced.

So, how can we tap into our creativity? There are more ways to stimulate creativity than the scope of this book allows, from visual stimuli to brain retraining, each has its own set of benefits, but here are just a few:

- **Visual stimuli** – create an intention board in your home or office. Social psychologists have conducted numerous experiments that demonstrate how behaviour and performance is affected by visual stimuli. One study found that participants primed with images associated with business, such as briefcases, pens, and people dressed in suits, became more competitive. In a 'Bright Ideas' study, social psychologist and assistant professor at Colombia Business School Michael Slepian, found that participants primed to a simple exposed light bulb became more insightful and creative. An intention board works by stimulating the subconscious mind to come up with creative ways to achieve goals. When you set goals, find somewhere to position an intention board (somewhere you look often) and pin visual reminders of the goal on it. This will stimulate your mind to work for your goal.

- **Daydream** – allow your mind to roam freely. Daydreaming triggers creative thinking by allowing us to rehearse the future and imagine our ideal life and adventures without risks. In effect, daydreaming is a more creative state than methodically reasoning through problems, because the unfocused mind actually allows new ideas and unexpected associations to form. Neuroscientists have identified this process as the brain's default network. However, daydreaming only helps if you pay attention to the content of your mind's wanderings and use initiative to apply and act on it.

- **Lateral thinking** – step sideways from your usual way of thinking. Coined by brain-training pioneer Edward de Bono, the term means actively and consciously breaking away from logical thinking strategies and becoming less constrained by traditional problem-solving methods. Lateral thinking encourages the question, 'Why not?' This requires a willingness to suspend judgement, self-censorship, and self-doubt until we break free from our normal habitual patterns of thinking. For example – if there are six eggs in a basket, and six people each take one of the eggs, how can there be one egg left in the basket? The answer – the last person took the basket with one egg in it. That's lateral thinking. If you want to explore this more, check out Edward de Bono's website and books, or look up lateral-thinking exercises and puzzles online.

- **Passion** – focus on what you're passionate about. It's difficult to spend time and energy on things we do not have a strong interest in, which leads to stop-start efforts that start with enthusiasm but burn out before success is achieved. Remember, creativity is enhanced by passion, whether at home, work, or in our relationships. Passion is the key that unlocks the hard work needed for us to achieve true creative-driven success.

- **Collaborate** – share and borrow ideas. Creativity doesn't happen in a vacuum and you don't always have to reinvent the wheel. Many the amazing successes have come from someone else's errors or half-achieved dreams (or ideas appropriated from entirely different situations). Creativity can be a lonely process (especially when we think we're the only ones to have a certain kind of problem), but it doesn't always have to be. Other people can be invaluable to your success. And on the flip side, contributing to others' creative ideas helps you think outside the square and build awareness of what is happening around you (such as opportunities).

Whatever technique/s you use, remember that creative solutions don't usually come in one go. Instead, moments of insight come as one part of the puzzle (and one piece of the complete answer). How do you keep hold of these puzzle pieces until you can fit them together? Some people write notes in a journal. Others have a shoebox to collect the pieces. When I'm writing, my way is to write on slips of paper and clip them together until I'm ready to craft them into a book. Any ideas for my book, I write down. Any articles I write, I keep with this collection. I do this even when I can't see how the words, phrases, ideas, and articles fit in exactly with my overall concept. But by not rejecting ideas, no matter how random they seem at the start, I eventually end up creating a picture. Now, not all ideas bear fruit. There always comes a time when I have to cull my pieces and dispose of ideas that aren't useful. However, when I know what to give up and what to pursue, my good ideas come together, and things start to make sense.

Creativity is crucial to a successful and productive life. It's about taking risks, looking at the world with new eyes, and then reaping the vast rewards of this new way of being. A successful life is rich with diverse experiences, and the more you practise creative ways of looking at similar and familiar situations, the more your experience of the world will be enhanced. One good idea has the ability to completely transform your life.

Consciousness and success

'Every one of us is the sum total of our thoughts.'
Earl Nightingale

Every thought we have is our consciousness, but our conscious experiences are constantly shifting and changing. Right now, you're focused on reading *Impossible to Fail*, but in time, your conscious experience will shift. Perhaps you'll remember a conversation you had with a family member or friend, or you'll notice that you need to stretch. Perhaps you'll start making mental notes for that holiday you've been thinking about. Your conscious experience can range from zero, when we are in deep sleep, to a very high level of consciousness, to Enlightenment, which is a total awareness of everything that exists around us and inside of us. These shifting streams of thoughts change dramatically from one moment to another, yet your experience of them seems smooth and effortless.

How does this relate to success?

> *'The secret is to become more aware,*
> *to adopt a conscious lifestyle.'*
> **Deepak Chopra**

In his article 'Why consciousness is the biggest secret to success', Chopra said success comes from being as aware as possible. That means, tapping into your consciousness, and constantly asking, 'What am I creating through my thoughts and awareness?' By being aware of, and responsive to, your surroundings, you're being shaped from the inside out, but when you react to outside circumstances, you're operating from a lower level of awareness.

Researcher Dr David Hawkins (author of *Transcending the Levels of Consciousness*) has conducted extensive research on consciousness. In his book *Power VS. Force – The Hidden Determinants of Human Behavior*, he said human personality can be described in a scoring system that ranges from 0 to 1000, with 0 being the lowest score and 1000 representing absolute enlightenment or pure awareness. Where a person is on the scale dictates how they relate to their life experiences. To Hawkins, the purpose of life is to move upward to higher states of consciousness – in fact, he said it was the only way to make meaningful progress in life.

Hawkins found that a focused effort to shift into higher states of consciousness, led to massive leaps of awareness very quickly. And when people successfully accessed a high state of consciousness, they were able to answer their mind's questions (such as 'Who am I, what do I want, and what do I need?) with 100 per cent certainty. Hawkins also said individuals who maintained the highest level of consciousness, counterbalanced a large number of people operating from lower levels of consciousness. Such people have extremely powerful influences over the wellbeing of their communities, and even on a wider scale. Why? A person who operates from a high level of consciousness will live in harmony and naturally have lots of synchronicity, so their work becomes effortless and fruitful, and success becomes continuous and ever-expanding. By default, this implies that if you are constantly struggling in life, there is a very good possibility you are operating at a low level of consciousness.

Many people achieve a high level of success and attribute it to hard work, willpower, and dedication. However, consciousness is more than intellect, according to Hawkins. While intellect was a result of higher states of awareness, he argued that its power was limited, and highly successful people were a natural manifestation of elevated consciousness.

Hawkins' research has massive implications for us in understanding ourselves, our relationship with the universe, and the relationship between our awareness and success. We have more power to exert control over our circumstances than we think. It's a lot more complicated than this, so if you are keen to know more, I suggest getting hold of his books or looking up 'levels of consciousness + Hawkins' online.

When we operate from a low level of consciousness, it feels like life is happening *to* us. When we operate from a high level of consciousness, life happens *through* us.

Want to be more successful? Stop trying to fix, change, resist, and control life. Instead, work on a consciousness evolution – become curious about what is happening, rather than going for the quick fix. Observe. Be willing instead of resistant. Be transparent and truthful with yourself. And treat yourself with love and respect. You're embarking on a huge journey of growth.

Want to raise your consciousness right now? Try these things:
- walk in nature
- move your body
- meditate
- do something that brings you joy
- set an intention to experience a consciousness evolution.
- Let success happen *through* you today.

What we have covered in this chapter

In this chapter we have covered:
- spiritual awareness
- connecting with your heart's intelligence
- tapping into your creativity
- the link between consciousness and success.

What do successful people do? Successful people understand the connection between consciousness and success. They know the difference between instinct and operating from the heart's intuitive intelligence. Successful people understand the importance of creativity and deliberately engage in practices that will enhance their lateral thinking.

CHAPTER 15
Maximising your potential

Maximising your potential is all about how you can think bigger than you have before. It's about the things you can do to activate a bigger vision and for you to live into more of your potential.

Millions of people are suffering worldwide from indifference and under achievement. The problem isn't necessarily lack of skills, education, or global competition, or even a lack of resources. The fact is, most people lack the required amount of *resourcefulness* needed to maximise their potential in life.

What we're going to cover in this chapter are topics to support you to maximise your personal potential, find inspiration and discover the power of the mastermind.

Maximising your personal potential

One of the key reasons people don't maximise their potential in life, is not because of their inability to cope with setbacks and challenges, it's because of their inability to tap into their resilience, purpose, drive and ambition. Maximising our potential is not something we learn at school. You can't read it from a book, and you can't learn something like this at a seminar. It is something you develop, in the form of resilience in the face of controversy and criticism. We know life will test us repeatedly to determine if we're worthy of success. Unfortunately, only a small percentage of people will ever achieve a high level of success and greatness. This is because of their inability to understand and maximise their potential. Now here are some key steps on how you can maximise your potential.

Firstly, well you've got to recognise your potential. To determine how best to utilise your potential, you must first recognise you have a lot more than you think you have. The greatest people in the world are no more exceptional or different than you and me. We all start out in life on the same track, and except for a few bumps in the road, we create the highway of success with the same pavement. To keep up with the most successful people requires us to go along the journey by seeing ourselves as a potential difference maker. Or perhaps a potential change maker, a potential millionaire, a billionaire, an entrepreneur, an innovator, a leader, a guru or anything similar, just to say, "You know what, it is possible for me." You've got to first understand the possibility you can be a lot more than you're currently being. That's not just a cliché. You can and will evolve into the person you think you aspire to become, if you first recognise your potential.

I love the quote by Carol Dweck. She said,

"Becoming is more important than just being."

The second step is to trust the process. That means once you're committed to maximising your potential and you recognise maximising happens when you take calculated risks with unpopular or unconventional actions. The reason only one percent of the world is at the top, isn't because they're necessarily brilliant, it's because they went against popular opinion. They went against the grind, and made tough decisions based on their faith in the process.

The story of David and Goliath sums this up perfectly.

Dave is the founder of Warby Parker, a company that sells spectacles. One day, he was waiting in line at the Apple store to buy an iPhone, when he compared the cost of an iPhone with glasses he needed to buy. Dave thought about how the cost of his glasses, which was really a necessity and not a luxury item, had hardly changed from the time his grandfather used to wear them. He wondered why glasses required such a hefty price tag.

Why did such a fundamentally simple product cost more than a complex smartphone? The thing is, anyone could have asked those questions and arrived at the same answers he did, but most people don't ask the question. They just accept things at face value. So, once he became curious about why the price was so steep, he began to do some research into the eyewear industry. He learned a European company called Luxottica dominated the industry, and they'd raked in over 7,000,000,000 pounds in revenue the previous year. He understood the same company provided licenses for the major well-known brand suppliers like Pearle Vision, Ray-Ban, Oakley and even the licenses for Chanel and Prada. It made sense to him why the glasses were so expensive. He realised nothing in the cost of goods justified the price. Luxottica was taking advantage of its dominant position as the key supplier, and charging twenty times the cost. Because *no one* questioned the cost of glasses in their whole lifetime.

This thing went unchecked for a long time, and Dave realised he could do something about it. He realised rules and systems are created by people. If a particular role or policy was manmade, then it had the potential to be reversible. Although Dave didn't have a background in e-commerce or technology, let alone in business, he trusted there was an opportunity for him to start a company. He sold eyeglasses that normally cost $500.00 in a store, for $95.00 online. His business success depended on a functioning website. He knew without a website it would be impossible for customers to view or buy his products.

Now, at this point, Dave was told many times he was crazy, that people would never buy glasses over the Internet without trying them on first. But Dave trusted the process. He launched his website in February 2010, and called his company Warby Parker. He expected he would sell a pair or two of glasses each day. It shocked him when he hit the entire financial target for the year in less than a month. They sold out so fast they needed to put 20,000 customers on a waiting list. It took them nine months to stock enough inventory to meet the demand.

Now fast forward this a few years later, to 2015. Fast Company released a list of the world's most innovative companies and Warby Parker didn't just make the list, they came in first. The previous winners were Google, Nike, and Apple and they all had over 50,000 employees. Warby Parker's start up, was just Dave, a new kid on the block and very little support. At that stage, when he was listed as the top company, he only had 500 staff compared to the 50,000 plus staff the other companies had. In five years, Dave, along with his team, built one of the most fashionable brands on the planet, and then donated 1,000,000 pairs of glasses to people in need.

The company cleared $100,000,000 in annual revenues and was valued at over $1,000,000,000. This possibly happened because Dave went against popular opinion and made tough decisions, based on his unwavering faith in the process. So, stepping out on a belief that tells your conscience the reward is far greater than the risk, can be a great thing. That's why sometimes you have to follow your gut, despite the lack of supporting evidence.

This is one of the key differences between vision and sight. Most people in the world know how to use sight. Leaders who are the change makers, the difference makers, the innovators, the destructors, the entrepreneurs, the gurus, the experts of the world, use their vision to see beyond what most people see. Realise you have the potential. If you don't recognise it, you won't tap into it. This is an amazing story which I love sharing. It demonstrates recognising your potential and knowing sometimes it pays to act on your gut, even when your intellect tells you it's not possible.

Another way to maximise your potential is to be okay with being criticised. This is something that can be very difficult for most people. Fear of rejection and fear of judgment is one of our primal fears, and it's conditioned most people to believe that being criticised is something to be avoided.

Understand, if people like Henry Ford, Thomas Edison, Alexander Bell, The Wright Brothers, Bill Gates, and Steve Jobs feared criticism because they feared failure, we wouldn't have access to the great inventions we have today.

'Realistic' people limit themselves with traditional dogma and they follow what society expects of them. They're more concerned about surviving and pleasing people. Because of this, they never maximise their life. They rely on their intellect and their past to determine possibilities for their future. In doing so, they under-estimate the power of their imagination. They genuinely believe looking at old data is sensible, and the realistic thing to do.

To maximise your potential, think big. You must dream big, visualise big, and sometimes be prepared to be the only person who believes in your vision.

If you think of some of the best leaders and role models in the world, they're people who were condemned, criticised, judged and ostracised. To share a few examples, think of Nelson Mandela, Abraham Lincoln, Martin Luther King or even Jesus Christ in Christianity. It's almost like a price you pay for greatness. To maximise your potential is to be okay with it, and to be in acceptance of the fact it's a natural part of the process.

Not everyone will have the same vision as you, but that doesn't mean you should give up on your vision. People may try to shoot you down, or 'protect' you, by stopping you from taking massive action. It could be family members who may even ridicule or laugh at you. People can get scared about a big vision, and because of this, they don't take action if an exaggerated sense of risk is involved. Remember, most people don't mean any harm, they're just trained to be 'realistic.' Being criticised and ostracised on your journey of success will happen, but you need to be okay with it, if you really want to maximise your potential.

Another step to maximising your potential, is to do an audit on your life. If you're not happy with your life right now, audit yourself and understand it's the quality of your thinking driving the quality of your actions, and the quality of your decisions. You must understand, success doesn't happen because of one or two good decisions. Success, is a consequence of a series of good decisions, made consistently over the long term. Failure in life, is a series of consistently bad decisions made over the long term.

You may recall me telling you in the previous chapters, that the quality of your thinking determines your feelings. These feelings determine your behaviour, and your decisions, and that, in turn, drives your results. So the people who never tap into their full potential during their lifetime lack the quality of thinking necessary for successful outcomes. Many neglect the importance of developing their mindset.

We each have massive potential and genius within us, but whether that genius is cultivated will come down to what takes place in our thinking on a regular basis. Are you monitoring your thoughts? Are you paying attention to the images you're painting in your mind?

Do you know what happens when people worry? When you worry what you're doing is bringing a negative imagined event forward into your mind. As you know, the subconscious mind thinks in images, and the language of the subconscious mind is emotions. Whatever you constantly imagine and visualise in your mind, or whatever feeling you continually nurture, is what will occur in your life because your subconscious mind will heighten your awareness towards those things. This again relates back to your mindset. Don't be fooled, just because you've understood all the mindset stuff at a conscious level, doesn't mean you're ready to apply it.

Information must become experience for you to achieve sustainable results. You can read this whole book and say to yourself, 'I understand all of this stuff,' but you must ensure you have understood it at the deepest possible level. If your behaviours have not changed and become automated (habitual), then you've only comprehended the information at an intellectual level.

The key step to building a bigger future, and maximising your potential, is to not immediately limit what's possible. Many people reach out to me and claim they wish to be successful, but when I offer them solutions, possibilities, or opportunities, they say "No," "Not right now," "This is not the right time," "I'm too busy," or some version of it.

If you observe carefully, you will find people literally say "No" to so many things without even knowing what's involved. The reality, in most cases, is people have no way of knowing if they can undertake something unless they jump into it. But, because of pre-conceived ideas or inherited limiting beliefs, they cannot perceive the possibilities. They close their door to so many new experiences and opportunities.

Many times people limit themselves. They tell themselves,
- "I won't apply for that degree this year"
- "I won't apply for that high paid job yet"
- "This is not the right time."

Basically, a lot of negativity and blocks in our lives, are disguised as 'practical' considerations. We are deluded into believing we are being sensible. The fact is, we are afraid of the unknown and trust our intellect more than we trust our imagination.

If you want more out of life, one thing you can do, is to say "Yes" more often. Experience it first because you can't fully understand and comprehend the consequences of your actions until you've said "Yes" to certain things in life. Of course, you've got to make sure those things correspond to your purpose, passion, and goals. If they do, say "Yes" more often, instead of saying "No."

Some of your best moments, will occur when your mind is stretched to its limits to accomplish something difficult and worthwhile. I believe it's in our innate spiritual nature to want to maximise our potential. The benefits are tremendous. When you maximise your potential, you will see many changes happen.

First, you will feel energised on a regular basis and you won't wait to get out of bed. You'll feel a bit of fear, but also a bit of excitement too, together in a good way. You'll feel high levels of motivation to do whatever it takes to figure it out. And you'll stop thinking about other jobs in a different life, or distractions and daydreaming about things that provide you with a quick fix. That's because it's almost like you'll love the things most people hate.

So, what do most people hate? Most people hate hard work. They hate the grind, the slog, the criticism, the embarrassment, the failures, the setbacks, the challenges, and the problems. Most people want the destination, but they don't love the climb. If you love the things other people hate, and love the climb, you train your mind to love the process. If you can do that, you will become one of the most successful people. I promise you that. It's about tricking your mind to love all the things we naturally avoid, which is a symptom of a mediocrity-based culture.

Pain, problems and challenges, adversity and setbacks, are not enemies. Those things are our friends. You must see problems, challenges and setbacks as things to help you, serve you, support you, and help you grow. It's the comfort zone that is the enemy, but looks like the friend. Because most people don't have vision and give too much regard to their feelings, they don't fully understand this. The things which feel bad in the short term, because they show up as friction, are good for us in the long term. The stronger the emotion, the higher the friction. Don't resist the friction.

Start loving the things other people hate and maybe avoid some things people love.

Mark Twain said,

> **"When you find yourself on the side of the majority,**
> **it is time to pause and reflect."**

I understand it's not realistic to spend every waking moment at high octane performance, but it is possible to tap into your talents and potential, to be the best you can, every single day. When you experience all this, you will know how exhilarating work and life can be. I want you to experience that because I've experienced it, and I want you to know it's absolutely possible. In addition, having met and interviewed so many successful people, they all claim to feel this. Once you recognise your potential and let the intent in, you'll tap into it. You'll stop limiting yourself, and you'll find you'll start living into your potential.

If you're not already living into your potential, then it's probably a wakeup call to know there is more you could be getting out of life. We all have limitless potential. If we aren't stretching that potential, we will end up being bored. We will waste our true potential and deny the world of the impact we can have. People talk about the wasted resources in the world, the environmental resources, and they talk about climate change. Hardly anyone talks about the wastage of human resources. Human beings can make things happen, but so many of us waste our potential, and there's no outcry about this. If every single human being decided they would maximise their potential, we wouldn't have the world problems we do. That's why it becomes incredibly important to set the intention and understand maximising your potential is not just about you. When you are at your best, you benefit others and the world. Those who are inspired have purpose, are invested in their development, and have more to give, compared to those living lives of frustration, limitation and scarcity.

I hope this gives you some great insights into the fact that maximising your potential doesn't happen by chance. It's something that happens when you're aware of it, and set an intention to live into your potential. Our potential is indeed limitless. In every area whether it's music, sport, or technology, you will find records are being broken, and as I mentioned, if you think things will stay the same as they are today, they won't.

Can you imagine our cars ten years from now, do you think they'll be the same? Or the way we live, our lifestyles, how we think about things; do you think they'll stay the same? No, obviously they won't. So, in ten years' time, we know things will be different. But why? Because somebody is thinking ahead. Somebody is not accepting the status quo. The question is, "Why isn't that somebody you?" Why can't you be at the forefront of change, as opposed to resisting change?

That is truly, the essence of maximising your potential.

Finding inspiration

We can describe inspiration as a new and better way of answering a question or solving a problem. It's a feeling we get, a feeling of elation and elevation when we are on the right track in life. It happens naturally and it's beautiful to experience, and beautiful to watch. Inspired people do not need extrinsic motivation. Rather than having to push themselves, they're pulled by something far more superior and greater than just their day-to-day struggles.

People who live in an inspired state are people who have achieved a level of self-actualisation and think beyond their own survival. Unlike other people who are bogged down by "busy-ness," and being stuck in autopilot patterns, inspired people spend a lot of their time thinking of insightful ideas. They create solutions that can make their life, the lives of others, and the world, a better place.

Eleanor Roosevelt said,

"Great minds discuss ideas, average minds discuss events and small minds discuss people."

Inspiration is the energy that enables us to become creative. It helps us unleash our most powerful self, and it helps position our best self to the world.

Here are some things you can do to arouse feelings of inspiration.

1. Read or watch biographies of inspiring and creative people. Inspiration is contagious. In your search for inspiration, you can read or watch biographies of those whose creativity, personality, abilities or ingenuity has influenced you.

I love this quote by Steve Jobs,

"Your time is limited so don't waste it living someone else's life."

Don't be trapped by dogma, which is living with the results of other people's thinking. Don't let the noise of other people drown out your own inner voice. Have the courage to follow your heart and your intuition. They somehow already know what you truly want to become. Everything else is secondary.

When certain people inspire us, it indicates who we can become. We can only admire in others what's inside of us. Learning and being inspired by role models can be an indicator of the traits we're hiding within ourselves, and we possibly haven't taken the time to nurture. We all need external triggers for inspiration from time to time, and other people can be a prime source of that. Our role models show us what's possible for ourselves, and they also can help us increase our confidence. But the thing is, role models don't just fall into our laps, we have to seek them out. Think of the top three or five people who inspire you. People who, when you watch them or hear their words, give you goosebumps. Write down what it is that inspires you about these people. See if those qualities inherently reside inside of you and ask yourself, "What can I do to cultivate these qualities further?"

2. Change your "I don't know," or "I can't" statements, to "What if?" and "How can I?"

Sometimes our own fixed patterns can become a massive barrier to inspiration. When we think closed-ended thoughts like "I can't," or "I don't know how," or "It won't work," we go into a negative self-fulfilling prophecy. We can remain stuck there for a long time without any awareness.

When you replace those statements and questions with statements like, "I have what it takes to figure this out," "I'm open to the possibility solutions will come up," or "There has to be a way to fix this," you'll unleash the inspiration and energy reserved within you.

When you are open to possibility there's always a way. This open-ended thinking and self-questioning can become your way of tapping into your inspiration.

And remember, you don't have to come up with the answers immediately.

To begin with, just empty your mind and engage yourself on more questioning. Then let the answers come to you. Inspiration can sometimes emerge naturally and spontaneously. You must understand, your subconscious mind will eventually provide you with the solutions, as long as you maintain a state of expectation, they'll come to you at some stage. Suspend un-belief or too much scepticism.

Instead of constantly making negative statements or even actively seeking answers, engage in asking yourself good, intelligent questions. Let your mind wonder about possibilities rather than just shutting them down.

Albert Einstein once said,

"To raise new questions, new possibilities and to regard all problems from a new angle requires creative imagination."

3. Take a break from your routine. When you get outside of your normal routine you give yourself permission to think and act outside of the box. Give yourself a day or even a few hours, when almost everything you do, in that time, is a departure from your normal routine. Things like taking a different route to a destination, or listening to unfamiliar music, trying unusual foods or visiting an interesting store. Perhaps problem solving in new environments, brainstorming with your non-dominant hand or watching a TEDx video on an innovative idea you are normally not interested in. See what that does to your thought patterns. This departure from routine preferences can help add to your existing patterns of thinking.

Now and then, breaking from your everyday routine can help you experience the world in brand new ways. This can inspire you to come up with fresh perspectives. The new stimulus might give you a breakthrough in your personal life or business.

4. Listen to some complex music. The connection between music, intelligence, and creativity have been well studied and established. Research has proven listening to Mozart's Sonata can temporarily increase special intelligence. So find stimulating and enjoyable complex music to listen to, because it has the potential to refresh your mind.

Staying consistent with who you are and your core values is one of the best ways to feel inspired. Don't enter relationships, transactions or partnerships inconsistent with your values, because these things kill authentic inspiration.

When it comes to finding your inspiration, don't pretend to be someone you're not! Own your space in the world, become highly clear on who you are, and magnify the elements of you, that make you uniquely you.

Here are some questions that can help you achieve further clarity on who you are;

- **If you were an animal, which animal would you be and why?**

In my case, I consider myself to be a lion. Why? Because I have the key qualities of courage and risk taking that closely resemble that of a lion.

- **If you were a song, what song would you be and why?**

For me, my favourite songs that make me feel really inspired are 'Feeling Good by Michael Bublé' and 'Crazy by Seal.'

- **If you were a colour, what colour would you be?**

Me, I would be navy blue, because to me, it demonstrates strength, reliability, power and quality.

- **If you were a car, what car would you be?**

I would be a Mercedes Benz. Why? Because Mercedes Benz is synonymous with reliability. It's recognisable, it's prestigious, and it's powerful.

Now, don't get me wrong, I'm not just picking the best ultra-luxury brands here, because I could pick a Rolls Royce. But I'm not a Rolls Royce. Mercedes Benz is something the average person can reach and acquire, by stretching themselves a bit, and that's where I want to be. I don't want to be average, but I don't want to be completely unreachable. For me it makes sense. I drive a Mercedes Benz and I feel like there is a reason I am attracted to that brand.

- **If you were a food, what food would you be?**

In my case, I would be Thai, something that's healthy, nutritious and combines protein with vegetables and a little spice.

- **If you were a celebrity, who would you be and why?**

I would be someone like Brian Tracy. Why? Because I really respect his knowledge, his influence, his entrepreneurial nature and his ability to inspire.

These questions are all sources of great inspiration, designed to help you understand yourself better and live more in alignment.

There are several key actions you can take to feel inspired. For example, you can do things that push you further outside of your comfort zone. Focusing on the future and its possibilities can make you feel inspired. Being focused on your accomplishments and how far you've come, instead of how far you have to go, can also give you amazing feelings of inspiration, combined with gratitude. Helping somebody or delighting somebody can also be a great source of inspiration for us.

Forgiving someone who has done something wrong by us can create strong feelings of inspiration. Appreciating a piece of art or architecture, or visiting a new town or restaurant, are things that can help us feel inspired. And for me, inspiration is standing by what I believe, even if it means there'll be consequences I don't want to deal with. There is just something amazing about believing in something, standing by it, and having the courage to be authentic in the face of criticism, opposition, and resistance.

When you know and own your place in the world, when you are uniquely you, you will stand out in an increasingly commoditised and distracted world.

So, inspiration is like a butterfly, we have to chase it sometimes. If you want to live a life that is not ordinary, you must seek inspiration out. You will also realise inspiration is one of the best ways to maximise your potential, because when you're inspired, you do not need motivation. Motivation is just automatically unleashed inside of you.

The power of the mastermind

You can either hang around people who will pull you down and mock you for going after your big goals and thinking differently, or you can spend time with people who inspire you. The people you want in your corner are people who will support your dreams, raise your standards, and believe in your ability to make the impossible possible. You can select a powerhouse team, forming a tight-knit group of individuals you respect, to accomplish personal and business goals in the best way. Do this by surrounding yourself with people who will lift you up, and want the same things you want.

Never ask people for directions who are not going in the same direction as you, or have never been in that same direction. Don't ask people for advice who don't want the same things you want. This is the essence of a mastermind alliance. A successful mastermind is one which operates in complete harmony and cooperation, for the success of each individual member, and for the success of the group.

Jim Rohn once said,

"You are the average of the 5 people you spend the most time with."

In his book, *Think and Grow Rich*, Napoleon Hill introduced the concept of the mastermind for the first time. He defined a mastermind group as the coordination of knowledge and effort, of two or more people, who work toward a definite purpose in a period of harmony. People from all walks of life can come together in masterminds for many reasons. These reasons include things like personal growth, motivation, emotional support, business growth, financial success, to work on specific projects, or even to develop a sense of community and bonding.

Masterminds go far beyond just networking. They require commitment, and they require a desire to learn, grow, support others, and to receive support. There are several significant benefits that have been proven as part of joining a mastermind, or even creating one. Many well-known millionaires swear by the benefits of a mastermind, and how instrumental the masterminds have been in their professional and personal success.

Here are some benefits of having, creating, or even joining an existing mastermind.

1. Professional Support.

Masterminds can help you develop business skills and provide you with insights and feedback on projects and ideas. They can stimulate your thinking and encourage you to do things you haven't considered. They can help you support or critique your vision, get clear on your plan of action, and point you towards reliable resources, supplies, leads, or even referrals.

2. Emotional Support.

Finding support can be difficult, especially when you're on the journey of big success, and especially if people are self-employed. Business owners and entrepreneurs struggle in silence because people don't understand them. Masterminds can provide a safe environment for you to be vulnerable and share your ideas, dreams, victories, and defeats, with others. They help you deal with stress and can eliminate distracting internal dialogue.

3. Clarity.

Knowing where you are and where you want to be is important, but knowing how you'll get there, is critical. It can mean the difference between success and failure. A mastermind group can help you with fresh perspectives, pointing out your blind spots, and reminding you of your priorities. They can highlight the most efficient path, identifying opportunities and pitfalls and help you create a clear, efficient action plan.

4. Efficiency.

Masterminding with other skilled people can dramatically shorten your learning curve. New ideas and solutions can arise effortlessly.

5. Focus.

Most people struggle, not because of what they know, but because of what they don't know. A mastermind group is essentially borrowing other people's brains, so it can help you focus on the tasks and priorities you need for success. Sometimes these things may not be in your current level of awareness.

Many models exist, and there are multiple ways in which you can run a mastermind. You can have one that has a very democratic nature, or you can have one where a leader decides, then makes the rules. Some masterminds are casual, and some run like a business.

So, starting out, you will need to know what kind of format suits you and your group. When people get together and join a mastermind for a social purpose, there may not be a specific objective. However, in order for you to become successful, it is good to outline some specific objectives for the mastermind.

Here are a few things I recommend you consider, in identifying which mastermind to join or even setting one up.

- **Group size.** Large groups can provide you with a deeper pool of resources, but developing intimacy can be difficult. A good size may be between eight to twelve people, and small groups can be easier to coordinate. It can be difficult if one or two members are regularly absent, and that's why you need some rules.
- **Admission policies.** Decide whether you want to admit new members and if you do, what kind of approval process they need to go through. Decide if the approval process is something everyone decides and everyone gets to vote on. Is there a trial period or any other qualifying criteria for new members?
- **Meeting format.** Does the group meet in person or by conference call using technology? If it's a conference call, do they hold periodic retreats? Do the people ever get together in person? How often do people meet? Where do they meet? These are just some considerations for a mastermind group.
- **Commitment.** How long will the group work together?
- **Policies.** How will your group handle things like confidentiality agreements, absence, conflict of interest, or how would you remove somebody who is not a good fit?
- **Mission statement.** Last but not least, the mission statement of the mastermind is critical. What is the group's focus? What is its intention and what is the direction it's looking to undertake? Who does this group serve? And do the members share a group vision?

Mastermind meetings don't have to be complicated, a simple agenda usually works best. Most groups start with a basic check in. Each person takes one or two minutes to tell how they're doing, what's new, and any important issues they may want to cover during the meeting.

An alternative method involves deciding in advance which person's needs and goals will be the focus of the next meeting. That person usually will submit any information that needs reviewing to the group before the meeting, to give the group a chance to help. At the end of the meeting, the group will work together to create an agenda and assignment for the next meeting.

All great successful people know the synergy value of collaborating regularly with a carefully selected group of peers. You'll find people at the top all have close-knit masterminds of people, who regularly come together to discuss business, achievements, policies, decisions, and so forth.

It will surprise you how much a carefully selected group of peers and their encouragement, insights, and strategies, can propel, inspire, and enable you to reach greater heights than you thought possible. Most average people, unfortunately, will try to work out things on their own. Highly successful people understand it's best to leverage off other people's expertise, time, and experience. This is where masterminds are unbelievably powerful.

Either look for a mastermind who can help you achieve your goals, or if you can't find one, create one and start looking for people who will be the right fit. You'll be surprised at how quickly a mastermind can propel your success and results.

What we have covered in this chapter?

In this chapter we have covered, how to:
- maximise your personal potential
- find inspiration
- discover the power of the mastermind.

What do successful people do? Successful people understand the importance of achieving and maximising their potential. They know how important it is to stay inspired, how to seek inspiration and also how to find inspiration within themselves.

Successful people understand the power of the mastermind and collaboration, for creation and growth of ideas

CONCLUSION

We're at the end of *Impossible to Fail*, but the beginning of your success journey.

As you can see life mastery requires an understanding of multiple concepts that connect to and provide mental models for dealing with life's situations. Continual success (the ability to design the life and lifestyle you truly want to live) is the consequence of a series of good decisions. At the same time, continual failure to achieve your desired life and lifestyle is the consequence of a series of bad decisions. How do we improve the quality of our decisions? By understanding the concepts that contribute to life success and applying mental models that relate to those concepts.

Everyone faces some limitations, setbacks, and challenges. But those limitations, setbacks, and challenges do not cause failure. Factors that contribute to continual failures are:

- Lack of self-awareness
- Lack of clarity about your purpose and goals
- Not understanding cause and effect
- Not understanding how the mind works
- Lack of alignment between values and goals
- Lack of ability to persist, persevere and bounce back (resilience)
- Not understanding your inner power
- Not knowing the fundamentals that drive financial, career or business success.

Eliminate these factors and it will be impossible to fail. Remember, your life cannot be transformed until you have embodied the concepts in this book. Surface level understanding or simple exposure will not drive change. So, you need to:

- emotionally and repetitively engage with the concepts
- apply them in your life.

That's how information is converted into a habit or belief. Again, if you do this, it's impossible to fail.

I know this for certain. I failed in school, in many jobs and relationships, but I didn't *fail in life*. Why? Because the failures I mentioned weren't failures at all. They were lessons, stepping-stones, and strengthening experiences. They made me wiser and stronger, and enabled me to succeed.

It comes back to how you perceive failure. The universe is benevolent. It wants you to succeed, but it gives you tests to pass so you don't fail at the next level. When you shift your perception about failure, you will realise, like me, that it is truly impossible to fail.

Don't just be inspired by *why*. Be inspired by *how*. How you do something will guarantee your success. Bring passion, joy, and enthusiasm to whatever you want to get results in, and success will be guaranteed.

Find something you care about and commit deeply to it. To succeed, you will have to commit and go all the way. And when you attempt to go all the way, you will fail sometimes (but they are lessons). If you are not failing, you are not succeeding. This is important. Failures are temporary. Failure is the only way to succeed. Avoid failure and you avoid success. Make mistakes but don't make the same mistake more than twice.

And remember this: you cannot succeed if you quit. Quitting comes down to perspective (in most cases). Often, a setback is simply a reminder to change course, to take a detour. Not to stop, but to change strategy. Change plan. Change perspective.

The difference between the right and wrong perspective is everything. Especially when it comes to failure. Don't just lie there and take it. Shift perspective. Why? Because the right action follows the right perspective.

Don't forget. Defeat is inevitable, but quitting is optional. Don't quit and you can guarantee your success.

Impossible To Fail? You bet!

And one last thing – if you decide to start over again, remember, you're not starting from scratch. You're starting from experience.

That's an advantage!

> *'It's impossible for me to fail, because even*
> *when I do, I grow in learning and character.'*
> **Ron Malhotra**

OTHER TITLES BY RON MALHOTRA

8 Wealth Habits of Financially Successful People (2014)

Move Forward or Move Aside (2015)

The Little Black Book of Investment Success (2016)

Magnify: Make Your Life Matter (2018)

ABOUT THE AUTHOR

RON MALHOTRA is the author of five books, entrepreneur, award-winning wealth planner, success coach, business advisor, and thought-leadership mentor. Ron speaks internationally on topics including success, wealth, influence, and business. His views are highly sought after and have been published across a range of mainstream media. Ron's online content has been viewed more than fifty million times. Ron lives with his wife and daughter in Melbourne, Australia.

Lightning Source UK Ltd.
Milton Keynes UK
UKHW011833040621
384966UK00007B/741/J